Thinking through French Philosophy

LEONARD LAWLOR

Thinking through French Philosophy

The Being of the Question

INDIANA
University Press
Bloomington & Indianapolis

Publication of this book is made possible in part with the assistance of a Challenge Grant from the National Endowment for the Humanities, a federal agency that supports research, education, and public programming in the humanities.

This book is a publication of

Indiana University Press
601 North Morton Street
Bloomington, IN 47404-3797 USA

http://iupress.indiana.edu

Telephone orders   800-842-6796
Fax orders   812-855-7931
Orders by e-mail   iuporder@indiana.edu

© 2003 by Leonard Lawlor

The paper used in this publication meets the minimum requirements of American National Standard for Information Sciences—Permanence of Paper for Printed Library Materials, ANSI Z39.48-1984.

Manufactured in the United States of America

Library of Congress Cataloging-in-Publication Data

Lawlor, Leonard, date
Thinking through French philosophy : the being of the question / Leonard Lawlor.
    p.   cm. — (Studies in Continental thought)
Includes bibliographical references and index.
    ISBN 0-253-34225-2 (cloth : alk. paper) — ISBN 0-253-21591-9 (pbk. : alk. paper)
    1. Poststructuralism. 2. Philosophy, French—20th century. 3. Merleau-Ponty, Maurice, 1908–1961.
I. Title. II. Series.
    B2424.S75 L39 2003
    194—dc21

                                                                                            2002013860

1 2 3 4 5   08 07 06 05 04 03

For Jennifer

Contents

Acknowledgments

Although this book is much more than an investigation of Merleau-Ponty's philosophy, I have always referred to it as my "Merleau-Ponty book." Thus I must acknowledge the help and inspiration from my friends in the Merleau-Ponty world. First and foremost, I must thank Ted Toadvine, whose 1996 Ph.D. dissertation at the University of Memphis (*Contradiction, Expression, and Chiasm: The Development of Intersubjectivity in Maurice Merleau-Ponty*) made me reflect on Merleau-Ponty's philosophy seriously for the first time. Then I must thank my friends at *Chiasmi International,* Renaud Barbaras and Mauro Carbone. And finally I must thank these perennial Merleau-Ponteans: Pat Burke, Edward S. Casey, Mike Dillon, Fred Evans, and Hugh J. Silverman. I am especially grateful for the comments David Pettigrew and François Raffoul gave to me concerning an earlier draft of this book; their comments really allowed me to clarify what I was doing in this book. My thanks also to Jay Julian, who proofread the manuscript and composed the index. As always, I appreciate the support my colleagues and students in the Department of Philosophy at the University of Memphis have always given to me.

All of the essays collected here have been revised for this volume. The order of the chapters does not correspond to the chronology of the essays. The chronological order of the writing is the following: spring 1994: "Eliminating Some Confusion"; summer 1995: "The End of Phenomenology"; winter 1998: "The End of Ontology"; summer 1998: "If Theory Is Gray"; winter 1999: "The Beginnings of Post-modernism"; autumn 1999: "The Legacy of Husserl's 'The Origin of Geometry'"; spring 2001: "The Chiasm and the Fold"; summer 2001: "The Beginnings of Thought"; summer 2001: Interview for *Journal Phänomenologie.* The revision of all the essays occurred during the autumn of 2001.

"'If Theory Is Gray, Green Is the Golden Tree of Life'": Philosophy and Nonphilosophy since Hyppolite" has never been published before.

"The Chiasm and the Fold: An Introduction to the Philosophical Concept of Archeology" is an expanded version of an article in *Chiasmi International* 4 (2002), pp. 105–16. It was first presented at the conference "Phenomenology in the Nordic Countries" in Copenhagen, Denmark, May 31, 2001. It was presented again at the annual meeting of the Society for Phenomenology and Existential Philosophy, October 5, 2001, in Baltimore, Maryland. And it was presented a third time at the conference "Merleau-Ponty aux Frontières de l'Invisible," held at the Université Jean Moulin Lyon 3, March 1–2, 2002. "The Chiasm and the Fold" is reprinted here with the permission of the Associazione Culturale Mimesis, Milan.

"Eliminating Some Confusion: The Relation of Being and Writing in Merleau-Ponty and Derrida" first appeared in *Écart and Différance: Merleau-Ponty and Derrida on Seeing and Writing,* edited by M. C. Dillon (Atlantic Highlands, N.J.: Humanities Press, 1997), pp. 71–93. "Eliminating Some Confusion" is reprinted here with the permission of Humanity Books (Prometheus Books).

"The Legacy of Husserl's 'The Origin of Geometry': The Limits of Phenomenology in Merleau-Ponty and Derrida" first appeared in *Merleau-Ponty's Reading of Husserl,* edited by Ted Toadvine and Lester Embree (Dordrecht: Kluwer), pp. 201–26. It was first presented at a Center for Advanced Research in Phenomenology Symposium on Merleau-Ponty and Husserl, Florida Atlantic University, Delray Beach, Florida, November 19, 1999. Then it was presented at the British Society for Phenomenology, Oxford, England, April 7–9, 2000. It was presented a third time at the Centre National de la Recherche Scientifique, École Normale Supérieure, Paris, April 28, 2000. And finally it was presented at the International Phenomenology Symposium, Perugia, Italy, July 20, 2000. "The Legacy of Husserl's 'The Origin of Geometry'" is reprinted here with the permission of Kluwer Academic Publishers.

"The End of Phenomenology: Expressionism in Merleau-Ponty and Deleuze" first appeared in *Continental Philosophy Review* (formerly *Man and World*) 31, no. 1 (January 1998), pp. 15–34. An earlier version of this essay was first presented at the Merleau-Ponty Circle, Duquesne University, Pittsburgh, Pennsylvania, September 23, 1995. "The End of Phenomenology" is reprinted here with the permission of Kluwer Academic Publishers.

"The End of Ontology: Interrogation in Merleau-Ponty and Deleuze" first appeared in *Chiasmi International: Trilingual Studies Concerning the Thought of Merleau-Ponty* 1 (1999), pp. 233–52. It was first presented at the conference L'Eredita delle Filosofia di Maurice Merleau-Ponty nel Pensiero Contemporaneo, held March 12–14, 1998, at the Università degli Studi di Milano, Italy, and then for a second time at the Annual Meeting of the Society for Phenomenology and Existential Philosophy, Denver, Colorado, October 9, 1998. "The End of Ontology" is reprinted here with the permission of the Associazione Culturale Mimesis, Milan.

"The Beginnings of Post-modernism: Phenomenology and Bergsonism, Derrida and Deleuze" first appeared in *Confluences: Phenomenology and Postmodernity, Environment, Race, Gender,* Simon Silverman Phenomenology Center, Duquesne University, Pittsburgh (1999), pp. 53–68. It was first presented at the "Confluences: Phenomenology and Postmodernity, Environment, Race, Gender," at the Simon Silverman Phenomenology Center at Duquesne University, Pittsburgh, Pennsylvania, March 12, 1999. It was then presented at the conference Rhizomatics, Genealogy, and Deconstruction at Trent University, Peterborough, Ontario, May 22, 1999. "The Beginnings of Post-modernism" is reprinted here with the permission of the Simon Silverman Phenomenology Center, Duquesne University.

"The Beginnings of Thought: The Fundamental Experience in Derrida and Deleuze" is an expanded version of an essay that is forthcoming in *Between Deleuze and Derrida,* edited by Paul Patton and John Protevi (Continuum Press, 2003). A shorter and simplified version of this essay was first presented as a lecture at the Universiteit voor Humanistiek, Utrecht, Netherlands, on May 30, 2001, with the title "The Experience of Force, the Experience of the Other: The Philosophy of Difference in Deleuze and Derrida," then at the University of Vienna on March 5, 2002, for the Grüppe Phänomenologie, and finally at Central European University, Budapest, on March 6, 2002. This essay is based on the three Deleuze lectures that I have given in my Introduction to Philosophy classes at the University of Memphis since autumn 1996.

Appendix 1 was originally published in German as "Ende der Phänomenologie? Interview mit Leonard Lawlor," conducted by Silvia Stoller and Gerhard Unterthurner for *Journal Phänomenologie* (Vienna) 16 (2001), pp. 27–44. The English version of the interview is reprinted here with the permission of *Journal Phänomenologie.*

Appendix 2, Gilles Deleuze's "Reversing Platonism," has been translated specifically for this book by Heath Massey. "Renverser le platonisme" originally appeared in *Revue de Métaphysique et de Morale* 71, no. 4 (Oct.–Dec. 1966), pp. 426–38. Presses Universitaires de France has granted permission for this English translation, and Columbia University Press has granted permission for the use of portions of Mark Lester's English translation of "Plato and the Simulacrum" found in *The Logic of Sense* (New York: Columbia University Press, 1990), pp. 253–66.

Abbreviations

The citations used in this book refer first to the original French, then to the English translation. At times the translations have been modified

Books by Gilles Deleuze

BER   *Bergsonisme.* Paris: Presses Universitaires de France, 1966. English translation by Hugh Tomlinson and Barbara Habberjam as *Bergsonism.* New York: Zone Books, 1991.

DR   *Différence et répétition.* Paris: Presses Universitaires de France, 1968. English translation by Paul Patton as *Difference and Repetition.* New York: Columbia University Press, 1994.

F   *Foucault.* Paris: Minuit, 1986. English translation by Paul Bové as *Foucault.* Minneapolis: University of Minnesota Press, 1988.

LS   *Logique du sens.* Paris: Minuit, 1969. English translation by Mark Lester with Charles Stivale as *The Logic of Sense,* edited by Constantin Boundas. New York: Columbia University Press, 1990.

NP   *Nietzsche et la philosophie.* Paris: Presses Universitaires de France, 1962. English translation by Hugh Tomlinson as *Nietzsche and Philosophy.* New York: Columbia University Press, 1983.

QPH   *Qu'est-ce que la philosophie?* Co-authored with Félix Guattari. Paris: Minuit, 1991. English translation by Hugh Tomlinson and Graham Burchell as *What Is Philosophy?* New York: Columbia University Press, 1994.

SPE   *Spinoza et le problème de l'expression.* Paris: Minuit, 1968. English translation by Martin Joughin as *Expressionism in Philosophy: Spinoza.* New York: Zone Books, 1990.

Books by Jacques Derrida

LOG   Edmund Husserl, *L'Origine de la géométrie,* translation and introduction by Jacques Derrida. Paris: Presses Universitaires de France, 1974 [1962]. English translation by John P. Leavey as *Edmund Husserl's Origin of Geometry: An Introduction.* Lincoln: University of Nebraska Press, 1989 [1978].

DIS   *Dissemination.* Paris: Seuil, 1972. English translation by Barbara

Johnson as *Dissemination*. Chicago: University of Chicago Press, 1981.

DLG   *De la grammatologie*. Paris: Minuit, 1967. English translation by Gayatri Spivak as *Of Grammatology*. Baltimore: Johns Hopkins University Press, 1974.

ED   *L'Écriture et la différence*. Paris: Minuit, 1967. English translation by Alan Bass as *Writing and Difference*. Chicago: University of Chicago Press, 1978.

MP   *Marges de la philosophie*. Paris: Minuit, 1972. English translation by Alan Bass as *Margins of Philosophy*. Chicago: University of Chicago Press, 1982.

VP   *La Voix et le phénomène*. Paris: Presses Universitaires de France, 1967. English translation by David B. Allison as *Speech and Phenomena*. Evanston: Northwestern University Press, 1973. Throughout I use the title "Voice and Phenomenon," instead of "Speech and Phenomena," for reasons explained in the Preface to my *Derrida and Husserl* (Bloomington: Indiana University Press, 2002).

Books by Michel Foucault

AS   *L'Archéologie du savoir*. Paris: Gallimard, 1969. English translation by Alan Sheridan as *The Archeology of Knowledge*. New York: Pantheon, 1972.

EU   "Jean Hyppolite. 1907–1968," originally published in *Revue de Métaphysique et de Morale*, no. 2 (1969), pp. 131–34; collected in Michel Foucault, *Dits et écrits, 1954–1988* (Paris: Gallimard, 1994), pp. 779–85. All citations are to the Gallimard edition. All translations are my own.

MC   *Les Mots et les choses*. Paris: Gallimard, 1966. English translation as *The Order of Things*, no translator listed. New York: Random House, 1970.

NGH   "Nietzsche, la généalogie, l'histoire," in *Homage à Jean Hyppolite*. Paris: Presses Universitaires de France, 1971, pp. 145–72. English translation by Donald F. Bouchard and Sherry Simon as "Nietzsche, Genealogy, History," in *Language, Counter-memory, Practice*. Ithaca: Cornell University Press, 1977, pp. 139–64.

OD   *L'Ordre du discours*. Paris: Gallimard, 1971. English translation by A. M. Sheridan Smith as "The Discourse on Language," in *The Archeology of Knowledge*, pp. 235–37.

PD   "La Pensée du dehors," *Critique*, no. 229 (June 1966), pp. 523–46; collected in Michel Foucault, *Dits et écrits, 1954–1988* (Paris: Gallimard, 1994), pp. 518–39. English translation by Brian Massumi as "Maurice Blanchot: The Thought from the Outside," in *Foucault/Blanchot*. New York: Zone Books, 1987. Reference will be made to *Dits et écrits*.

RR   *Raymond Roussel*. Paris: Gallimard, 1963. English translation by Charles Ruas as *Death and the Labyrinth: The World of Raymond Roussel*. Berkeley: University of California Press, 1986.

Books by Jean Hyppolite

LE   *Logique et existence*. Paris: Presses Universitaires de France, 1952. English translation by Leonard Lawlor and Amit Sen as *Logic and Existence*. Albany: State University of New York Press, 1997.

Books by Maurice Merleau-Ponty

BN   See HL below.

HES   A. Hesnard, *L'Œuvre de Freud*, Preface by Maurice Merleau-Ponty. Paris: Payot, 1960. All translations are my own.

HL   *Notes de cours sur L'origine de la géométrie de Husserl suivi de Recherches sur la phénoménologie de Merleau-Ponty,* under the direction of R. Barbaras. Paris: Presses Universitaires de France, 1998. English translation by Leonard Lawlor with Bettina Bergo as *Husserl at the Limits of Phenomenology: Including Texts by Edmund Husserl*. Evanston: Northwestern University Press, 2002. Reference is made to the pagination of the Bibliothéque Nationale; so there is a second abbreviation in the references: BN.

NC   *Notes de cours, 1959–1961,* edited by Stéphanie Ménasé, Preface by Claude Lefort. Paris: Gallimard, 1996. All English translation are my own, except when referring to "Philosophie et non-philosophie depuis Hegel," which has been translated by Hugh J. Silverman as "Philosophy and Non-philosophy since Hegel," in *Philosophy and Non-philosophy since Merleau-Ponty*. New York: Routledge, 1989. References to "Philosophie et non-philosophie" have been correlated to the English translation. All other translations from these course notes are my own.

PHP   *Phénoménologie de la perception*. Paris: Gallimard, 1945. English translation by Colin Smith, revised by Forrest Williams as *Phenomenology of Perception*. London: Routledge and Kegan Paul, 1962.

RC   *Résumés de cours, Collège de France, 1952–60*. Paris: Gallimard, 1968. English translation by John Wild, James Edie, and John O'Neill as

"Themes from the Lectures at the Collège de France, 1952–60," in *In Praise of Philosophy and Other Essays*. Evanston: Northwestern University Press, 1970.

S   *Signes*. Paris: Gallimard, 1960. English translation by Richard C. McCleary as *Signs*. Evanston: Northwestern University Press, 1964.

VI   *Le Visible et l'invisible*. Paris: Gallimard, 1964. English translation by Alphonso Lingis as *The Visible and the Invisible*. Evanston: Northwestern University Press, 1968.

Thinking through French Philosophy

Introduction

The Being of the Question

—

The essays collected in this volume attempt to determine the philosophical system that arose in France during the 1960s. While this moment in recent philosophical history includes many philosophers, I have selected only three: Deleuze, Derrida, and Foucault.[1] Although I have limited myself in this way, the system I have constructed probably—this claim could be tested—accounts for the variety of philosophical positions during this period. But even if my system turns out not to correspond to the facts, even if my system turns out to be false, this lack of truth may be what is most philosophically interesting here. I was not trying to determine a statistical average of terms used or of ideas in circulation during the Sixties in France. I was not trying to determine the "ideal type" of French philosopher of the Sixties.[2] I was trying to do much more. I was seeking the "point of diffraction" in this Sixties thinking, perhaps in thinking as such.[3] I was seeking a point—like a glimmering star—on which to focus; I was seeking a point—like a knot—to disentangle. The point that I found has, I think, to speak like Deleuze, the power on the basis of which one creates new concepts. Because of this power concentrated in this point, I have come to call this system of thought "the great French philosophy of the Sixties."

The point of diffraction in the great French philosophy of the Sixties is the experience of the question. Thus this moment refers back to the great German philosophy of the Twenties. When Heidegger re-opens the question of being, he defines being itself as a question: the question of being is the being of the question. In the famous Introduction to *Being and Time,* Heidegger, of course, did not have in mind the kind of question that is posed in school, where the teacher, knowing the answer to the question in advance, relinquishes the students of all responsibility for thinking. A genuine question has two characteristics. On the one hand, a genuine question demands to be left open, even left without a response. A genuine question must be a quest; this openness is why the question can account for the universality of being. On the other hand, a genuine question demands to be closed off, even answered once and for all. A genuine question must be able to be finished; this closure is why the question can account for the determination of being. A question therefore is fundamentally differentiated between openness and closure, between irresponsibility and responsibility. Difference therefore defines the being of the question. But this difference is not all. The experience of being interrogated is the experience of powerlessness. Thus it is always the experience of death; to answer the question is to bring the interrogation to an *end*. Yet, at that very *moment* of interrogation, a *space* opens up in which it is possible to find more answers, to live. In this paradoxical space, powerlessness and power, lack and excess, life and death are doubled. Only in the experience of the double is it possible to think. As the later Heidegger says, "what is most thought-provoking is that we are still not thinking."[4]

If the point of diffraction in the great French philosophy of the Sixties is the experience of the question, then the philosophy of Derrida, Deleuze, and Foucault is a philosophy of interrogation.[5] Throughout the essays collected here, I have deliberately chosen to call the great French philosophy of the Sixties—what one usually calls post-structuralism or post-modernism or deconstructionism or genealogy—"the philosophy of interrogation." I have done this because it seems to me that Merleau-Ponty, at the end of his life in 1961, had already found the point of diffraction in the experience of the question. We do not know how he would have completed *The Visible and the Invisible*. We do not know the direction that his thinking would have taken. But three things are clear. First, as is particularly evident in his 1960 course notes for Husserl's "The Origin of Geometry," Merleau-Ponty was conceiving his own philosophy as the "convergence" of phenomenology and ontology. This convergence explains the structure of *The Visible and the Invisible*. At once, Merleau-Ponty maintains a reduction to perceptual faith (Husserl), and he interprets the perceptual faith as interrogation (Heidegger). This convergence is most at work in Chapter 3, "Interrogation and Intuition." Second, Merleau-Ponty is about to make, in the Fifties, what we now commonly call "the linguistic turn." His investigation of Saussure's linguistics is well known. Thus we could say that he was on the verge, as well, of a convergence between phenomenology and structuralism. But, more importantly, like Derrida at virtually the same time, Merleau-Ponty had, as a result of his last investigation of Husserl's "The Origin of Geometry," come to recognize the constitutive role of language. Consequently, it looks as though Merleau-Ponty was about accept Heidegger's controversial claim that it is not man who speaks, but "die Sprache spricht." Again, it is not clear in what direction Merleau-Ponty would have taken his thinking. But it seems to me that there is one last thing that is clear. I think this is what makes Merleau-Ponty's final philosophy great. So, third, the "point of diffraction" appears "in person," "in the flesh" (*leibhaftig*), we might say, in Chapter 4 of *The Visible and the Invisible*, "The

Intertwining—The Chiasm." The fold of the chiasm is the paradox of the double. Perhaps this is the most important thing Merleau-Ponty wrote:

> Once we have entered this strange domain [of ideality], one does not see how there could be any question of *leaving* it. . . . [If] the thin pellicule of the quale, the surface of the visible, is doubled up [*doublée*] over its whole extension with an invisible reserve; and if finally, in our flesh as in the flesh of things, the actual, empirical, ontic visible, by a sort of folding back [*repliement*], invagination, or padding, exhibits a visibility, a possibility that is not the shadow of the actual but is its principle, that is not the proper contribution of a "thought" but is its condition, . . . then . . . there is to be sure a question as to how the "ideas of the intelligence" are initiated over and beyond, how from the ideality of the horizon one passes to the "pure" ideality, and in particular by what miracle a created generality, a culture, a knowledge come to add to and recapture and rectify the natural generality of my body and of the world. (VI 199–200/152, Merleau-Ponty's emphasis)

Because this "doubling up," "this folding back," is the point of diffraction of the great French philosophy of the Sixties, all of the essays collected here take place either explicitly or implicitly in dialogue with Merleau-Ponty.[6] Already in Merleau-Ponty, what is at stake in the philosophy of interrogation is thinking.

Thus, the purpose of *Thinking through French Philosophy* consists in establishing what *options* of thinking the philosophy of interrogation still makes available to us today. As the phrase "the point of diffraction" suggests, I have tried to develop a sort of *optics*. The first step in the development of this optics was to construct the system of thought of the great French philosophy of the Sixties in a schematic form. This schema always focuses on a lack (powerlessness). It is from this lack that the diffraction takes place. The attempt then at developing the diffraction (a second step) means that I established *oppositions* between Foucault and Derrida, between Derrida and Deleuze, between Merleau-Ponty and Derrida, Merleau-Ponty and Deleuze. Although I have established oppositions, I have tried never to take sides. Instead, I was interested in that fine point where one kind of thought turns into its opposite just as white turns into black. But, and this is truly what was difficult to do, I tried as well (a third step) to determine, with precision, the gradual change of the "more and less." Deleuze is more immanent, less transcendent, than Derrida. If the presence or absence of the dative relation—in French the preposition "à," in English "to"—defines the opposition between transcendence and immanence, then the French idiom "à même"—"à" plus "même," the other and the same—is the point where the transition occurs. This "à même" shows how gradual, how infinitesimal, the change occurs.

In the essays collected here, these three steps are not clearly delineated. Some of the essays are more oppositional; some are more infinitesimal. The first two essays—"'If Theory Is Gray, Green Is the Golden Tree of Life'" and "The Chiasm and the Fold"—attempt to develop the Foucault option of thinking. To do this, "'If Theory Is Gray, Green is the Golden Tree of Life'" presents an opposition between Foucault and Derrida from the standpoint of metaphysics, language, and time. "The Chiasm and the Fold," however, sets up a diffraction between Foucault and Merleau-Ponty through the concept of archeology. "The Chiasm and the Fold," in particular, presents us with the pre-history of the philosophical concept of archeology in Kant, Freud, and Husserl (or Fink). But, more importantly, it leads us to the spatialization of time, to a place, to two places: the earth and the archive. And these two places are different, the earth in Merleau-Ponty being the place of the fold (*le pli*) or the *mi-lieu* or the homoclite whereas the archive in Foucault being the place of the unfold (*le dépli*) or the *non-lieu* or the heteroclite. Moreover, the two Foucault essays themselves seem to be opposed since "If Theory Is Gray" concerns Foucault's genealogy, while "The Chiasm and the Fold" concerns his archeology. The assertion, however, that relates the two Foucault essays is unstated; despite the periodization that Foucault himself endorsed, Foucault's archeology and his genealogy are continuous. As he says in "What Is Enlightenment?" "[critique] is genealogical in its design and archeological in its method."[7] The archeological method for Foucault consists in locating the space of the "heteroclite," literally the "other-fold." Within this space, archeology is able to show us "the dispersion that we are" (AS 173/131); it enacts the destruction of the subject of knowledge (man) (NGH 170–72/162–64), and then allows—this is the genealogical purpose of archeology—new forms of subjectivity to be constituted through the care of the self. Indeed, in the final published volume of the *History of Sexuality*, Foucault shows that the relation between a man and a woman (marriage), the heterosexual relation, is actually a "homoclite," whereas the relation between a man and a boy (education), the homosexual relation, is actually a "heteroclite." It seems to me that we cannot understand the later Foucault without understanding the first Foucault.

In "The Chiasm and the Fold" Derrida's name does not appear, but the descriptions of Merleau-Ponty there allude to him. Thus, the next two essays —"Eliminating Some Confusion" and "The Legacy of Husserl's 'The Origin of Geometry'"—compare Derrida and Merleau-Ponty. In "Eliminating Some Confusion," an attempt is made to oppose Merleau-Ponty and Derrida by means of the concept of form. Formalization is really the ineradicable opposition between Merleau-Ponty and Derrida. By means of this opposition, we are able to eliminate the confusion between Merleau-Ponty and Derrida. Whereas Merleau-Ponty in "Indirect Language and the Voices of Silence" claims that the museum is the inauthentic historicity—because only the forms of the paintings remain and not the lived experience of the single task of painting—Derrida claims, as in *Voice and Phenomenon* (VP 24–25/ 23–24), that the relation between authentic and inauthentic, proper and improper, are always interwoven. Yet, now we have the course notes for one of Merleau-Ponty's final courses at the Collège du France, a course on Husserl's last fragmentary writings: "Husserl at the Limits of Phenomenology." These notes are complicated and ambiguous. Yet, it seems that, if we compare them with the chapter on Husserl in *La Nature* and "The Philosopher and His Shadow," we can see that the really important final Husserl text for Merleau-Ponty is "The Earth Does Not Move," and not "The Origin of Geometry." That it looks as though "The Earth Does Not Move" is the more important text provides more evidence for the difference between Merleau-Ponty and Derrida, a difference focused on formalization or even "technologization." The earth that does not move, for Merleau-Ponty, precedes formalization; it is *soil* (*Boden*). This difference between soil and form means that "Eliminating Some Confusion" is, if we can say this, the more "accurate" of the two essays collected here on Merleau-Ponty and Derrida, even though the second essay is more mature and more interesting philosophically. Thus "The Legacy of Husserl's 'Origin of Geometry'" starts from the recognition that, when Merleau-Ponty lectures on "The Origin of Geometry" in "Husserl at the Limits of Phenomenology," he, like Derrida, recognizes the essential necessity of writing. This necessity allows us to consider again a confusion between Merleau-Ponty and Derrida. Thus "The Legacy of Husserl's 'The Origin of Geometry'" establishes an infinitesimal difference between Derrida and Merleau-Ponty across the concepts of interrogation and faith. This gradual transition from Merleau-Ponty to Derrida is possible because both accept and extend Husserl's greatest phenomenological insight from the Fifth Cartesian Meditation, that is, that I can never have a presentation (a *Gegenwärtigung*) of the other's interior life, but only ever a representation (a *Vergegenwärtigung*). Indeed, the generalization of this phenomenological insight is Derrida's most defining principle.

We can see both this opposition and gradual differentiation again, if we look at Derrida's most recent (2000) and most detailed investigation of Merleau-Ponty in *Le Toucher—Jean-Luc Nancy.*[8] Here in "Tangente III," the focus is on *Fremderfahrung*. Derrida stresses that Merleau-Ponty in "The Philosopher and His Shadow" seems to succumb to an "intuitionism," which would consist in thinking that I could have immediate access to the other.[9] Derrida even claims that Merleau-Ponty's intuitionism is unfaithful to Husserl.[10] Here we have the ineradicable opposition between Derrida and Merleau-Ponty—and this "dry" question of form is also how one could explain Derrida's early criticisms of Merleau-Ponty in his Introduction to "The Origin of Geometry" (see LOG 114–20/110–14). For Derrida, the *Vergegenwärtigung* is always formal, whereas for Merleau-Ponty it is a content (like an intuition) demanding to be put into a form. Yet, in the same "Tangente," Derrida also suggests an infinitesimal difference. He quotes a working note to *The Visible and the Invisible* from 1960 (VI 307–8/254), in which Merleau-Ponty claims that "something other than the body" is needed to make the junction of the touching and the touched, a "something other" that is not "mind" or "consciousness," that is "untouchable" and also "invisible." In other words, this "something other" is "not presentable" due to an irreducible mediation. Derrida then comments on the quote by saying, "What is Merleau-Ponty designating with this 'something other than the body,' and which is not mind or consciousness? Never will we be closer to what [Jean-Luc] Nancy . . . shares here with Merleau-Ponty. Nor will we ever be closer to that on the basis of which other things they share, other proximities and other distributions are also to be delineated."[11] Needless to say, if this quote about the untouchable brings us closer to what Merleau-Ponty shares with Nancy, it also brings us closer to what Merleau-Ponty shares with Derrida.

But it is perhaps possible that Merleau-Ponty shares more with Deleuze than Derrida, and this is what the next essay considers. The critique that Deleuze makes of phenomenology presents us with the defining principle of Deleuze's philosophy: the foundation can never resemble what it founds. This principle allows us to see a gradual differentiation between Deleuze and Merleau-Ponty. Like Deleuze, Merleau-Ponty in *Phenomenology of Perception,* as is well known, speaks of expression and uses the phrase "a past that was never present" (at the end of the "Sentir" chapter). Through a certain interpretation of these concepts, which attempts to define them without any concept of resemblance, it is possible to claim that the transcendental field in Merleau-Ponty's *Phenomenology of Perception* is composed of what Deleuze calls pre-personal singularities. If this claim is true, then Merleau-Ponty's transcendental field is an infinite plane of immanence. And then the following claim from "Everywhere and Nowhere" becomes important:

> The extraordinary harmony of external and internal is possible only
> through the mediation of a *positive infinite* or (since every restriction to
> a certain kind of infinity would be a seed of negation) an infinite infinite.
> It is in this positive infinite that the actual existence of things *partes extra*

partes and extension as we think of it (which on the contrary is continuous and infinite) communicate or are joined together. If, at the center and so to speak in the kernel of Being, there is an infinite infinite, every partial being directly or indirectly presupposes it, and is in return really or eminently contained in it. (S 187/148–49, Merleau-Ponty's emphasis)

But the claim that Merleau-Ponty's transcendental field is an infinite plane of immanence is limited. Merleau-Ponty's *Phenomenology of Perception,* like his entire philosophy including *The Visible and the Invisible,* is based in a decentering of subjectivity by means of intersubjectivity: it consists in a dative relation. We return again to the insight of the Fifth Cartesian Meditation. The very insight that allows us to draw Merleau-Ponty and Derrida together is, however, the very thing that allows us to oppose Merleau-Ponty and Deleuze. The following comment from Deleuze has been, in these essays, the principle by means of which many of the oppositions were established:

> Knowledge [in Foucault] is Being, the first figure of Being, but Being lies between two forms. Is this not precisely what Heidegger called the "between-two" or Merleau-Ponty termed the "interlacing or chiasmus"? *In fact, they are not at all the same.* For Merleau-Ponty, the interlacing or the between-two merges with the fold. But not for Foucault. . . . Everything takes place as though Foucault were reproaching Heidegger and Merleau-Ponty for going too fast. (F 119/111–12, my emphasis)

"The End of Ontology," the second essay on Deleuze and Merleau-Ponty, relies on this comment, but also attempts to follow another comment that Deleuze makes in his Foucault book, that is, that Foucault's "major conversion" is the conversion of phenomenology into epistemology (F 117/109). The result of following this comment is that "The End of Ontology" is the most controversial essay in this volume. It seems to me that it is controversial in at least two ways. On the one hand, it is controversial in light of the recent renewal of interest in classical phenomenological research. Its first sentence announces that "the phenomenological philosophy of Edmund Husserl is at an end."[12] It seems to me that this claim should not be so controversial since, as we have known for a long time from Heidegger, phenomenology ends in ontology. Extending this Heideggerian development, "The End of Ontology" shows that ontology has two possible and opposed ends. Merleau-Ponty's idea of perceptual faith is one end, the end of ontology in religion. And here we must recognize a very Derridean (and perhaps Levinasian) interpretation of Merleau-Ponty. The other end of ontology is Deleuze's idea of learning, the end of ontology in epistemology. We have before us then the opposition of faith and knowledge. We arrive at both of these ends by means of a reflection on interrogation. Interrogation on the Merleau-Ponty side is sympathy for the weakness of the other, whereas interrogation on the Deleuze side is cruelty in relation to the weakness of the other. I think that this claim about cruelty is also what makes "The End of Ontology" controversial. Yet, it is important to keep in mind that cruelty is *only* one of the expressions of power. As Deleuze stressed as early as *Nietzsche and Philosophy,* power can always be transmuted; it can always be expressed in multiple ways. As Nietzsche says,

> The justice that began with, "everything is dischargeable, everything must be discharged," ends [*endet*] by winking and letting those incapable of discharging their debt go free: it ends, as does every good thing on earth, by *overcoming itself.* This self-overcoming of justice: one knows the beautiful name it has given itself—*mercy;* it goes without saying that mercy remains the privilege of the most powerful man, or better, his—beyond the law.[13]

Mercy is perhaps the greatest expression of power.

Because Merleau-Ponty is opposed to Deleuze by means of faith and religion, we are able to oppose Derrida to Deleuze. The opposition between Derrida and Deleuze is an opposition that begins with their respective first philosophical inspirations: Husserl and Bergson. But, within their own philosophies, the opposition extends along four trajectories: destruction versus deconstruction; purity versus contamination; fiction understood as the virtual image versus fiction understood as the trace; and intuition versus language. The first term of each couple represents Deleuze's position, while the second represents that of Derrida. This last opposition, between intuition and language, which I adopted from Derrida's *Voice and Phenomenon* (see VP 16/16), suggests that Deleuze (unlike Foucault and Derrida) does not have his starting point in the experience of language. Yet, this suggestion is incorrect. With intuition here what I am trying to show is that Deleuze experiences language first as a formless immediacy (again we find only an infinitesimal difference from Merleau-Ponty), a formless immediacy of sense: noise. And in the Deleuzian experience of noise, there is death. Thus we are again at the point of diffraction, which brings us to the final essay, "The Beginnings of Thought." This essay attempts to investigate the point in its finest differentiation, taking note of all the similarities in the thought of Derrida and Deleuze: the paradox of the double; the appropriations and critiques of Husserl's phenomenology; the appropriations of Lévi-Strauss's concept of a floating signifier; the connection of the concept of sense to time; and finally the experience of death in interrogation. Because, between Derrida and Deleuze, we have the smallest of differences, we have had to construct difficult formulas for the options that each of them represent. Derrida's option is a thought of mediated unity, whereas Deleuze's option is a thought of immediate duality. Derrida's option is the thought of self-interrogation, which the other contaminates, whereas Deleuze's option is the thought of interrogation by an other, which dissolves the self. The similarity of these formulas indicates that the diffraction between Derrida and Deleuze keeps threatening to disappear into the point.

As I said, all of the essays collected here take place either explicitly or implicitly in dialogue with Merleau-Ponty. Thus throughout the writing of these essays, I have always tried to keep firmly in mind this comment from Merleau-Ponty's "Indirect Language and the Voices of Silence":

> Husserl has used the fine word *Stiftung*—foundation or establishment—to designate first of all the unlimited fecundity of each present which, precisely, because it is singular and passes, can never stop having been and thus being universally; but above all to designate that fecundity of the products of a culture which continue to have value after their appearance and which open a field of investigations in which they perpetually come to life again [*où ils revivent perpétuellement*]. It is thus that the world as soon as he has seen it, his first attempt at painting, and the whole past of painting all deliver up a *tradition* to the painter—*that is,* Husserl remarks, *the power to forget origins* and to give to the past not a survival [*une survie*], which is the hypocritical form of forgetfulness, but a new life, which is the noble form of memory. (S 73–74/59, Merleau-Ponty's emphasis)

But it is not just Merleau-Ponty's shadow that is cast across each of these pages. I have also taken seriously Foucault's comment at the end of his inaugural address to the Collège de France in 1970: "Jean Hyppolite has formulated the most fundamental problems of our epoch" (OD 80/237; cf. EU 136). Although the point of diffraction appears in person in Merleau-Ponty, this point finds its highest condensation in Hyppolite, in his 1952 *Logic and Existence.* At the beginning of Part II of *Logic and Existence,* Hyppolite stresses that Hegel's thought is really similar to that of Nietzsche. The proclamation that "God is dead" means that there is no second intelligible world behind the first phenomenal world; there is no transcendent "beyond." Hyppolite says,

> Hegelian logic recognizes neither the thing-in-itself nor the intelligible world. The Absolute is not thought anywhere else than in the phenomenal world. Absolute thought thinks itself in our thought. In our thought, being presents itself as thought and as sense. And Hegel's dialectical logic, like the logic of philosophy, is the expression of complete immanence. (LE 70/58–59)

But Hyppolite even condenses the point down to one sentence: "Immanence is complete" (LE 230/176).[14] We might say that this sentence is the most perfect expression of the paradox of the double, of the point of diffraction. But we could also express it by borrowing a quote from Goethe's *Faust*: "If theory is gray, green is the golden tree of life."

1 "If Theory Is Gray, Green Is the Golden Tree of Life"

Philosophy and Non-philosophy since Hyppolite

Derrida's claim that "the problem of language will never [be] simply one problem among others" (DLG 15/6) could be used to define what we are calling "French philosophy of the Sixties."[1] In the Fifties, however, there were three signs heralding the approach of this philosophical movement. The first sign is Jean Hyppolite's *Logic and Existence*, which being a book on Hegel's logic begins with philosophy of language; indeed, Hyppolite calls Hegel's logic a "logic of sense" (LE 221/170, 228/175).[2] The second sign is Maurice Merleau-Ponty's "Indirect Language and the Voices of Silence," which being one of the first discussions of Saussure's linguistics ends up investigating silence; indeed, Merleau-Ponty claims that language expresses as much by what it does not say as by what it does say (S 56/45). Lastly, there is Martial Gueroult's *Descartes's Philosophy Interpreted According to the Order of Reasons*, which aiming to respect both the soul and style of Descartes's *Meditations* ends up analyzing the structure of the work; indeed, Gueroult calls the work a "monument."[3] Hyppolite's book, Merleau-Ponty's essay, and Gueroult's study, all three of which appeared in 1952, provided a spectrum of philosophical possibilities. In 1969 Michel Foucault places Hyppolite in the middle of it:

> Hyppolite intentionally put his own project into confrontation with two of the great works which were contemporaneous with him . . . : that of Merleau-Ponty, which was the investigation of the originary articulation of sense and existence and that of Gueroult, which was the axiomatic analysis of coherence and philosophical structures. Between these two benchmarks, Hyppolite's work has always been, from the beginning, the attempt to name and to bring to light—in a discourse at once philosophical and historical—the point where the tragedy of life makes sense in a *Logos*, where the genesis of a thought becomes the structure of a system, where existence finds itself articulated in a Logic. Between a phenomenology of pre-discursive experience—à la Merleau-Ponty—and an epistemology of philosophical systems—as we find in Gueroult—Hyppolite's work can be

read as a phenomenology of philosophical rigor as well as an epistemology of philosophically reflected existence. (EU 782–83)

Foucault is giving us here a spectrum, a diffraction, of philosophical options with Hyppolite in the middle. The "middle" that Hyppolite's name represents is expressed by one comment from *Logic and Existence:* "immanence is complete" (LE 230/176). The announcement of the completion of immanence is why Foucault states (again in 1969) that Hyppolite's *Logic and Existence* formulates "all the problems which are ours" (EU 785). The most basic problem is this: how to conceive, within immanence, the difference between logic and existence (the Logos and time), structure and genesis, thought and experience, the said and the unsaid, monument and soul, philosophy and non-philosophy. All of the great French philosophy from the Sixties amounts to a series of solutions to this most basic problem. Therefore, while in the Fifties Hyppolite occupied a middle between a phenomenology of pre-discursive experience and an epistemology of philosophical systems, in the the Sixties, the spectrum, so to speak, narrows to a point with the result that Derrida, Deleuze, and Foucault themselves form a spectrum *across* the "middle" called "Hyppolite." Thirty years later, our task is clear: in order to construct new philosophical concepts—beyond *différance,* the trace, and deconstruction; beyond difference, repetition, and construction; beyond the statement, force, and genealogy—we must determine the philosophical options that expand across the "Hyppolite" middle. We are going to begin with Foucault.

I. Only If Theory Is Gray, Then the Golden Tree of Life Is Green

It is possible to determine with some confidence the philosophical connection between Foucault and Hyppolite since Foucault has written, at least briefly, about Hyppolite explicitly: his 1969 eulogy "Jean Hyppolite. 1907–1968" (from which I quoted above) and the end of his 1970 inaugural address at the Collège de France, *L'Ordre du discourse.* These two works reinforce one another in their attempt to define Hyppolite's "philosophical and historical discourse." Hyppolite's enterprise, according to Foucault, is not that of a historian of philosophy (EU 780) and not that of a historian of Hegel's philosophy (OD 76/236). Instead, Hyppolite is a historian of "philosophic thought" (EU 780); as such, he brings about "displacements" in Hegel's philosophy (OD 77/236). The displacements come about as responses to the one question that guides this history of philosophic thought: "what is philosophical finitude?" (EU 781). For Foucault, philosophical finitude refers to the limits that particular philosophies fix and always trangress, the limits of their beginnings and of their ends (EU 781). Hegel's philosophy, in particular, marks for Hyppolite the moment when philosophy "became entitled to the problem of its beginning and its completion" (*achèvement*) (EU 784). Particular philosophies always transgress the limits of beginning and end because of the type of relation that philosophy has with non-philosophy. Foucault claims that philosophy maintains a relation with what it is not—science or everyday life, religion or justice, desire or death (EU 783)—that is at once interior, already there silently inhabiting non-philosophy, and exterior, never necessarily implicated by any science or practice (EU 783). This very specific sort of relation means that philosophy itself never actualizes itself in any discourse or system (EU 780). Either a philosophic discourse is interior to non-philosophy and therefore is not yet itself but still death; or it is exterior to non-philosophy, and therefore it is itself, but as philosophy it loses contact with what gave it life (EU 784). Since philosophy itself never actualizes itself in any particular discourse or work, philosophy for Hyppolite becomes a "task without endpoint [*sans terme*]" (OD 77/236). Never complete, philosophic thought is devoted to the "paradox of repetition,"[4] and the paradox, according to Foucault, takes the form of a "question that is constantly taken up again in life, death, and memory" (OD 77/236).[5] According to Foucault, therefore, Hyppolite transforms "the Hegelian theme of the completion of self-consciousness into a theme of repetitive interrogation" (OD 77/236).

When Foucault states that Hyppolite transforms Hegel's conception of philosophy into a "task without endpoint," Foucault interprets this task as "a task always rebegun [*recommencée*]" (OD 77/236). Moreover, he says that philosophy in Hyppolite "re-establishes contact with non-philosophy," approaches "as close as possible not to what completes it but to what precedes" (OD 78/236; cf. EU 782). What is at issue, therefore, in Foucault's own philosophy is the re-beginning of philosophy (and not its end or ends); hence the importance of the word "archeology" in Foucault (and not eschatology). The archeological concern is why he asks, "What is the beginning of philosophy?" (OD 78/236). In the eulogy, Foucault answers this question by saying that philosophic thought in Hyppolite is the "moment when philosophic discourse makes up its mind, uproots itself from its refusal to speak [*mutism*], and distances itself from what henceforth is going to appear as non-philosophy" (EU 780, cf. 783). What the historian of philosophic thought must do is enter into this moment. When that happens, one enters into the space of philosophy itself, which systematically erases one's own subjectivity (EU 781). The historian of philosophic thought remembers in the Bergsonian sense; "one has to form the sharp point, actual and free, of a past which has lost nothing of its being; one regrasps one's shadow by a sort of self-torsion" (EU 782). This memorial moment, in which one loses one's subjectivity and thus turns this memorial moment into a moment of counter-memory, is when discourse becomes the voice of no one (*personne*) (EU 779; OD 7/215, 81/237; LE 6/5); it becomes gray, and *then* it is possible "to open [a philosophic work up and] . . . deploy it" so that it lives (EU 781). Foucault therefore concludes his eulogy by saying that, with Hyppolite, it is always necessary to recall that "if theory is gray, green is the golden tree of life" (EU 785).

This sentence—"If theory is gray, green is the golden tree of life"—alludes to lines 2038–39 from Goethe's *Faust* (Part I, "Study"). Hegel quotes these lines in the chapter on Reason in *The Phenomenology of Spirit* (in particular, paragraph 360), and Hyppolite emphasizes them in his analysis of Hegel's so-called "philosophy of language" in *Logic and Existence*, Part 1. But, what is most important is that Foucault changes the structure of the sentence. In the Goethe original and in Hegel and in Hyppolite, the sentence is a conjunction: "theory is gray and green is the golden tree of life"; in Foucault's reformulation, it is a conditional: "if theory is gray, green is the golden tree of life." For Hyppolite, interpreting Hegel, this sentence, uttered by Faust, represents a decision to attempt "a turn back" (*un retour en arrière*) from knowledge, mediation, and language to experience, immediacy, and silence (LE 19–21/16–18). Gretchen and Faust, in other words, represent the type of consciousness that despises "the understanding and science, the supreme gifts of man" (lines 1850–51). For Hyppolite, by "turning back" to the immediacy of pleasure, as Mephisto recommends, this type of consciousness thinks that it is plunging headfirst from dead theory into life itself, but, as Hegel shows, actually it is rushing straight into mute experience, into the ineffable, into indeterminateness. In short, this consciousness goes into the ground: *zu Grunde gehen*. Instead of plunging into concrete particularity, this consciousness ends up in abstract universality; instead of ending up in life, it ends up in death. For Foucault, however, changing the structure from a conjunction to a conditional, this sentence represents a necessity to attempt to re-begin, to return (cf. PD 534/34). For Foucault, it is necessary that theory be gray; *if* theory is gray, *then* the golden tree of life is green. In other words, in this formulation, life's enhancement depends necessarily on theory being gray; theory must become gray. In order for theory to become gray, for Foucault, one must enter into the ineffable experience that Foucault in *Histoire de la folie à l'âge classique* called madness. The truth of Hegel's discussion, as presented by Hyppolite, is that the subject goes into the ground in such a moment of pleasure. In his 1966 essay on Blanchot, "The Thought from the Outside," Foucault, speaking of Ulysses, describes the moment in the following way:

> In order for the narrative that will never die to be born, one must listen but remain at the mast, wrists and ankles tied; one must vanquish all desire by

a ruse that does violence to itself; one must experience all suffering by remaining at the threshold of the alluring abyss; one must finally find oneself beyond song, as if one had crossed death while still alive only to restore it in a second language. (PD 538/42)

Madness alone occurs if one only rushes to the sirens and does not remain tied to the mast; not to remain tied is stupidity and even suicide (cf. DR 197–98/152). What Ulysses experiences instead, as he remains tied to the mast and listening, is madness bent into thought. He experiences philosophic thought or the thought from the outside. The silence into which Ulysses enters is not subjective and interior; it is a "mutism," a refusal to speak, which allows one to listen. This "ruse" or experiment which problematizes desire places one "this side" (not beyond) the limit of discourse, in "the placeless place" (PD 537/52), in "the interstices" (OD 7/215), in forces (PD 525/27), in what must be called the "informal" (*informel*) (F 120/112–13, 129/121). In the placeless place, death is partial and continuous with life; here, one dies, *on meurt* (F 102/95). Only by crossing death in this sense, only by living as the set of functions which resist death (RR 71/54; F 102/95),[6] can one hear the voice of "no one," *personne* (which is not the voice of the subject called "Ulysses"). Only then will the narrative that will never die be born. Only then, subjectless, does discourse become a monument of this singular moment; only then do forces get folded, pleasure used, ethics invented.[7] Only if theory is gray, then the golden tree of life is green.

II. Foucault's Three Great Concepts:
Metaphysics, the Actual, and Genealogy

Any attempt to determine the Foucaultian option of the "Hyppolite" middle must include a discussion of Foucault's famous 1971 essay "Nietzsche, Genealogy, History," which was first published in a volume entitled *Hommage à Jean Hyppolite*. In fact, the color gray can be used to define the three great concepts that Foucault presents in this essay. The first great concept is that of metaphysics. Metaphysics is not gray; it is blue. To say that the color of metaphysics is blue for Foucault means that its gaze is skyward, "lofty and profound" (NGH 146/140), toward "distances and heights" (NGH 162/155). In regard to history, metaphysics adopts a supra-historical perspective (NGH 159/152, 167/160). Foucault provides two names for the supra-historical perspective: Platonism (NGH 167/160) and Egyptianism (NGH 159/152, 163/156). What joins these two together, for Foucault (following Nietzsche), is Socrates. Egyptianism is the belief in the immortality of the soul, the proclamation of the existence of a "beyond" as a promise of a reward (NGH

162/156), a "millennial end" (NGH 160/154). Socrates accepts this Egyptian religious belief. What then defines Platonism, according to Foucault, is its success in "founding" the religious belief (*d'être parvenu à la* [*la croyance à l'immortalité*] *fonder*) (NGH 167/160). Platonism founds the belief in the immortality of the soul by means of universals (NGH 165/158), objectivity (NGH 165/158), and the certainty of absolutes (NGH 159/153). Relying on universals, objectivity, and the certainty of absolutes, metaphysics conceives history in a number of ways: "the meta-historical deployment of ideal meaning and indefinite teleologies" (NGH 146/140); "monotonous purposiveness" (NHG 145/139); "to bring to light slowly a meaning buried within the origin (NGH 158/151); "a teleological movement or natural structuration" (NGH 161/154); "the obscure work of a destination . . . the anticipatory power of sense" (NGH 155/148). Foucault specifies these formulations by examining the historian's concept of origin (exact essence or identity of things, greatest perfection, purest possibility, site where truth corresponded to discourse) (NGH 148–49/142–43), the historian's concepts of event (recognition, reconciliation, successive forms of a primordial intention, and ideal continuity) (NGH 159/152, 161/154), and the historian's conception of end (result, totality fully closed in on itself) (NGH 161/154, 159/152). These conceptions of origin, event, and end imply what Foucault calls an "inversion of the relationship of will and knowledge" (NGH 165/158). This inversion is "hypocritical" because it hides a perspective behind a fiction or lie of eternal truth. The inversion takes place by "bridling," "by fighting relentlessly against" one's individual will (silencing preferences, surmounting distaste, miming death) in order to show to others the inevitable law of a superior will (NGH 165/158). This inevitable law of a superior will—"Providence, . . . final causes" (NGH 165/158)—is that toward which metaphysics gazes. Metaphysics therefore for Foucault supports history with an "apocalyptic objectivity"; in other words, it gives support to history from "outside of time" (NGH 159/152).

Foucault's second great concept is what Nietzsche calls the "historical sense" or "actual history" (*l'histoire effective, wirkliche Historie*). Actual history takes no support from the outside of time; it is, as the phrase suggests, actual, not ideal or possible or universal history. Insofar as actual, this history without support from the outside of time "can escape from metaphysics" (NGH 159/152–53; cf. also NGH 167/160). In other words, actual history is history without a foundation and in this regard is anti-Platonistic; actual history, Foucault says, "hollows out that upon which we like to make history rest" (NGH 160/154). It inserts all of what we believed immortal in man back into mortality and in this regard is anti-Egyptianistic (NGH 159/160). Lacking a foundation and the immortality of the soul, actual history, for Foucault, allows for no consoling play of self-recognitions (*reconnaissances, nous retrouver*) (NGH 160/153). Rather than understanding (*Verstehen*), actual history is concerned with "slicing," that is, with making discontinuities. The traditional relation between necessary continuity and the irruption of an event then is inverted in actual history; an event is always a reversal of the relations of forces, the usurpation of power, the appropriation of a vocabulary turned against those who used it: events are chance, accidental, or aleatory conflicts and not modifications of an ideal meaning (NGH 161/154). The result of the inversion in favor of chance events is that actual history consists, instead of origin, in descent—unentangleable systems of racial traits and inscribed bodies—and, instead of end, it consists in emergence—the current episode in a series of subjugations or in diverse systems of subjugation. Actual history also inverts the relation of distance and proximity. Actual history consists in the close—the body, the nervous system, nutrition, digestion, and energies. Like a doctor, it has no fear of looking down, instead of gazing upward like the metaphysician (NGH 162/155–56). Being unafraid of looking down, actual history is also unafraid of being perspectival knowledge (NGH 163/156–57). Unlike the historian influenced by metaphysics, the historical sense in Nietzsche, according to Foucault, does not "bridle" its will in favor of the form of an eternal will. It looks from a certain angle, with the deliberate purpose of appreciating, of saying "yes" or "no." It does not reject the system of its own injustice (NGH 163/157). Supporting itself therefore on no constants, actual history, for Foucault, systematically shatters all of that with which we back ourselves in order to grasp history in its totality (NGH 160/153; cf. also NGH 167/160).

Genealogy, the third great concept of "Nietzsche, Genealogy, History," does not, of course, attempt to grasp history in its totality. In fact, genealogy, for Foucault, makes a "use of history which frees [*affranchisse*] history forever from the simultaneously metaphysical and anthropological model of memory"; it produces "a wholly other form of time in history" (NGH 167/ 160).[8] A "wholly other form of time," for Foucault, has two characteristics. On the one hand, a wholly other form of time is time not grasped from the outside of time; instead, there is only becoming (or immanence). Everything becomes actual, not ideal or possible; that everything becomes actual means that everything is presence. Presence here must be understood on the basis of the second characteristics of a wholly other form of time, discontinuity. As actual, that is, as *wirklich* or *effective*, presence is what effectuates discontinuity. To say that presence is understood on the basis of the second characteristic, discontinuity, means that presence is not based on the form of the present.[9] Here presence is not the being that metaphysics "lies" into becoming. The metaphysical lie consists in the belief that the form of the present is the means of measurement and comparison of all experiences: the form of the present determines all experience, which allows for the recognition of the same object from the past in the present and for the anticipation of the same object from the past in the future. The myth is that the form of the present produces continuity by mediating all experience, by relativizing present and future experience to what has been experienced within the boundaries of this form. In contrast, the wholly other form of time is time which has no form (cf. F 120/113);[10] it is time as the "non-place" (cf. NGH 156/150). The informality of time—its grayness—is why Foucault says that what is at issue in genealogy is to turn history into a "counter-memory" (NGH 167/160); what is at issue in genealogy is to forget the form of the present.

Foucault specifies this forgetting in his discussion of the three genealogical uses of history with which he closes "Nietzsche, Genealogy, History." Foucault is clear that he is charting a change in Nietzsche's thinking from an earlier position expressed in the 1874 *On the Use and Abuse of History for Life* in which Nietzsche criticized the three modes of historical investigations for having "barred access to the present intensities and creations of life" (NGH 168/161) to a later position in the 1880s in which genealogy amounts to an extreme "bending" (*ployer*) of the modes of historical investigations to a new use (NGH 158/151–52). Based on this change in Nietzsche's thinking, genealogy, for Foucault, must "bend" history into another form of time and at the same time "unbend" (*déployer*) another form of time in history (NGH 167/160). This *ployer* and *déployer* is why Foucault designates the three specific genealogical uses of history with a positive name—parodic, dissociative, and sacrificial—and why he also calls each use "destructive" (NGH 167/160). To use history positively, to bend it into a wholly other form of time, history must unbend; its metaphysical foundation must be destroyed. Each of the three uses of history, according to Foucault, extends the mode of history—monumental, antiquarian, and critical—so far that it destroys itself.

The parodic and destructive use enacts this "bending-unbending" of history insofar as it is concerned with the past. It opposes the theme of reminiscence and recognition (*reconnaissance*); to be opposed to the theme of recognition means to be opposed to recognition of a reality from the past. In other words, parodying the figures of the past "irrealizes" them or strips them of their past present in order that they "do not stop returning" (NGH 168/161). If history aimed at remembering only a past reality, the past would never be able to return since it would be merely a past present, over and done with; if history aimed at remembering an "essence" lost at the origin (NGH 168/161), the essence would be able to return only once since it would be a perpetual present. "The great carnival of time" (NGH 168/161), however, allows the past to return eternally. Indeed, what Foucault is discussing at the end of "Nietzsche, Genealogy, History" is Nietzsche's doctrine of eternal return, a doctrine in which forgetfulness becomes synonymous with absolute memory (cf. F 115/107). Only a memory not relative to a past reality, as in the parodic use of history, can open the future.

The dissociative and destructive use enacts the "bending-unbending" of history insofar as it concerns the present. It opposes continuity and tradition; to be opposed to continuity and tradition means to be opposed to the continuity of identity. In other words, dissociation "de-synthesizes" the past identities establishing continuity in the present in order to pluralize them (NGH 169/161). In the dissociative use of history, these identities are constituted by heterogeneous and complex systems of elements which are in turn multiple and distinct; our fellow creatures from the past are determined since they were produced necessarily by these systems and are modifiable since they were produced by countless numbers of systems. The heterogeneous and complex systems in which past identities consist forbid us all identity in the present. So, although metaphysical history promises a return to a first fatherland because it recognizes the continuities of soil, language, and urban life in which our present is rooted (NGH 169/162), the dissociative use of history "is bent" (*s'acharner*) on dissipating the land, scattering the roots, without any promise of a return.

Finally, the sacrificial and destructive use enacts the "bending-unbending" of history insofar as it concerns the future. It opposes history as *connaissance*, that is, history as a history of conscious science and scientists. To be opposed to history as *connaissance* then means to be opposed to the subject of *connaissance* (NGH 170/162). In other words, sacrificing "interrogates" the subject to discover the forms and transformations of the will to knowledge (*la volonté de savoir*) (NGH 170/162). The sacrificial use of history brings to light that *connaissance* rests upon the will to *savoir*, which is injustice—cruel subtlety, the inquisitor's tenacity (*acharnement*)—and that the instinct for *connaissance*, the will to *savoir*, is bad (NGH 170/163). The will to *savoir* carries with it an always greater tenacity, and the instinctive violence in it is always accelerating and growing (NGH 171/163). The always greater tenacity and always growing violence in which the will to *savoir* consists forbids the subject of *connaissance* from being neutral, from being devoid of passion, from being tenaciously attached (*acharnée*) to truth. So, while metaphysical history believes that *savoir* slowly detaches itself from its empirical roots (in needs) in order to become pure speculation subject only to the requirements of reason, the sacrificial use of history calls upon the subject to experiment on itself with the result that it, that is, we, may end up perishing for *connaissance*. Here Foucault quotes the following comment from Nietzsche's *Beyond Good and Evil:* "to perish [Foucault's French is *perir,* but Nietzsche's German is *zu Grunde gehen*] through absolute knowledge may well form a part of the foundation of being" (NGH 171/163–64). On the basis of this quote, we can see why Foucault included this essay in a volume devoted to the memory of Jean Hyppolite. "Nietzsche, Genealogy, History" bends and unbends Hegelianism toward a "going into the ground," into the experience of the informal, into the experience of immediacy, into madness,[11] into death so that "the narrative that will never die is born." Indeed, the sentence with which Foucault closed his eulogy for Hyppolite, "if theory is gray, green is the golden tree of life," could have been this essay's epigram because the essay's first sentence is "Genealogy is gray" (NGH 145/139).[12]

III. The Diffraction between Foucault and Derrida

Foucault chooses to write about Nietzsche in order to pay homage to Hyppolite because Hyppolite had claimed that with Hegel's philosophy "immanence is complete" (LE 230/176) and the completion of immanence (or the elimination of transcendence), as Hyppolite himself knew (LE 69/57), is what Nietzsche's saying "God is dead" means. Hyppolite expresses Hegel's completion of immanence, however, in the following way (from the Conclusion to *Logic and Existence*): "This passage from history to absolute knowledge, the passage from the temporal to the eternal is Hegelianism's most obscure dialectical synthesis. . . . The Logos is absolute genesis, and time is the image of this mediation, not the reverse" (LE 246/188). All of the solutions developed in the Sixties to the problem of how to conceive difference within immanence consist in *reversing* this relation of the Logos and time. The different ways in which one can reverse the relation of Logos and time (the relation of logic and existence) define the diffraction of philosophical options that the name "Hyppolite" represents. If we briefly look now at Foucault in comparison to Derrida, we can construct two of the different logics of the reversal of the Logos and time. As we shall see, it is not insignificant that Derrida chose to honor Hyppolite with an essay on Hegel—his "The Pit and the Pyramid: Introduction to Hegel's Semiology"—rather than an essay on Nietzsche.[13]

We can begin to see the different logics of reversal most clearly if we examine how Foucault and Derrida define metaphysics. For both Derrida and Foucault, Hegel's philosophy counts as metaphysics insofar as it maintains the priority of the Logos as the original over time as the image. For Derrida, however, Hegel's philosophy belongs to "the metaphysics of presence" (MP 82/71). The Logos is defined as knowledge of presence, even pure presence (logocentrism), while time is defined as non-presence. For Derrida therefore, to reverse the priority of the Logos and time is to prioritize temporal mediation. In contrast, for Foucault, as we have seen, Hegel's philosophy (still related to Plato-nism) belongs to the metaphysics of a supra-historical perspective. The Logos is defined as belief in non-presence, while time is defined as presence. For Foucault, therefore, to reverse the priority of the Logos and time is to priori-tize temporal immediacy.

As is well known, Derrida in his early writings always defines metaphysics in terms of what happens to the sign. For Derrida, metaphysics is defined by the sign being considered as a mere passage for presence (MP 82/71). The prioritization of temporal mediation for Derrida then means the prioritization of the sign. Through a reflection therefore on language oriented by *écriture*—whose primary characteristic is indefinite iterability—Derrida transforms the metaphysical concept of the sign into that of the trace. The trace (as in Levinas) is the trace of the other or others. For Derrida, the trace does not present the interior life of the other; to use the language of phenomenology, the trace's mode of presentation is always that of *Vergegenwärtigung* (repre-sentation) (cf. VP 54/49), a kind of intuition of absence (cf. MP 96/83). For Derrida, because the trace is always an intuition of an absent life, the trace is always a funerary monument. As is well known, this funerary monument, hieroglyphics, is both the condition for the possibility of life and its condition of impossibility. The monument is necessary—for anything to be or live it must be indefinitely iterable in the sign—and yet is contingent—the sign al-ways brings death and non-being. This necessary contingency, for Derrida, is the enigma of the pyramid (MP 95–96/82–83). And the enigma of the pyramid, connected to death and life, is why Derrida speaks of specters and hauntology.[14]

For Foucault, too, the reversal of the relation of Logos and time priori-tizes the sign. But, for him unlike for Derrida, the concept of the sign is not transformed into that of the trace insofar as the trace is understood as the representation of non-presence and non-being. Foucault's consideration of language is not oriented by *écriture*.[15] Instead, for Foucault, the sign is a state-ment (*énoncé*) and a statement is a "modality of existence" of signs (AS 140/107). In other words, it is precisely being and presence therefore that define the statement. Moreover, it is precisely their being that turns them into monu-ments; Foucault says,

> [Archeology] seeks to define not the thoughts, representations, images, themes, *haunting* ideas [*les hantises*, my emphasis] which are hidden or revealed in discourse; but those discourses themselves, those discourses as practices obeying certain rules. It does not treat discourse as *document* [Foucault's emphasis], as a sign of something else, as an element that ought

to be transparent, but whose unfortunate opacity must often be pierced if one is to reach at last the depth of the essential in the place in which it is held in reserve; it is concerned with discourse in its own volume, as a *monument* [Foucault's emphasis]. (AS 182/138–39)

For Foucault, therefore, Derrida's hauntology would be Egyptianism, a promise of *psyche*, of spirit, of specter;[16] the form of the trace can be "reactivated" (AS 138/105). The monument in Foucault can be repeated but only because it is material (AS 138/105); it is the monument of non-formed forces. The presence of forces—life—is what makes the monument effective.

We can therefore insert into the diffractional relation between Derrida and Foucault a strict opposition: between presence and non-presence, between trace of non-present spirit and monument of present matter. Nevertheless, in the project of reversing the relation between Logos and time both prioritize time. In fact, both focus on the form of the present. But, for Derrida, the form of present, of the living present, is such that time is always formal and productive of forms (MP 90–91/78–79): Derrida's philosophy is a formalism (DLG 92/63; MP 206–7/172).[17] For Derrida, time is the absolute form. Because time is the absolute form, Derrida's thought concerns passage. The indefinite iterability of the form of the present extends beyond the limit of the present's content, and yet, since it is the form of the present, it limits everything. For Derrida, there is no informal that is not formed, no outside that is not inside; everything is immanent. This conception of immanence is why he says in *Of Grammatology* that "there is no outside the text" (DLG 227/158), and immanence in Derrida always results in the contamination of opposites. Derrida's concept of contamination is inspired by Hegel's conception of the absolute form (cf. LE 208/158). This inspiration is why it is significant that Derrida chose to honor Hyppolite with an essay on Hegel. In his 1964 essay on Levinas, "Violence and Metaphysics," Derrida says, "Pure difference is not absolutely different (from nondifference). Hegel's critique of the concept of pure difference is for us here, doubtless, the most uncircumventable theme. Hegel thought absolute difference, and showed that it can be pure only by being impure" (ED 227n1/320n91). This comment still defines Derrida's philosophy, even today. Purity always has a formal limit which also de-limits it and makes purity mix with the unpure. Contamination allows us to define Derrida's thought, deconstruction, in terms of the aporia:[18] it is an attempt to be on the outside while remaining on the inside. This way of "constraining" (MP 127/108) the outside to be inside can never be complete for Derrida; there is no end. Therefore, deconstruction is always re-deconstruction; and, to coin a word, we can characterize it as *refinition*. Deconstruction attempts to be at the end, death, while surviving.

In contrast, for Foucault, time is not the absolute form but rather the absolute non-form; his philosophy is an informalism. As we have seen, genealogy attempts to make us forget the form of the present in order to remember the "non-place" (*non-lieu*). Because genealogy makes us return to the non-place below or between—the interstices in—the form of the present, Foucault's thought too concerns passage. But, here, it is the passage of the mad in their ship—*Stultifera Navis*[19]—floating on water. Water is informed force, the "gray dimension" (RR 133/103) of the surface. For Foucault, everything is in water, immanent in matter. Foucault's concept of immanence, being profoundly inspired by Nietzsche (F 78/71), results in us being purely on the outside, in pure immediacy, in pure presence. Only being in this gray dimension at the surface can re-form the forms and make them be "green" again. Only this gray dimension can select certain forms and make them return eternally. Because it goes into the ground, genealogy for Foucault is a way of remaining on the outside while being on the inside. It is problematization, which is not an attempt to survive the end in order to re-end; by going into the ground, it attempts to survive the beginning in order to re-begin. As "recommencement," genealogy is not eschatological (in any sense of this word). Its focus is life (not death) insofar as life consists in the set of functions which resist death.

So, starting from the Hyppolite "middle," we can see that both Derrida and Foucault attempt to reverse the Hegelian relation between logic and existence, the Logos and time. And in this reversal, prioritizing time,[20] they are led to consider the sign. Hence, "the problem of language will never [be] simply one problem among others." But they differ insofar as they conceive the relation between the Logos and time—philosophy and non-philosophy since Hyppolite—on the one hand, as prioritizing time as non-presence, trace, and form; for Derrida, deconstruction concerns the aporia of the end and aims at refinition. On the other, the relation is conceived as prioritizing time as presence, monument, and inform; for Foucault, genealogy concerns the problem of the beginning and aims at re-beginning. But, if the difference between deconstruction and genealogy amounts to a difference between aporia and problem, then we must take up the concept which is more fundamental than that of aporia and problem, the concept of the question. And to take up the question of the question, we will have to turn to Merleau-Ponty, for whom, following Heidegger, being is interrogation.

2   The Chiasm and the Fold

An Introduction to the Philosophical
Concept of Archeology

Two systems of thought still determine what we, especially as Continental philosophers, think: on the one hand, the system of thought that arose in Germany in the Twenties and Thirties, and, on the other, the French philosophy of the Sixties. While referring to the phenomenology of the Twenties and Thirties, the essay that follows attempts to determine the logic of and therefore the philosophical options available from the system of thought established in France during the Sixties. It attempts to determine its "point of diffraction." Many things are well known about the system of thought deriving from the French philosophy of the Sixties.[1] At that moment, in the Sixties, a need is felt to re-conceive history without end and without origin. This need motivates a convergence between phenomenology and structuralism.[2] The convergence consists in a reduction of subjectivity or sense, since sense implies directionality and thus end and origin. Sense is reduced down to something non-subjective or non-sensical, that is, to a structure whose elements themselves do not signify (cf. MP 161–62/134). The reduction to a non-signifying structure prioritizes spatiality over temporality, that is, it prioritizes a non-mundane space, a profound space. And what is discovered in this strange space is a lack, *un manque*,[3] a lack that produces excess. The point of diffraction in Sixties French philosophy is precisely this excessive lack. In light of the profound spatiality in which one finds the lack or defect, we could call this entire system of thought "transcendental topology."[4] We could also, however, call it "archeology."[5]

Obviously, the word "archeology" belongs to Foucault. Yet, at the end of his life, Merleau-Ponty, and thus virtually at the same time as Foucault, was characterizing his own thinking as an "archeology." These two names more than any other pair, it seems to me, define the philosophical concept of archeology. Thus, what I am going to do here is take stock of the proximity and distance between Merleau-Ponty and Foucault's concepts of archeology. As we shall see, the proximity lies in a concern for the profound spatiality that we have already mentioned, with its lack, gap, hollow, and divergence. The distance between them, however, will lie in the characterization of this lack in terms of transcendence and immanence, or, more precisely in terms of an impure immanence and pure immanence, than in terms of negative and positive, and finally in terms of the archive and the museum. This distance between Foucault and Merleau-Ponty will be at its greatest when we see them characterize the spatiality as the chiasm and the fold, which will turn out to be a difference between a milieu and a non-place, between a *mi-lieu* and a *non-lieu,* between a homoclite and a heteroclite, between finally a jointure and a disjointure. Despite this distance, the archeologies of Merleau-Ponty and Foucault always focus on one thing: a past, a past that is still effective, a past that is still present, a past that has always already been present, and thus, a past that was never present. This past is a past that is free for the future. In other words, these archeologies are always focused on what Freud called "the unconscious," what Husserl called "transcendental subjectivity," and what Kant called "the a priori." Thus we are starting this investigation with the pre-history of the philosophical concept of archeology: Freud, Husserl, and Kant.

I. The Pre-history of the Philosophical Concept of Archeology: Freud, Husserl, and Kant

What motivates the Sixties philosophical appropriation of the term "archeology" is its etymology, which is double.[6] On the one hand, the term refers to the commencement or the beginning, that is, it refers to the principle, in nature or history, where things begin: the *arche.* On the other hand, "archeology" refers to the commandment, that is, it refers to the principle according to which order is given, the place from which gods and men command: the *archon.* Thus we have in the one word two orders, that of the sequential and that of the jussive, we might say, succession and simultaneity. At once, "archeology" designates the past—the sequential order—and yet a past that still commands in the present—the jussive order, a past that is always present.

When Foucault defines his archeology, he plays on this etymology, and, of course, we associate the term "archeology" with Foucault. However, as I already pointed out, Merleau-Ponty was using it as well in the Fifties.[7] It is significant that Merleau-Ponty used the term not only in the Preface that he wrote for Hesnard's 1960 book on Freud (HES 9), but also in his last essay on Husserl "The Philosopher and His Shadow" (S 208/165) and his last course on Husserl (HL BN 29n44). These two contexts tell us something of the philosophical pre-history of the term: Freud and Husserl. In a late manuscript, Husserl was speaking of a "phenomenological archeology,"[8] and it is possible that Merleau-Ponty read this manuscript during his studies in Louvain in 1939. But it is more probable that Merleau-Ponty borrowed the term from Fink's writings on Husserl, in particular from his essay "Das Problem der Phänomenologie Edmund Husserls," which appeared in the *Revue Internationale de Philosophie* in 1939.[9] We can isolate one more aspect of the pre-history of the concept of archeology in Merleau-Ponty, although this discovery would not have been possible without Foucault. In a 1971 essay, "Monstrosities in Criticism," Foucault claims that his use of the word "archeology" comes from Kant.[10] Although Foucault does not explain this comment, it seems clear that he must be referring to the thesis he wrote on Kant's *Anthropology* in 1961 since Foucault calls what he is doing in this thesis an archeology.[11] Yet in Part 2 of *The Critique of Judgment* on teleological judgment, Kant refers to an "archeology of nature."[12] Although, as far as I know, Merleau-Ponty never explicitly associates his use of "archeology" with Kant, in the 1956–57 lectures called *La Nature,* Merleau-Ponty discusses teleological judgment in Kant and (almost) refers to the exact page on which Kant speaks of an archeology of nature.[13] So, it is possible that Kant provided some inspiration for Merleau-Ponty's use of "archeology." Nevertheless, it is Foucault who explicitly states that Kant is his source of the term. Foucault does not, however, reject the idea that he may have adopted the term from Freud and from phenomenology as well. In his 1954 Introduction to the French translation of Binswanger's *Traum und Existenz,* Foucault not only sets up a confrontation between phenomenology and psychoanalysis, not only mentions Husserl's "The Origin of Geometry," but also cites Fink's 1947 lecture on the essence of enthusiasm.[14] Thus, although this claim is a little speculative, we can say that Foucault and Merleau-Ponty share the same pre-history of the philosophical concept: Freud, Husserl (or more precisely Fink), and Kant.

The most important characteristics of the philosophical concept of archeology comes from psychoanalysis. Because psychoanalysis is concerned with curing the hysteric, its archeology is always interested; it is *not* an investigation of the past for its own sake. By means of an investigation of the past, archeology concerns itself with the transformation of the present; indeed, and perhaps paradoxically, archeology is really concerned with the future. This concern with the future implies two other characteristics of archeology. On the one hand, as Freud's 1905 "Dora case" indicates, the past to which one returns, while preserved, is always incomplete. Since the past is always incomplete, the solution to the hysterical symptom is always incomplete. Thus, as Freud says there, since long buried, priceless relics of antiquity are mutilated when they are brought back to light, one must restore what is missing, and not fail to mention in each case, "like a conscientious archeologist," "where the authentic parts end and [the] constructions begin." Thus the future cure is based on a past that is incomplete—it is past and no longer there—and a reconstruction that is inventive.

On the other hand, for a future cure to be found, it must be the case that the past is conserved. The past must be simultaneous with the present; it must therefore not be past, but rather still be present. We can see this conservative conception of the past, a past still present, always present, if we start with the well-known discussion of archeology from the opening of Freud's 1930 *Civilization and Its Discontents*.[15] Here, while discussing "the general problem of preservation in the sphere of the mind," Freud compares the mind to "the history of the Eternal City," Rome. The comparison goes like this: when a visitor equipped with the most complete historical and topological knowledge—"more," Freud says, "than present-day archeology"—tours "the great metropolis which has grown up in the last few centuries since the Renaissance," he will be able to see the ruins of the Aurelian walls from the time of the early Caesars, he will also be able to see sections of the Servian walls "where they have been excavated and brought to light," and finally he will be able to trace out the outline of the oldest settlement, the *Roma Quadrata*. Since Rome preserves the past alongside the present, the Eternal City then, for Freud, is like the psychical entity "in which nothing that has once come into existence will have passed away and all the earlier phases of development continue to exist alongside the latest ones." In other words, as in Rome, the historical sequence of the psychic entity will be represented by juxtaposition in space, that is, by simultaneity.[16] Now, the image of the eternal city, for Freud, is not a perfect image of the psychic entity, because there are *intentional* demolitions and constructions in a city, whereas a psychic entity only undergoes *unintentional* traumas that can destroy remains of the past. Although this description confirms the incomplete nature of the past, the implication is clear: aside from traumatic destructions, the past is preserved intact in the place called the psychic entity or more precisely in the unconscious. As Freud says in his 1915 essay "The Unconscious," "the processes of the unconscious are timeless; that is, they are not ordered temporally, are not altered by the passage of time, in fact bear no relation to time at all."[17] The philosophical concept of archeology always implies, as Freud says in this essay, an "overcoming of an error"; the error is this: "supposing that the forgetting we are familiar with signifies a destruction of the memory-trace—that is, its annihilation." This comment means that "the forgetting we are familiar with" refers to our or my personal memory, a memory relative to me, to my consciousness. Thus, the overcoming of this error implies that we accept that there is an absolute memory, a memory not relative to an individual's ability to remember, that is, a memory not relative to consciousness.

The characteristic of an absolute memory implies the fourth characteristic of philosophical archeology: the displacement of the conscious subject. We can see this fourth characteristic in Freud's 1896 essay "The Aetiology of

Hysteria."[18] Here he compares the analyst to an explorer who "arrives in a little-known region where his interest is aroused by an expanse of ruins, with remains of walls, fragments of columns, and tablets with half-effaced and unreadable inscriptions." At this moment, according to Freud, the "explorer" could proceed in two ways. On the one hand, the explorer could inspect what lies in view and question the inhabitants living in the vicinity about what their tradition tells them of the history and meaning of these archeological remains. On the other hand, "he may act differently." Instead of questioning the inhabitants about what tradition says about the ruins, he puts them to work excavating them. Freud says, "If his work is crowned with success, the discoveries are self-explanatory"; in particular, the numerous inscriptions are bilingual and reveal an alphabet and a language, "and when they have been deciphered and translated, yield undreamed-of information about the events of the remote past, to commemorate which the monuments were built." Freud concludes: "Saxa loquuntur!" This exclamation "Stones talk!" brings us to the fifth characteristic of philosophical archeology: the non-living or dead monument that nevertheless speaks.

On the basis of this brief investigation of Freudian psychoanalysis, we have been able to assemble five characteristics of the philosophical concept of archeology. Its investigation of the past concerns the future; the past it investigates is incomplete; and yet, the past is conserved, juxtaposed to, and simultaneous with the present; present consciousness is not the object of archeological investigation; and finally, what is the object is the monument that speaks for itself. Now, Ricoeur in his work on Freud, *De l'interpretation* (published in English as *Freud and Philosophy*) claims that Freudian archeology is an "anti-phenomenology,"[19] precisely because, as we just noted, psychoanalysis undoes the evidence of consciousness. But Husserl himself had spoken of a "phenomenological archeology," and Fink had made this idea known in his writings on Husserl, in particular, in the essay that we have already mentioned above, the 1939 "Problem of Edmund Husserl's Phenomenology."[20] So we now turn to Fink's interpretation of Husserl.

Fink defines Husserl's phenomenology in terms of the problem of being, the problem of "the originary state of human access to being."[21] In other words, phenomenology investigates the originary ontological experiences that institute—here Fink uses the verb "stiften"[22]—the sense of being that we possess naturally today. Fink stresses that these experiences are not nearby and are not given to the phenomenologist immediately. They are mediated by tradition and forgetfulness. According to Fink, in order to overcome the distance and forgetfulness, phenomenology engages in a *Zurückfragen*, a regressive inquiry or, more literally, a questioning back.[23] This term is well known from Husserl's "The Origin of Geometry" and from Fink's *Sixth Cartesian*

Meditation. Regressive inquiry aims at "re-establishing" what Fink calls "the initial knowledge forgotten in the buried traditions," and it even aims at "returning to the immediate knowledge of the being from which the traditions, even though they obscure, derived."[24] It is important that Fink insists here that the regressive inquiry is not the well-known psychological question of the psychical origin of our representations.[25] It does not concern an empirically verifiable real genesis of human thought from infancy up to maturity; it is not at all a question of psychological development. Instead, according to Fink, the phenomenological regressive inquiry "wants to bring to light knowledge in its struggle with the being."[26] In other words, "the phenomenological regressive question concerning the beginnings of knowledge attempts to grasp the human intellect in its movement towards the being."[27] Fink concludes this description of *Zurückfragen* by saying that one can call this theoretic endeavor *Erkenntnistheorie*, since Husserl himself did call it that. But, Fink adds, "Husserl always regretted that the term 'archeology,' a term perfectly appropriate to the essence of philosophy, was already reserved for a positive science."[28] Phenomenology then would be defined as the return to what Fink calls "the archi-beginnings of knowledge," *die Uranfänge des Wissens.* Now, even though Fink is ontologizing Husserl's phenomenology, even though he is stressing that phenomenological archeology is not investigating psychological genesis, he is careful to say that "Husserl interrogates the being in such a way that the decision of this question is for him an analysis of consciousness."[29] As always with Fink, however, the consciousness or subjectivity that phenomenology interrogates is transcendental; in the phenomenological reduction, the concept of *Geist,* he says, undergoes a fundamental transformation.[30] This transformation means that consciousness is not taken in the strict sense; "the unconscious," as Fink also says, "is therefore always included."[31] And the transformation means that transcendental consciousness does not exist somewhere in the world or in metaphysical space.[32] Yet, this non-mundane non-spatial subjectivity opens out onto what Fink calls "the problematic *space* of phenomenological philosophy."[33] It seems that this description of phenomenological archeology is not entirely incompatible with that of psychoanalytic archeology. Regressive inquiry overcomes forgetfulness and thus consists in a kind of memory. And, since Fink stresses that regressive inquiry is not concerned with psychological genesis, we must define this memory as an absolute memory, that is, one not relative to psychological memory. Moreover, the memory is directed at a non-mundane space, like the strange space of Freud's eternal city in which all past constructions are preserved side by side. Even phenomenology's inseparable connection to consciousness does not seem entirely incompatible with psychoanalysis, since Fink insists that the concept of *Geist* undergoes a radical transformation in the reduction. In his Preface to Hesnard's book on Freud, Merleau-Ponty himself recognized this near compatibility between psychoanalysis and phenomenology; he speaks there of a "convergence" between phenomenology and Freud's investigation (HES 8). Yet, one thinks not only of Merleau-Ponty when reading Fink. Foucault too quickly comes to mind since Fink seems to be defining Husserl's phenomenology as *l'archéologie du savoir* when he is speaking of the *die Uranfänge des Wissens*. Fink even distinguishes *Wissen* from *Erkenntnis,* thereby anticipating Foucault's own distinction between *savoir* and *connaissance.*

In Foucault, *connaissance* refers to the conscious opinions and debates among scientists, whereas *savoir* refers to unconscious discursive practices that determine the conscious opinions (AS 239/183). *Savoir* therefore refers to what Foucault calls "historical a priori," and he claims, as we have already noted, that he borrowed this idea from Kant, which brings us to the last aspect of the pre-history of philosophical archeology. Here we must look at three passages in Kant, one from *Anthropology from a Pragmatic Point of View,*[34] one from *The Critique of Judgment* (paragraphs 79 and 82 in Part 2), and a fragment from *Progress in Metaphysics.*[35] We must say that the passage from the *Anthropology* is the most important since, as is well known, Foucault translated this text into French.[36] Yet, each of the three passages contributes to the idea of philosophical archeology. The context of the passage from the *Anthropology* is important; it occurs in a section on the "faculty of designation," and thus it concerns the sign. Kant speaks of an "archeology of nature" that reads "traces of volcanoes that no longer erupt." In the passage from *The Critique of Judgment* (to which we have already referred above) Kant elaborates on this idea that an archeology of nature concerns signs or traces. Here Kant distinguishes an archeology of nature from natural history, that is, from the description of *present* genera and species. Natural history's description would take place by means of intuition since it describes nature in its present form. In contrast, an archeology of nature describes *past* genera and species, and thus it would necessarily pass through signs or traces, "petrifications" or "traces that remain of nature's most ancient revolutions."[37] Whereas the passage in *The Critique of Judgment* concerns natural history, the fragment included in *Progress in Metaphysics* concerns what Kant calls a "philosophizing history of philosophy," which he distinguishes from a mere history of philosophy. A mere history of philosophy would present the empirical and thus contingent order of how thinkers have philosophized up until the present. In contrast, a philosophizing history of philosophy would be rational and necessary, that is, it would be a priori. Kant says, "For whether or not [a philosophical history of philosophy] sets up facts of reason, it does not borrow them from historiography, but rather draws them from the nature of human reason as philosophical archeology." Thus, Kant's philosophical archeology would concern not the contingent, successive order of the history of philosophy. Rather, it would concern the rational and necessary order of philosophical concepts. Yet, this order would still be historical since it would account only for this factual or, we might say, singular set of concepts. Philosophical archeology would constitute, with this necessary and yet factual order, a historical a priori. And this archeology, like the archeology of nature, would proceed not by intuition but by means of signs. Thus Kant's concept of a philosophical archeology implies, as we already saw in Freud, that archeology is a method of reading signs.

Before we turn explicitly to the concept of archeology in Foucault and Merleau-Ponty, we can summarize what we have seen in this examination of archeology's pre-history. Although the three aspects of the pre-history have reinforced certain characteristics of the philosophical concept of archeology, they do not perfectly coincide. So here is the compilation of the characteristics. First, archeology concerns signs, traces, or sedimentations of the past, in a word, mediation; thus archeology is not a form of intuition, but a form of interpretation or regressive inquiry. Second, in the reading of signs, consciousness is displaced toward an unconscious that precedes it, that has been conserved and that is incomplete. In fact, this incompleteness of the unconscious implies that philosophical archeology is always a kind of an-archeology: the complete origin is missing. Third, archeology investigates then the space of the unconscious, that is, a spatial order or simultaneity that is prior to consciousness or empirical or psychological genesis. This prior order we can call an a priori. Fourth, although this order is prior, it is not an abstract a priori; it is an a priori for these singular historical facts or signs. The fifth characteristic is that, in the investigation of this historical a priori, archeology overcomes a kind of forgetfulness, which implies that it consists in a kind of memory. And then finally, this memory is not really a memory of the past, that is, it is not interested in the past for its own sake; its interest is the future. With this summary in mind we can now turn to the concepts of archeology in Foucault and Merleau-Ponty.

II. The Concepts of Archeology

What is clearest in Foucault's *Archeology of Knowledge* is that Foucault is differentiating himself from Merleau-Ponty (AS 265/203). We must take this explicit differentiation seriously if we are going to determine the philosophical concept of archeology developed during the Sixties. If we examine the three different texts in which Merleau-Ponty, at the end of his life, speaks of archeology—that is, the Preface to Hesnard's 1960 book on Freud, and the two texts on Husserl, "The Philosopher and His Shadow" and the course called "Husserl at the Limits of Phenomenology"[38]—we can assemble six characteristics of his conception of archeology. These six characteristics are roughly parallel to the ones we just listed on the basis of the pre-history.

First, archeology, for Merleau-Ponty, investigates the originary "soil" of corporeal experience (S 227/180).[39] If we look at the résumés for the course on nature and for the course on interrogation, we see that Merleau-Ponty was investigating nature as this "originary soil" (RC 125/156, 156/180; VI 320–21/267). But, if we look at the Husserl discussion in *La Nature* (as well as *Husserl at the Limits of Phenomenology*), we see that Merleau-Ponty was interpreting this natural space through Husserl's descriptions of terrestrial kinesthesia in "The Earth, the Originary Ark, Does Not Move" fragment (S 22/180; HL BN 45).[40] Therefore we can refer to natural originary soil as the soil of the earth. Merleau-Ponty himself, however, also refers to it as latent intentionality (S 209/165), and also to latency in the Freudian sense (HES 9), which means that this originary soil is the unconscious. Merleau-Ponty insists in both "The Philosopher and His Shadow" and in the Preface to Hesnard that phenomenology is not "a new philosophy of consciousness" (HES 7). That phenomenology is not a new philosophy of consciousness is why Merleau-Ponty speaks of a "convergence" or "consonance" between phenomenology and psychoanalysis. But this is also why, in "Husserl at the Limits of Phenomenology," he will speak of a "convergence" between phenomenology and ontology, that is, a convergence with Heideggerian ontology (HL BN 33). Following Heidegger, Merleau-Ponty will also call this originary soil "the unthought" (S 202/160) or *Denkmöglichkeiten* (HL BN 46), or, as in *The Visible and the Invisible*, "*Wesen* in the sense . . . [of a] verb" (VI 154/115). This reference to *Wesen* is indicative of Merleau-Ponty's later thinking. The originary soil consists in a presenc*ing* (*west*) of an essence or ideality. This presencing, as we shall see, is at the literal center of Merleau-Ponty's chiasm. Second, since, in the Preface to Hesnard, Merleau-Ponty refers to this originary soil as the unconscious, he also attributes to it the characteristics of the unconscious that we saw earlier: intemporality and indestructibility. In "Husserl at the Limits of Phenomenology," Merleau-Ponty's reproduces, of course, his favorite Husserlian quote from paragraph 16 of *Cartesian Meditations*—"the beginning . . . is . . . mute experience which must be brought to the pure expression of its own sense"—but he also emphasizes this quote from "The Origin of Geometry": "from a historical perspective, what is really first is our present." This present, according to Merleau-Ponty, "designates a presence that is richer than what is visible of it" (HL BN 14), a "deep present," a present that includes the past, that includes therefore the intemporal and thus still present unconscious (cf. VI 320–21/267). Thus, for Merleau-Ponty, archeology investigates a past that is *simultaneous* with the present and yet not visible. This invisible but still present past brings us to the third characteristic of Merleau-Ponty's archeology. Archeology must proceed by means of the mediation of signs. In "The Philosopher and His Shadow" and in "Husserl at the Limits of Phenomenology," Merleau-Ponty engages in a way of reading texts that brings to light what is "unthought" in them; on the basis of this unthought, he is able to establish his own philosophy (S 209/166). Interpretation obviously works on the mediation of language, and in the Preface to Hesnard, Merleau-Ponty calls psychoanalysis an "unpitying hermeneutics" (HES 6). The idea of a hermeneutics leads to the fourth characteristic. Archeology for Merleau-Ponty is defined as a dialogue or a *Rückfragen*. As in Husserl, in Merleau-Ponty, archeology questions back across sedimentation and forgetfulness (S 218/173, 115/92). According to Merleau-Ponty, this dialogue or regressive questioning enters into a milieu between subject and object, between me and the other who is being questioned. And this milieu brings us to the fifth characteristic. Although the milieu implies immanence, a "being halfway between," a "mi-lieu," and thus a "staying *within*" rather than a "going *out*," in fact, what Merleau-Ponty sees in the middle is transcendence. For Merleau-Ponty, being is always *être-à*. And here, perhaps, we must reflect on the French idiom "à même," which suggests a very close relation, "right on." This relation of something being right on the other is why we are speaking of an impure immanence in Merleau-Ponty rather than transcendence. The milieu for Merleau-Ponty is defined by a relation of "to," a question *to* the other, *right on* the other, or a question from the other *to* me, *right on* me. Following Husserl, Merleau-Ponty always stresses that, in the experience of the other (as in interrogation), it is impossible for me to experience the interior life of the other (VI 303/249); it is always mediated by the *à même*. And, as is well known, Merleau-Ponty extends this impossibility of the presentation of the other's interior life to my experience of my own body, as in the touching–touched relation (S 210/166). This impossibility of presence implies that the dialogue always includes moments of silence and thus of non-sense. Indeed, that my speaking arises from the other's silence is the basis for Merleau-Ponty's own interpretation of Heidegger's famous saying "Die Sprache spricht" in "Husserl at the Limits of Phenomenology" (HL BN 36). For Merleau-Ponty, it is not me who speaks, but it is the silence of the other that comes to speech in me; thus in "The Philosopher and His Shadow," Merleau-Ponty speaks of a "primordial *On*" at whose level "communication is no problem" (S 221/175). This silence, non-sense, or absence brings us to the sixth characteristic of Merleau-Ponty's archeology. Merleau-Ponty himself defines this silence as a negativity or lack (HL BN 3). Like the *Wesen* we just mentioned, this negativity is at the literal center of Merleau-Ponty's chiasm. Because of this point of negativity at the center of the dialogue, my response to the interrogation is creative. Because I do not have the inventory of the other's thought, I must create that thought on the other side. I must create an answer and speak. As Merleau-Ponty says in "The Philosopher and His Shadow," "to think is *not* to possess the objects of thought" (S 202/160, my emphasis; cf. HL BN 13). This creativity is why Merleau-Ponty, following Husserl himself, can call his way of interpreting "a poetizing of the history of philosophy" (HN BN 3).[41] This creativity based in non-presence is also what Merleau-Ponty calls expression. Now, if we keep this silence, this absence, this non-sense, this *Nichturpräsentierbarkeit* (VI 286/233), this negativity or lack, in mind, then we must conclude that, for Merleau-Ponty, archeology is not a positivism but rather a kind of "negativism."

"Negativism" is a rather unfortunate word, and with it I am not suggesting anything like pessimism or nihilism. Yet, it is clear throughout Merleau-Ponty's final writings and courses, and especially in the chapter of *The Visible and the Invisible* called "Interrogation and Dialectic," that he is trying to develop a concept of negation that is internal to being. Thus, this word "negativism" is a roughly accurate characterization of Merleau-Ponty's final philosophy. More importantly for our purposes, it will allow us to see, more clearly, Foucault's relationship to Merleau-Ponty. As I said, what is clearest in Foucault's *Archeology of Knowledge* is that Foucault is differentiating himself from Merleau-Ponty's archeology: Foucault characterizes his own archeology as a positivism (AS 164–65/125). Here, as with Merleau-Ponty, we can assemble six characteristics of Foucault's archeology. First, Foucault's archeology is a positivism because it is concerned with the positivity of discourse (AS 147/112); this positivity of discourse means that discourse is not related to anything other than itself, to *nothing* other than itself, especially, as is well known, not to a constituting subjectivity or consciousness. Thus, like Merleau-Ponty, Foucault speaks of an *on dit*, an anonymous voice, the voice of no one (AS 161/122). Yet, this *on dit* in Foucault, unlike Merleau-Ponty, is precisely the patency of language (not its latency or what is implicit in language) (AS 144/109, 90/67); it is precisely the said (not the unsaid, the "not yet said," prediscursive silence, or the unthought) (AS 144/110, 90/67, 100/76).[42] Archeology, for Foucault, investigates the "singularity" of things that have been said, and precisely as they have been said (AS 143/109). Yet, although not related to anything other than itself, discourse, a singular discourse, contains what Foucault calls "historical a priori," an idea which, we saw, he seems to take from Kant. The Foucaultian notion of historical a priori must be distinguished, on the one hand, from what we saw in Merleau-Ponty; it must be distinguished from "the primary soil of an experience" (*au premier sol d'une expérience*) (AS 105/79, 65/48). On the other hand, historical a priori must be distinguished from "the a priori agency of *connaissance*" (AS 105/79). So historical a priori refer neither to originary experience (or speaking speech) nor to the conditions of the possibility of a kind of knowledge. For Foucault, historical a priori are the rules that conditioned the very existence (not possibility) of these singular things said; these conditions are only as wide as this singular set of things said.[43] Foucaultian archeology is investigating the actual conditions that gave rise to this singular system of statements. This a priori of discourse brings us to the second characteristic of Foucault's archeology. As with Merleau-Ponty, the pastness or a priori that archeology investigates is a past that is still present. If we look at Foucault's "Forward to the English Translation" of *Les Mots et les choses,* we can see that the aim of this book is the "positive unconscious" of the human sciences (MC xi). Thus we can say that the historical a priori possesses the characteristic of being "untemporal." Moreover, according to Foucault, the historical a priori are a priori of a history "of things actually said" (*des choses effectivement dites*) (AS 167/127).[44] The historical a priori therefore are actual; they still rule the discourse that is present; they are simultaneous with the present. The third characteristic of Foucaultian archeology is the one that is parallel to mediation and sedimentation in Merleau-Ponty. Foucault does not accept either of these notions since his archeology aims at the positivity of discourse; it does not aim at anything buried or hidden, at any secret or negative side of discourse (AS 143/79). Nevertheless, discourse is not visible (AS 145/110). Foucault gives two reasons for this invisibility of discourse. On the one hand, it lies beneath "in a sort of vertical dimension" (AS 143/109) or "on this side of" (*en deçà*) "terminal" constructions or unities such as books and authors (AS 100/75, 145/111). On the other hand, discourse is not visible because "the signifying structure of language always refers *to* something" (AS 145–46/111, my emphasis): to the object, the sense, and the subject. As Foucault says, "Language always seems to be inhabited by the other, the elsewhere, the distant, the far; it is hollowed by absence" (AS 146/111). This inhabitation of language by the other means that discourse looks to be a transparent passage to something other than itself. Thus if one conceives it only as a passage, one never sees it for itself; one never sees it all. Its assumed transparency makes it invisible. As strange as this may sound—since Foucault is explicitly differentiating himself from phenomenology (AS 265/203)—the invisible but unhidden status of discourse "necessitates," as Foucault says, "a certain conversion of the look and of the attitude." This "reduction," however, is not a neutralization or a suspension of belief or a parenthesizing of all positing of existence, since archeology in Foucault investigates precisely the existence of discourse (AS 159/121). That archeology concerns the existence of discourse and its conditions bring us to the fourth characteristic. As Foucault says often, *The Archeology of Knowledge* is not presenting a theory of discourse but only a description (AS 149/114). Indeed, archeology for Foucault is not a *Rückfragen* or a dialogue but a description.[45] That Foucaultian archeology is a description means that it is not an interpretation or a hermeneutics that attempts to multiply the senses of the one thing that has been said or to show the commonality of one sense throughout many expressions (AS 155–56/118). In contrast, archeological description aims at discovering the "singular place" (*emplacement singulier*) that each thing said occupies; it aims to "map" (*réperer*) the localization of that thing said in its historical a priori (AS 157/119). This idea of mapping means that what Foucault is doing in *The Archeology of Knowledge* is opening up "a coherent *domain* of description" (AS 150/114, my emphasis). Thus as with Merleau-Ponty's archeology, here we are concerned with a certain *lieu*. Yet—and this brings us to the fifth characteristic—unlike Merleau-Ponty, Foucault conceives this place not as transcendence, but as immanence. Repeatedly, in *The Archeology of Knowledge*, Foucault claims that, as archeologists, we must remain *within* discourse (AS 98/74, 101/76, 105/79, 63/46), that we must be "intrinsic" to discourse (AS 89/67). Thus, as Foucault himself does, we can speak of "a surface of discourse" (AS 105/79) or a "plane of discourse" (AS 169/128); or we can speak like Deleuze: discourse in Foucault is "a plane of immanence."[46] There is no relating of this plane back *to* anything else, no transcendence (AS 148/ 113). Yet there are the historical a priori, which are within discourse, but which as well are not identical to the things said. They are neither internal to discourse, since they are below the level of the terminal constructions, and yet they are not external to discourse (AS 62–63/46). They are, "in a sense, at the limit of discourse" (AS 63/46). This limit is the place of archeology for Foucault. This idea of a limit of discourse within discourse brings us to the sixth and last characteristic of archeology in Foucault. Although Foucault never refers discourse to anything other than itself, he does speak of a lack correlative with the field of discourse (*un manque*) (AS 145/110). This lack is the center point of Foucault's fold. It is what Foucault himself calls a "point of diffraction" (AS 86/64). On the basis of the point of diffraction within a discourse, one can strategize—not create—and make new statements—not expressions.

III. The Archive and the Museum

At the point of this lack, we have come to the exact point at which Merleau-Ponty and Foucault divide from one another, their "point of diffraction." We can see the distance already: strategy or creativity, statement or expression. We know that Merleau-Ponty is going to characterize this lack as a negativity and that Foucault will characterize it as a positivity. Yet, both call it an *écart*, a divergence, indeed, a point of divergence (AS 87/66; S 217/172). The point of divergence refers us to a place. And now we shall see this distance take shape as two places: the archive and the museum. In short, the archive in Foucault is a place of statement (*l'énoncé*), whereas the museum in Merleau-Ponty is a place of expression. In *The Archeology of Knowledge*, Foucault explicitly opposes his concept of statement to a certain concept of expression (AS 74/55, 153/117, 272/209).

According to Foucault, the concept of expression always defines itself in relation to totality and plethora (AS 155/118).[47] The concept of expression always depends on a totality, like "some sort of great uniform text," which overflows any individual element of a discourse and to which each element of a discourse belongs. This great uniform text has never been articulated, and yet it brings to light what humans "had wanted to say" in all of their expressions, both linguistic and non-linguistic. Because the totality is what humans had wanted to say, Foucault calls this totality an "implicit sense" (*sens implicite*) (AS 155/118). We can see the word "pli," fold, inside the word "implicit." In effect, what Foucault is implying here is that "the whole is said" in this sense; the sense has all possible sayings folded up inside of itself. Thus we can say that the implicit sense consists in an internality; it contains the whole inside of itself, or it is the whole. If there is a lack in this whole, the lack consists in that which has not yet been ex-pressed or made ex-pli-cit, articulated, the unsaid. That the totality is an implicit sense means that either discourse is treated as a plethora of signifiers in relation to a unique signified, or discourse is treated as a plethora of signifieds in relation to a unique signifier. In either case, that of the signifier or of the signified, expression implies that discourse is the fulfillment—hence the word "plethora," fullness or plenitude—of the implicit sense. As Foucault says, "If we study discourse in this way, then discourse is at once plentitude and indefinite wealth" (AS 156/118).

If this concept of expression is based on the principle that the whole is said, for Foucault, the "principle" (*le principe*) of the archive is that "the whole is never said" (AS 156/118). This "never said" principle or origin *only* seems to resemble the "unsaid" of expression. The unsaid of the im-plicit sense allows for a plethora of signifiers that ex-press one unique signified or a plethora of signifieds that one unique signifier ex-presses. In contrast, Foucault says, things said, statements (*les énoncés*), "are always in deficit" (AS 156/119). This deficiency means not only that there are relatively few things that are said; statements are rare. But also this deficiency means that statements never have the support of a totality—no wealth of gold—that guarantees their value; thus they are also rare in the literal sense, that is, scattered or dispersed. And this dispersion is why there is no plethora: statements are scattered; they are not fulfillments of an implicit sense; they are not full by having been all folded up in an implicit sense. Because each statement or singularity is not related back *to* the implicit totality, it is entirely positive. For Foucault, there is no, so to speak, "implicity" in discourse, no interiority; rather, there is multiplicity (AS 171/130) and exteriority (AS 161/122). Therefore, Foucault defines the archive as the "level of a practice that makes a *multiplicity* of statements emerge as so many regular events and as well as so many things open to being treated and manipulated" (AS 171/130, my emphasis).

Merleau-Ponty's counter-concept to the archive is what he calls, in "Indirect Language and the Voices of Silence," the "museum." The museum is the counter-concept to Foucault's archive because, for Merleau-Ponty, the museum represents one kind of historicity, which is a "fallen image" of authentic historicity (S 79/63; cf. VI 203/154). The museum represents, as Merleau-Ponty says, "the historicity of death" (S 79/63), and he describes its space as a "necropole" (S 78/62). The museum consists in artworks detached from the lives of the painters. The result is that the space of the museum consists in oppositions of paintings, struggles between schools, and the denials of one painting by another; this space, Merleau-Ponty says explicitly, sounding like Foucault when he describes the archive, is a space of "exteriority" (S 75/60): the particular paintings do not look to be *inside* the single task of painting. Yet, by means of retrospection (S 74/59, 77/62), the museum is able to reconcile the paintings and make them look like "moments of one effort" (S 77/62). The reconciliation among the painters occurs only with death (S 76/60). The "necropole," however, is made possible by what Merleau-Ponty calls "the true milieu of art, the historicity of life." In the historicity of life, paintings are reconciled "insofar as each one expresses the *whole* of existence" (S 79/63, my emphasis). In other words, "each painter revises, recaptures, and renews the *entire* undertaking of painting in each new work" (S 75/60, my emphasis). There is, as Merleau-Ponty says, "a single task" in all painting (S 75/60). Each painting, therefore, is an expression of this single task. And, because each painting expresses the whole of painting, there is a "fraternity" of painters in the living historicity (S 77/62). Thus the living historicity is not a space in which each painting is exterior to each other but interior to the whole.

Now, we must recall here that, in "Indirect Language," Merleau-Ponty is appropriating Saussure in order to define his concept of expression. Thus, he speaks of a whole (as Foucault did when he contrasted statement with expression)—the system of a language—which precedes and determines each part or sign of a language; this whole is the single task of painting, indeed, of all language. Merleau-Ponty is quite precise about this prior whole. It is not composed of positive ideas (S 50/39); it does not consist in an "original text" (S 54/43); it is not a "logical totality" (S 50/39); and finally, one could not take its inventory (S 74/59). This prior whole is a kind of negativity or non-sense in language. This negativity is the differences between the signs, the divergences (*écarts*) between them, which literally mean nothing (S 49/39), and this "nothing" between the signs is why Merleau-Ponty says that all language is indirect, allusive, or silence (S 54/43). Yet, Merleau-Ponty defines this prior whole, which is nothing, as being imminent in each of its parts. Although the learning of a language must proceed from parts to the whole (even though all the senses of the signs depend on this whole), progress in learning is made, according to Merleau-Ponty, "by the internal articulation of a function which is in its own way already complete" (S 50/40); "the phonemes are from the beginning variations of a unique speech apparatus" (S 50/40). This "unique speech apparatus," this "one function," implies that Merleau-Ponty is conceiving this prior whole, this "single task," this negativity, as an empty intention, an empty intention that still commands possible fulfillments. In *The Visible and the Invisible*, Merleau-Ponty says that "all the possibilities of language" are given with the structure of the mute world (VI 203/155). Thus, this whole that is a single task is already possessed and yet it is not yet possessed; it is a "pre-possession," a *Vorhabe* as Husserl would say (cf. VI 242/188). Following Foucault, we might call it an implicit sense, except for the fact that the whole is unfilled and thus negative. In any case, for Merleau-Ponty, because the whole is imminent in any one part, in any one expression, in any one painting (S 77/62), "the cave paintings," as Merleau-Ponty says, already contained the whole of painting (S 75/60, 79/63). "All the possibilities" of painting occur in the very first painting.[48] These cave dwellers refer us once more back to the originary soil of the earth, which is, for Merleau-Ponty, the "true milieu" of expression.

IV. The Chiasm and the Fold

If it is true that the soil of the earth is the true milieu of expression, then it contains as if concentrated into a point all the possibilities of expression. This point is the central point of the chiasm. Although Merleau-Ponty describes the chiasm in two ways, once in relation to vision and once in relation to language, the two occasions are really the same; they are, as Merleau-Ponty would say, "interlaced." The first description is the chiasm of vision or of "perceptual faith." When Merleau-Ponty (in the opening chapter of *The Visible and the Invisible*) is describing the perceptual faith, he is always describing binocular vision. Vision is binocular because we have two eyes. Thus the perceptual faith refers to what I believe as soon as I open my eyes. According to Merleau-Ponty, when I open my eyes, what "we see [is] the thing itself" (VI 17/11). This comment means that, when I open my eyes, I do not think

I have a mental representation, but I believe I have the thing out there—at the end of my gaze (*regard*) (VI 21/7). If the thing is at the end of my gaze, then we can see already that vision, for Merleau-Ponty, is chiasmatic: the ends of the two intersecting lines of the chiasm for Merleau-Ponty symbolize two eyes looking out at a thing, like this: >. Clearly, this symbol is only half of the chiasm. We get the second half when we continue the description of the body in perception. According to Merleau-Ponty, "the body . . . has shattered the illusion of a coincidence between my perception and the things themselves" (VI 24/8). I am certain that my vision is out there in the thing, and yet the vision is mine, which makes me uncertain. If the vision is mine, then there are other gazes on the thing which are not mine and which are therefore absent from me. Merleau-Ponty demonstrates this fundamental absence in perception by describing the well-known touching–touched relation (VI 24/9).[49] What this description shows is that it is impossible to grasp the perceiving of another, even when that other is part of me, even when it is my other hand. Merleau-Ponty allows us to understand this fundamental non-presentability of the other's perception better when he explicitly describes "others who see as we do" (VI 25/9). The first thing I have to realize is that when I see, I cannot give others access to the vision I have; simply, it is mine. But, similarly, "by a sort of backlash, they also refuse me this access which I deny to them" (VI 25/9). This lack of access means that, although I say of myself that my vision is out there in the thing, I say of the other's vision that his is behind his body, actually, behind his eyes, in there. And this relation is reversible just as the touching–touched relation is: the other too says that his vision is out there in the thing, whereas my vision, for him, is behind my eyes, "behind his body," as Merleau-Ponty says (VI 25/9). This reversible relation gives us the second half of the figure of the chiasm. When I say that my vision is out there in the thing, I can symbolize it like this: >. The ends of the lines here are my two eyes looking out and ending up in the thing at the point of intersection. But, when I say that the other's vision is behind his eyes, I can symbolize it like this: <. The ends of the lines are his eyes looking out at the world, but the *point of intersection*, which previously symbolized the thing itself at the end of my vision, now symbolizes the representation in his head behind the eyes (cf. VI 24 marginal note/9 marginal note). Now, of course, if we put these two symbols—><—together, we get an "X," we get the chiasm. And notice that the point of intersection, or, we might say, the point of diffraction, is at once objective—I see the thing itself—and subjective—the other's perception is "drawn inward" (*vers le dedans*), "behind his body" (VI 25/9). In other words, to use Platonic language, the point of intersection is at once the idea—I see the thing itself—and image—the other's perception is inside his head. Thus, we can see that the halfway point in the middle of the X, the mi-lieu, is precisely nothing, since it refers back to my vision and to that of the other; yet is it something since it is what is seen. As we have already noted, Merleau-Ponty calls this something a "Wesen in the sense of a verb," or it is the whole imminent in each of its parts.

The chiasm of language works in the same way as the chiasm of vision. As we already noted, for Merleau-Ponty, the mi-lieu is defined by the dative relation, speaking *to*. Thus, in a dialogue, someone is interrogating, we might say, *to* me, asking a question *to* me. When someone is questioning to me, I always encounter the non-presence of the other. I cannot live your stream of consciousness. I lack your, so to speak, soul. So, no matter what you say to me, I encounter it as a question, a question lacking an answer, lacking a sense. Therefore, no matter what you say, it sounds like silence to me. But what you have expressed is there right in the middle, halfway between you and me. Separated from you, I can repeat your expression. So it consists in a kind of ideality or sense. But, since I have only the ideality and not its, so to speak, "soul," I must create an other "side" of the ideality, express it. Thus, what is in the middle, halfway, is not nothing, but a "something," an "Etwas," as Merleau-Ponty says, "upon which these two sides are articulated"; it is the pivot of the "to," a pivot—Merleau-Ponty also uses the words "hinge" (HL BN 12, 13)[50] and "jointure" (HL BN 43)—that is, an invisible through which the visible holds (HL BN 12).

It is well known that Merleau-Ponty, before Foucault, used the image of the fold (e.g., S 53/42), and, indeed, the chiasm itself implies a fold, a four-fold. What we must conclude from our discussion of the chiasm is that, for Merleau-Ponty, the visible and the invisible, words and things, are interlaced, folded tightly together. Indeed, archeology for Merleau-Ponty questions back into this tightly woven knot. Yet, in *The Archeology of Knowledge,* Foucault says that by remaining at the level of discourse itself (which he describes as a "gray light"),[51] "by analyzing discourses themselves, one sees the loosening of the embrace, apparently so strong, of words and things" (AS 66/49). This comment obviously refers to Foucault's slightly earlier *Les Mots et les choses*. Indeed, *Les Mots et les choses* concerns precisely this loosening of the intertwining of words and things. It is not by accident, of course—and this is well known—that Foucault calls his chapter on the Renaissance "The Prose of the World," thereby appropriating the title of a work from the Fifties that Merleau-Ponty abandoned. In the Renaissance "up to the end of the 16th century," the "visible and the invisible," the entire universe "was rolled up upon itself" (MC 32/17). Words and things were so tightly folded together that there was a writing of the world and a world of writing. According to Foucault, this interlacing of words and things is so tight that (unlike the ternary system inherited from the Stoics) it resolves itself into "one unique figure"

(MC 57/42). With the Classical epoch, however, what we would call the modern epoch, this interlacing was to be analyzed, and this unique and absolute layer was to become binary. This Classical moment is crucial for Foucault's own thinking since it unties, "separates," words and things, leaving the eye to see and only to see and the ear to do nothing more than hear (MC 58/43). Words and things became separate when impressions were no longer considered as signs. But, as we know from Hume, taken on their own, impressions succeed one another in the most total differentiation and thus in perfect monotony (MC 83/68–69). It is here, for Foucault, in the Classical epoch with the monotony of impressions that the fold occurs. No impression would ever appear as either similar to or dissimilar from a previous one, if there were no power of recall, in a word, memory. This power of recall allows for representation, for, as Foucault says, "the always possible *refolding* [*repli*] of imagination" (MC 83/69, my emphasis). Based in this "refolding," representation *mediates* between things and words; indeed, representation in the Classical epoch defines being. Things would be determined by representations, and it would be possible to lay them out on a table, simultaneously; it would be possible to classify them. Words would be representations that would form their own table perfectly matched with the things. At the end of the eighteenth century the Classical epoch comes to an end, according to Foucault, because "the very being of what is represented is going to fall now outside of representation" (MC 253/240). According to Foucault, this discontinuity in which we now have two separate domains, representation and being, without mediation, allows for upsurge of the human sciences. Man occupies now the fold between words and things. And famously or infamously, Foucault announces at the end of *Les Mots et les choses* that the figure of man will come to an end; in fact, the void left by man's disappearance, for Foucault, does not prescribe a gap that must be filled. He says, "[This gap] is nothing more and nothing less than the unfolding [*dépli*] of a space in which it is once more possible to think" (MC 353/342).

In *Les Mots et les choses,* Foucault does not directly describe this unfolded space, but he certainly suggests it when he talks (in the Preface) about what inspired him to write this book. The inspiration came, he says, from Borges, when he invented, in one of his books, an entry for animal in a Chinese encyclopedia (MC 7/xv). Consisting in a series of kinds of animals, both real and fantastic, arranged arbitrarily with each designated by a letter of the Western alphabet, the encyclopedia entry has, according to Foucault, a monstrous quality. For Foucault, the monstrous quality of this taxonomy arises from the blanks that separate the categories from one another. This comment seems to be not very different from what we saw in Merleau-Ponty, since the prior whole is something that allows the wide diversity of expressions to be in a relation of "fraternity" inside a "single task." This single task would be "the common place [*lieu*]," *in* [*en*] which or *upon* [*sur*] which we could say this expression *and* this expression *and* this expression belong together (cf. MC 8/xvi). Yet, the entry that Borges reproduces contains a category that "ruins," according to Foucault, this common place. The category designated with the letter "h" is animals "included in this present classification" (MC 8/xvii). Thus, for Foucault, the monstrous quality of the taxonomy comes from a paradox. One of the categories contained in the classification itself contains all the other categories of the classification. We will therefore never be able to define a stable relation of container and contained. As Foucault says, "Absurdity destroys the *and* of the enumeration by making impossible the *in* where the things enumerated would be divided" (MC 9/xvii, Foucault's emphasis). Borges does away with the common place, the site, "the mute soil upon which it is possible for entities to be juxtaposed" (MC 9/xvii). In other words, there is no table that would allow us to lace words and things tightly together. This lack is a "disorder" or a "dimension without law or geometry," in which things are " 'laid,' 'posited,' or 'de-posited' in sites so different that it is impossible to find a space within which to welcome them" (MC 9/xvii–xviii). Foucault calls this unwelcoming space a "non-lieu" (MC 8/xvii), "the heteroclite," literally, the other-fold (MC 9/xvii). There is no "fraternity" in the heteroclite;[52] there is only "incompatibility" (MC 25/9). The Borges encyclopedia entry is a space of dispersion. This space of dispersion, for Foucault, is a purely unfolded space within which one can strategize, refold the statements, and make new statements, or even constitute new forms of subjectivity.

Conclusion: Absolute Memory

We can now see the distance between the archeologies of Merleau-Ponty and Foucault. In general, the philosophical concept of archeology concerns the past understood as still present, as actual or effective, as simultaneous with the present. Thus philosophical archeology concerns the spatialization of time; it concerns a kind of strange place. The spatial conditions outlined in archeology are in no way equivalent to mundane spatial relations such as one thing beside another or one thing outside another or one thing inside another. In these spatial conditions, the fundamental issue is the decision to conceive this non-mundane space as transcendence or immanence, or more precisely as impure immanence and pure immanence. If we follow Merleau-Ponty, then we are conceiving this spatialized time as impure immanence, as a sort of transcendence. If we are conceiving spatiality as a sort of transcendence, then the simultaneous past is transcendent to the present. If the simultaneous past is, however, transcendent to the present, then we need a strange (that is, non-mundane) connection to keep transcendence from being transcendent in the Platonic sense, that is, from being a pure heterogeneity. We must have a relation between the past and the present that holds the two together, and here perhaps we would have to take up a reflection on the *á même*. On the other hand, if we follow Foucault, then we are conceiving this spatialized time as immanence, or, better, as pure immanence, without any dative relation at all. If we are conceiving spatiality as immanence, then we are conceiving the simultaneous past as immanent in the present. If the past is immanent to the present, then we need a strange (that is, non-mundane) separation to keep immanence from being the immanence of consciousness as in the early Husserl, that is, a pure homogeneity. We must have a non-relation that holds the two apart, and again we would be led to a reflection on the *á même*. Despite this double development depending on how Merleau-Ponty and Foucault have decided to conceive spatiality of the past and present, they end up, as we saw, describing both the connection and the separation as a "lack"; the strangeness or non-mundane character of the relation demands this term. *This lack is precisely the point of diffraction between Merleau-Ponty and Foucault within the philosophical concept of archeology.*

We characterized the diffraction between them as a negativism and a positivism, since Merleau-Ponty calls the lack a negative and Foucault calls it a positive. Yet, we saw, as we pursued the difference between the archive and the museum, that Foucault's positivism really depends on the whole never being said, which, in turn, allows the statements to be entirely positive. They are not related to anything other than themselves; they are exterior. Their positivity consists in being dispersed. Historical a priori, for Foucault, are dis-positions of dispersion. What defines the archive is multiplicity. In contrast, Merleau-Ponty's negativism really depends on the whole being said, but never being said explicitly. The implicit but empty "single task" in turn allows the expressions to be entirely negative. They are related back to something other than themselves; they are interior to this task. Their negativity consists in being unified. Dispersion and exteriority belong to the museum; as a result, it is not, according to Merleau-Ponty, the true milieu of expression. Drawing on Merleau-Ponty's constant reference to the soil and cave dwellers, we called this true milieu the earth; the earth is the place of "implicity." This place of implicity is the chiasm. In the chiasm of vision or of dialogue, two halves, four eyes, your inside and outside and my inside and outside are related across a jointure. The chiasm is a "mi-lieu." We must say, therefore, that Merleau-Ponty's archeological space is a "homoclite." Here words and things, the visible and the invisible, are tightly folded together at the point. Divergence consists in following the reversals of the threads that were hidden inside; this hidden-ness is why one is able to create. In contrast, for Foucault, multiplicity is pre-cisely the unfold. In the unfold of discourse or description, statements are related across a disjointure. The unfold is a "non-lieu." Thus Foucault's ar-cheological space is a heteroclite. Here words and things, the visible and the invisible, are unhooked from one another, divergent. In fact, in Foucault, the point of divergence is not a point at all; this non-point is why one is able to strategize.

This disjunction between creation and strategizing points to the paradoxi-cal character of all philosophical archeology. Its interest in the past is never for the sake of the past. Its aim is always the future. Thus philosophical arche-ology is against a certain kind of forgetfulness and a certain kind of memory. It is against the kind of forgetfulness that accompanies the boisterous proc-lamation of the new. It is against the kind of memory that drones on about returning to the old. Instead, opposed to the droning memory, philosophi-cal archeology is a counter-memory. And opposed to boisterous forgetful-ness, philosophical archeology is a counter-forgetfulness. These "counters," of course, imply something else. Counter-forgetfulness becomes a new kind of memory. Perhaps Merleau-Ponty points to this new kind of memory when he says, in "Indirect Language and the Voices of Silence,"

> The world as soon as he has seen it, his first attempt at painting, and the whole past of painting all deliver up a *tradition* to the painter—*that is,* Husserl says, *the power to forget origins* and to give to the past not a sur-vival [*une survie*], which is the hypocritical form of forgetfulness, but a new life, which is the noble form of memory. (S 73–74/59, Merleau-Ponty's emphasis)

Or, perhaps, Foucault points to this new kind of memory when he says, com-paring Michel Leiris with Raymond Roussel,

> From so many things without social standing, from so many fantastic civic records, [Leiris] slowly accumulates his own identity, as if within folds of words there slept, with nightmares never completely extinguished, an abso-lute memory. These same folds Roussel parts with a studied gesture to find the stifling hollowness, the inexorable absence of being, which he disposes in complete sovereignty to create forms without parentage or species.[53]

Undoubtedly, if there is an urgency to my question of philosophical arche-ology, it arose from a need that I feel for this different kind of memory. Whether we call it noble or absolute, it is a memory identical to forgetfulness. This memory forgets (counter-memory) about totality and presence. It is a memory identical to the forgetfulness of the form of the present. Within this memory, forgetfulness will be a point of absence or dispersion. We shall have to symbolize it not just as a point but also as a question mark. Only if we remember the question will we be able to call this memory a "memory of the future."

3   Eliminating Some Confusion

The Relation of Being and Writing in Merleau-Ponty and Derrida

[Our life] is constantly enshrouded by those mists we call the sensible world or history, the one [*on*] of corporeal life and the one [*on*] of human life, the present and the past, as a pell-mell ensemble of bodies and minds, promiscuity of faces, words, actions, with, between them all, that cohesion which cannot be denied them since they are all differences, extreme *écarts* of one same something.
—Merleau-Ponty, *The Visible and the Invisible* (VI 116–17/84)

Does not this "dialectic"—in every sense of the term and before any speculative reconquest of this concept—open up living to différance, constituting in the pure immanence of lived experience the *écart* of indicative communication and even of signification in general?
—Derrida, *Voice and Phenomenon* (VP 77/69)

Perhaps more than anything else, this word *écart* has contributed to the belief that Merleau-Ponty's thought, especially that found in *The Visible and the Invisible,* anticipates, if not matches completely, Derrida's thought, especially that found in early texts such as *Voice and Phenomenon.* What is basic in each—*différance* in Derrida's case; the flesh in Merleau-Ponty's—is reversible. Both the flesh and *différance* are described in terms of contamination. There is ambiguity in Merleau-Ponty, undecidability in Derrida. Derrida and Merleau-Ponty share the same concern for difference and absence. It even seems possible to develop an ethics on the basis of their respective thoughts.[1] Yet, despite their undeniable proximity, one can establish distance between Merleau-Ponty and Derrida, first and foremost in the following way: Derrida is a grammatologist; Merleau-Ponty is an ontologist.

The decisive point is, as Derrida says, that "différance, in a certain and very strange way, [is] 'older' than the ontological difference or than the truth of Being (MP 23/22; cf. DLG 38/23). This comment makes two claims. On the one hand, it claims that *différance* cannot be defined in terms of being. *Différance* refers to an absolute non-being. Defined in this way, *différance* refers to a negation, a nothing that can be defined neither as a dimension of one sole something nor as a variant of the real. We can come to understand this "nothing" only if we recognize that the element that Derrida interrogates is logic, or more generally, language, and most precisely, writing. In contrast, the element that Merleau-Ponty interrogates is the visible, or more generally, experience, and most precisely, being. On the other hand, the comment claims, because of the strange sort of priority that Derrida mentions, that *différance*'s structure is supplementary: what is second is first and nothing returns to it. In contrast, for Merleau-Ponty, the structure of the flesh is circular: what is first is first and everything else turns within it.

To demonstrate this, I am going to proceed in two steps. First, starting from the element of being, I am going to try to reconstruct the ontology that animates *The Visible and the Invisible*. Merleau-Ponty's thought amounts to a monism, hence the circular structure of the flesh. The test of any monism lies in the relation of language to being. For Merleau-Ponty, speech is homogeneous with being because spoken language is one of being's possibilities. In contrast, language as a formalized system is separated from experience and seems to befall the homogeneity of being like an accident. Writing makes the transition to Derrida. Starting from the element of language, I am going to reconstruct the grammatology that animates Derrida's writings. We shall see here that Derrida's thought amounts to a dualism, hence the supplementary structure of *différance*. Because of writing's formality, the homogeneity of being already contains separation: the accident is necessary. In Derrida, the impossible can happen. Only if we clarify these two differences with as much precision as possible—that of Derrida's "grammatologism" versus Merleau-Ponty's ontologism, and the structure of supplementarity versus the structure of circularity—will we be able to eliminate at least some of the confusion concerning their relation. And only then will we truly be able to move to what seems to be the most pressing question: the question of alterity.

I. The Fall into Writing

From his earliest writings, Merleau-Ponty's project has consisted in the overcoming of the mind-body duality. In order to address this problem, Merleau-Ponty interrogates the visible, or more generally experience, and most precisely being. We can see that being is the interrogated element, for Merleau-Ponty, when, in *The Visible and the Invisible*'s fourth chapter, on the chiasm, he says that "the flesh is . . . an 'element' of Being" (VI 184/139). That this element must be understood in terms of experience can be seen in the opening chapter, when Merleau-Ponty defines perceptual faith in terms of experience (VI 48–49/28). And finally, returning again to *The Visible and the Invisible*'s ultimate chapter, we see Merleau-Ponty speak of the element as the visible (VI 184/140). Indeed, combining the terms, he says, "we would simply find again . . . scraps of this ontology of the visible mixed up *with* all our theories of knowledge" (VI 185/140, Merleau-Ponty's emphasis). Ontology, in *The Visible and the Invisible,* describes what Merleau-Ponty calls "ontological history" (VI 186/141) or "ontogenesis" (VI 30/14, 139/102, 266/213); it describes the genesis of meaning from experience (VI 146/109), from being (VI 148/110), or from being-in-the-world (VI 28/12). As Merleau-Ponty says, "Thought cannot ignore its apparent history, if it is not to install itself beneath the whole of our experience, in a pre-empirical order where it would no longer merit its name; it must put to itself the problem of the genesis of its own meaning" (VI 28/12).

The comparative plus *vieux que,* the adjectives *préalable* and *postérieure,* the preposition *avant,* the verb *précéder,* and the prefix *pré-*occur repeatedly in *The Visible and the Invisible.* They refer to a specific sort of priority, the key to which lies in the prepositions *au-dessous* and *sur.* Priority, for Merleau-Ponty, is not equivalent to "a transcendental, intemporal order, as a system of *a priori* conditions" (VI 117/85). In fact, this sort of system, according to Merleau-Ponty, "is in principle posterior to an actual experience" (VI 69/45). It is not the case that conditions for the possibility precede experience; rather, they "accompany" or "translate" or "express" experience (VI 69/45). Thus, the "originary," for Merleau-Ponty, while not excluding the "true past," cannot be reduced to what lies *derrière* us (VI 165/124). The originary is what is *below* and *over* us. Thus it is impossible to speak of logical or temporal priority (cf. VI 191/145); "before" means a lower level or tier (VI 153/114). Being is vertical, and that verticality is why Merleau-Ponty describes his final philosophy as an archeology.

Although Merleau-Ponty describes what is originary in terms of space, he forbids us to think of the "over" in terms of "superposition" (VI 177/134). This interdiction goes along with Merleau-Ponty's constant criticism, in *The Visible and the Invisible,* of "suveying thought" (*la pensée en survol*) and his sustained criticism of the notion of essence in the third chapter. Superposition, surveying thought, and essence imply a real or ideal rupture with experience (cf. VI 161/120). Experience, however, is "homogeneous" (VI 153/114). The "space of existence" (VI 150/111), the "milieu" (VI 154/114, 155/115, 156/117), the "atmosphere" (VI 116/84) is "undivided" (VI 162/121; cf. VI 157/117). The originary is "one same something" (VI 117/84), "the same world" (VI 64/41, 27/11), "one sole Being" (VI 148/110), "the unique Being" (VI 157/117; cf. VI 64/41); and oppositions "belong to the same Being" (VI 114/82) and to "one same body" (VI 185/141). Although Merleau-Ponty speaks of ambiguity (VI 129/94), this is an ambiguity—it is "good ambiguity" and not ambivalence (VI 127/93)—"not lacking in univocity." Although Merleau-Ponty speaks of a "hiatus" between touching and being touched, a hiatus that seems to imply a break or a cut, he adds immediately that this hiatus "is not an ontological void, a non-being" (VI 195/148). Perceptual faith "is not nothing" (VI 74/49; cf. VI 160/120); moreover, "one starts with an ontological relief where one can never say that the ground be nothing" (VI 121/88). Most importantly, "the negative . . . is borne by an infrastructure of being" (VI 160/120; cf. VI 134/98). That the negative is carried by being can be seen in the following expression: experience "is of [Being] but is *not* it" (*qui 'en est,' mais n'est pas lui*) (VI 164/123, my emphasis). The genitive *de* (or *en*) in such expressions (VI 92/63, 198/151, 200/153) is not an abyss.[2] Although, in the Introduction to *Signs*, Merleau-Ponty speaks of an "abyss" in what is fundamental, he adds immediately that we must not say that "this extremity is nothing" (S 29/21). In fact, in *The Visible and the Invisible*, Merleau-Ponty seems to think that the notion of an abyss represents a different way to conceive being than *écart* (VI 180/136–37). The genitive, we can even say, refers to an identity: the body "communicates this identity without superposition, this difference without contradiction, this divergence between the within and the without that constitutes its natal secret to the things upon which it closes" (VI 179/135–36); "my activity is identically [*identiquement*] passivity" (VI 183/139).

In the sense of an exterior relation between two individuals, there is no dualism in Merleau-Ponty nor is there a monism in the sense of one something containing individuals "as in a box" (VI 157/117, 182/138; cf. also VI 200/152, 53/32). The originary, he says, is "not of one sole type" (VI 165/124), of which other things would be mere instantiations or copies. Nevertheless, his ontology is a monism because of the notion of possibility. Everything in Merleau-Ponty, the Merleau-Ponty of *The Visible and the Invisible*, turns on the notion of possibility. Although Merleau-Ponty's ontology is not a materialism (cf. V1 184/139, 191/146), it is being's *content*, the real, which includes possibilities, and it is possibilities that generate differences, divergences, and negations. Possibility determines the very structure of the flesh. The flesh, Merleau-Ponty says, is not synthetic, which would imply a gap to be bridged (VI 23/8, 186/141). Rather, the flesh is "one sole body," "one sole tangible" (VI 186/141) "pregnant with all visions one *can* have of it" (VI 166/124, my emphasis). The flesh is the real (VI 150/112); and rather than the real being a simple variant of the possible, "it is the possible worlds and the possible beings that are variants and are like doubles of the actual world and actual Being" (VI 150/112). This comment clarifies the notion of doubling in *The Visible and the Invisible*. The double—the touched of the touching, for example—is the actualization of a possibility. As the flesh's "extension" (VI 153/114), as "a variant of one common world" (VI 27/11), the flesh is "relatively continuous" (VI 28/12). Doubles—touching and being touched —are opposites only when they have been transformed into theses, propositions, or significations (VI 30/13, 27/11). As Merleau-Ponty says, "The 'natural' man holds on to both ends of the chain, thinks *at the same time* that his perception enters into things and that it is formed this side of his body. Yet coexist as the two convictions do without difficulty in the exercise of life, once reduced to theses and to propositions they destroy one another and leave us in confusion" (VI 23–24/8, Merleau-Ponty's emphasis). When formulated, the compossibles appear as incompossibles (VI 49/29); since the compossibles appear as incompossible, Merleau-Ponty calls the world (or the flesh) the "impossible-possible" (VI 56/34).

Even though there is no contradiction in the flesh's reversibility, there is no coincidence (VI 162/122). The lack of coincidence is due to the fact that being is not the "immediate" (VI 162/122). Being is non-coincidence because it consists in a "double reference, the identity of returning into oneself with emergence from oneself, of lived experience with distance" (VI 165/124; cf. also VI 27/11, 130/95). This slogan—"to return into onself is to emerge from oneself" (VI 74/49)—implies that to actualize one possibility is to leave another possibility unactualized. As Merleau-Ponty says, I cannot "dominate all the implications of the spectacle" (VI 150/112). Opposed to *la pensée en survol,* for Merleau-Ponty, is *enlisé dans l'être.* Thus, stressing the spatiality of the flesh, one must say that every possibility of being is situated. So, as Merleau-Ponty points out, if perception is a fusion with the thing, the perception is extinguished and I cease to exist; conversely, if perception maintains distance, which preserves me, then I am no longer with the thing (VI 163/122). Similarly, if memory amounts to the process of preserving the past in the present, if it really allows me to "become again what I was," then "it becomes impossible to see how it could open to me the dimension of the past" (VI 163/122). For Merleau-Ponty, in either process—perception or memory—it is always necessary to begin again. This double reference—this identity—is why the image of the circle is appropriate for the notion of the flesh in *The Visible and the Invisible.* Such a spatial image implies that what is first is "the total situation" (VI 57/35, 74/49, 121/88), being. None of the positions within the circuit have priority (cf. VI 56–57/35); always referring back to the whole, all the positions are second. Making sense only in terms of each other, none of the positions makes sense independently. The lack of independence keeps the circle restless. As Merleau-Ponty says, "If one wants metaphors, it would be better to say that the body sensed and the body sentient are as the obverse and the reverse, or again, two segments of one sole circular course which goes above from left to right and below from right to left, but which is one sole movement in two phases" (VI 182/138; cf. also VI 125/91, 159/119, 185/140, 188/143).

Although one cannot, according to Merleau-Ponty, speak of "effective fusion" with being, which would bring the circular movement to rest, one can speak of "partial coincidence." This "good error" is made possible by language, but not by just any language (VI 166/124–25). The origin, Merleau-Ponty says repeatedly, is "silent" or "mute" (VI 17/3, 18/4, 57/35, 121/88, 138/102, 159/119, 167/125–26, 202/154). He says, for example, "language lives only from silence; everything we cast to the others has germinated in this great mute land" (VI 167/126). Moreover, he speaks of "the transition from the mute world to the speaking world" (VI 202/154). Finally, he says that "It is as though visibility . . . emigrated [*émigrait*] not outside of every body, but into another less heavy, more transparent body . . . that of language" (VI 200/153). Nevertheless silence is not the "contrary of language" (VI 233/ 179). He says that "lived experience is spoken lived experience [*vécu-parlé*], that, born at this depth, language is not a mask over Being . . . but the most valuable witness to Being" (VI 167/126). Being is not an "immediation that would be perfect without [language] . . . vision itself, the thought itself are . . . 'structured like a language'" (VI 168/126; cf. VI 169/127; S 53/44). Thus, somewhat paradoxically, Merleau-Ponty can speak of "mute language" and "voices of silence" (VI 168/126–27).

That silence is not the contrary of language means that "the structure of [our] mute world is such that all the possibilities of language are already given in it" (VI 203/155). From these possibilities arise an "operative language or speech" (VI 202/154). It is only operative speech, creative language, that allows for the partial coincidence with being. In order to capture the mute character of "authentic language" (S 53/44), Merleau-Ponty compares it to painting—Renoir's paintings "interrogated the visible and made something visible" (S 79/63)—and especially to music. Music such as the "little phrase" described by Proust in *Swann's Way* can sustain a meaning (*sens*) by means of its own arrangement (VI 201/153). Consequently, Merleau-Ponty describes operative language as one in which "sense and sound are in the same relationships as the 'little phrase'" (VI 201/153). This perfect unity of sense and sensible is the Merleau-Pontean *logos* (VI 168/126, 202/154). The Merleau-Pontean *logos* is

> a language of which [the speaker] would not be the organizer, words
> he would not assemble, that would combine through him by virtue of a
> natural intertwining of their meaning, through the occult trading of the
> metaphor—where what counts is no longer the manifest meaning of each

> word and of each image, but the lateral relations, the kinships that are implicated in their transfers and their exchanges. (VI 167/125)

Insofar as the *logos* makes the things themselves speak, it is not only the language of poets but also, according to Merleau-Ponty, the language of the philosopher: "It is by considering language that we would best see how we are to and how we are not to return to the things themselves" (VI 166/125).

We are not to return to the things themselves by means of the language of linguists, "an ideal system, a fragment of the intelligible world" (VI 201/154; S 53/44). While recognizing that such formal systems are the "occultation of the truth," "the reflective vice," "the first irretrievable lie," "forgetfulness of perceptual faith," for Merleau-Ponty, ideal systems arise from creative language. In other words, this "object of science" (VI 202/154)—theses, significations, propositions—is generated by means of an idealization of the real (VI 70/46). Similarly, "pure idealities"—as in geometry—are generated from the real. As always with Merleau-Ponty in *The Visible and the Invisible,* the issue in "the passage to ideality" (VI 51/30) is to describe an absence that would not be the contrary of the sensible (cf. VI 188/142–43), a negativity that would not be nothing (VI 198/151), an invisible that would be the possibility of the visible. Having, like and before Derrida, studied Husserl's *The Origin of Geometry,* Merleau-Ponty is well aware that the genesis of ideal objects—idealization—takes place through writing: books, museums, musical scores.[3] Nevertheless, Merleau-Ponty is also aware that writing becomes a "petrified meaning," that sense becomes "separated" or "detached" (*coupé*) (VI 126/92). Based in writing, the philosophy of essences, according to Merleau-Ponty, "succeeds in detaching itself from all beings" (*à se déprendre de tous les être*) (VI 145/108); writing is "a generalized warping of my landscape" (*un gauchissement général de mon paysage*) (VI 159/119). Most importantly, "Lived experience can no longer recognize itself [*se retrouver*] in the idealizations we draw from it" (VI 120/87). He even admits that pure ideality, made possible by writing, "will pass definitely beyond the circle of the visible" (VI 189/144, 30/14).

If it is indeed the case—and here we make the transition to Derrida—that writing brings about such an alterity, can we say the following: "When the silent vision *falls* [*tombe*] into speech, and when speech in turn, opening up a field of the nameable and the sayable, inscribes itself in that field, in its place, according to its truth—in short, when it metamorphoses the structures of the visible world and makes itself a gaze of the mind, *intuitus mentis,* this is always in virtue of the *same* fundamental phenomenon of reversibility" (VI 203/154–55, my emphasis)? Can we account for "spirit" without re-conceiving the fall into writing? Can we explain the "impossibility" of pure ideality by means of possibilities of the flesh? Mustn't we instead re-conceive the interrogative element in terms of non-phenomenality, in terms of the nothing?

II. A Dryer Question

In "Violence and Metaphysics," Derrida appropriates Levinas's thought (ED 161/109). Derrida's questions, however, break with those of Levinas. He asks, at the close of "Violence and Metaphysics," "Can one speak of an *experience* of the other or of difference? Has not the concept of experience always been determined by the metaphysics of presence? Is not experience always an encounter of an irreducible presence, the perception of a phenomenality?" (ED 225/152, Derrida's emphasis). Because of the sedimentation associated with the word "experience," for Derrida one must interrogate the element of logic, or more generally language. Most precisely, it is only through an interrogation of writing that one can gain access to the "beyond" of being, to what exceeds ontology (as well as phenomenology). As Derrida says in *Of Grammatology,* "Even before being determined as human . . . or nonhuman, the gramme—the grapheme—would thus name the element. An element without simplicity. An element, whether it is understood as the medium [*milieu*] or as the irreducible atom, of the archi-synthesis in general, of what one must forbid oneself to define within the system of oppositions of metaphysics, of what consequently one should not even call experience in general, indeed, the origin of *sense* in general" (DLG 19–20/9, Derrida's emphasis). We cannot, therefore, understand the element of writing either in terms of experience in the traditional sense or even in terms of sense. Nevertheless, Western metaphysics, "the metaphysics of presence," as Derrida has infamously summarized Western philosophy, has so defined writing; the metaphysics of presence is a logocentrism.

For Derrida, what defines logocentrism is the attempt to conceive reason—the *logos*—as essentially independent from linguistic mediation. Logocentric philosophy conceives reason as the complete and perfect mastery over whatever it reasons about. In other words, what reason reasons about is conceived as completely present. This conception of reason refers to an "absolute *logos*" (DLG 25/13). Consequently, language is relative. Language functions merely as a means of conveying already completed knowledge. In logocentrism—exemplified by Hegel, according to Derrida in "The Pit and the Pyramid"—language is a detour through which reason is able to return to itself (MP 82/71). Logocentrism, for Derrida, is defined by circularity. We cannot miss the obvious comparison of logocentrism to what we saw in Merleau-Ponty.

In any case, in a logocentric philosophy not all types of language are "provisional." Logocentrism must privilege the voice over writing, the phonic substance (that is, the phonic carrier of meaning) over the graphic substance. Only speech seems to be a diaphanous membrane; voice seems best to preserve presence and to enable its recovery. Nevertheless, logocentric philosophy recognizes that if knowledge is to be universal, it must be capable of being written down. Writing is a necessary supplement. Again, however, not every type of writing is well suited for this task. In order to ensure the passage's safety, knowledge must be written in a phonetic alphabet, which seems to maintain the animation of breath. In contrast, nonphonetic writing such as Chinese remains opaque; this type of writing is breathless because it is formalistic. As formalistic (or structural), each character, of course, derives its meaning from its difference from other characters (MP 122/104). Such formalistic writing would include mathematics—indeed, mathematical language is the model for nonphonetic writing (DLG 20/9)—where mere rote learning of the forms can lead to the manipulation of the signs without thought or content. Nonphonetic writings, therefore, are the death of speech (MP 123/105); in this case, writing functions as a mere supplement, something superfluous. Overall in logocentrism, writing, according to Derrida, is seen as derivative from speech; writing is even seen as an unfortunate accident afflicting speech from the outside.

For Derrida, grammatology, as the science of scienticity (DLG 43/27), is the science of logocentrism. Unlike Merleau-Ponty's ontology, grammatology is not primarily a genetic interrogation. Instead, it begins with the very "dry" (*seche*) question of essence (DLG 43/28),[4] which it then complicates through the question of genesis: "The grammatologist least of all can avoid questioning himself about the essence of his object in the form of a question of origin: 'What is writing?' means 'where and when does writing begin?'" (DLG 43/28). For Derrida, however, the genetic questions always disclose that language is constitutive for the generation of any object—natural or cultural—or of any thought. The genetic question always leads back to the structural question. Grammatology therefore begins with the structural question (or the naive ontological question, as Derrida also calls it [VP 26/25]), complicates it by means of genesis, only to return to structure, to the structure that makes genesis possible, in a word, language.

The grammatological movement can be seen already in Derrida's 1962 Introduction to Husserl's "The Origin of Geometry."[5] In order to understand the genesis of geometry and the method of reactivation of geometry's origin that Husserl describes here, it is necessary to investigate the structure of writing; writing, as Derrida shows (following Husserl), constitutes all ideal objects, indeed, all meaning, all truth, insofar as ideality must be intersubjective, onmispatial, and onmitemporal. As Derrida says, because the possibility of writing ensures the absolute traditionalization of the object, its absolute ideal objectivity, "the possibility or necessity of being incarnated in something graphic is no longer simply extrinsic and factual in comparison with ideal objectivity: it is the sine qua non condition of objectivity's internal completion" (LOG 86/89). Writing's ability to make ideal objectivity possible—the *sine qua non*—implies that "writing creates a kind of autonomous transcendental field from which every actual subject can be absent" (LOG 84/88). In other words, according to Derrida, writing implies the death of actual subjects; how else to virtualize dialogue? Nevertheless, in order to be what it is, writing must depend on a writer or reader in general; a text must be haunted by a virtual intentionality; in principle it must be intelligible for a transcendental subject in general. Otherwise, a text is unreadable, "a defunct designation" (LOG 85/88). Yet, and this is the crucial point for Derrida, there are silent prehistoric arcana, buried civilizations, intentions lost and secrets guarded in tombs, illegible inscriptions. Such imperfect unities of sense and sensible disclose that, even though we can see that death has a meaning (that is, death serves the purpose of making ideal objectivity possible), the fact that writing must be able—that is, in principle be able—to separate itself from its origin implies the failure of that meaning (*sens*) or purpose (LOG 85/88). The separation makes nonsense intrinsic to sense.

In "Signature Event Context," Derrida describes the same structure of writing. In SEC (as Derrida calls this essay in "Limited Inc."), in this very "dry" discourse, Derrida isolates certain characteristics of writing, which seem to be implied by writing's "usually accepted sense" (MP 369/311). He focuses especially on the characteristic of absence. According to Derrida, the absence of the actual sender or the intended receiver from writing is not an absence that happens sometimes, a factual absence. Rather, in order for writing to be what it is, absence must be able to "be brought to a certain absolute degree" (MP 374/315). Writing must be able to be legible, or more precisely, must be able to function "in the absolute absence of the addressee or of the empirically determined set of addressees" (MP 375/315). If absence is internal to the very constitution of what we call writing, then, as Derrida says, "this absence is not a continuous modification of presence; it is a break in presence, 'death,' or the possibility of the 'death' of the addressee, inscribed in the structure of the mark" (MP 375/316). Parenthetically, Derrida reminds us immediately of what we saw in the *Introduction,* that "the value or effect of transcendentality is linked necessarily to the possibility of writing and of 'death' analyzed in this way" (MP 375/316; cf. also VP 60–61/54).

The necessary link between the possibility of writing and transcendentality is precisely what Derrida calls *différance.* Or, to put this in another way, for Derrida in *Voice and Phenomenon* (and elsewhere), *différance* refers to the relation that holds between ideality and factuality. Facts exist as things in the world; in contrast, "authentic ideality" (VP 4/6) "is *nothing* existing in the world" (VP 8/10, my emphasis). Yet, while existing in a non-worldly sense, authentic ideality does not exist as something outside of the world; this externality—inauthentic ideality—was Platonism's mistake. Thus the relation (or passage or transition) between fact and essence is neither, for Derrida, a monism in the sense of one homogeneous being nor a dualism in the sense of two separate things. Yet, unlike the monistic relation in Merleau-Ponty, the relation in Derrida is a certain kind of dualism. As Derrida says, one must conceive the relation between fact and essence as "a radical difference . . . one having nothing in common with any other difference, a difference in fact distinguishing *nothing*, a difference separating no state, no experience, no determined signification—but a difference which, without altering anything, changes all the signs" (VP 10/11, my emphasis). As Derrida says, concerning the relation between the empirical (or psychological) ego and the transcendental ego, "my transcendental ego is radically different from my natural and human ego; and yet it is distinguished by nothing, nothing that can be determined in the natural sense of distinction" (VP 11/11–12; see also ED 245–46/164). This nothing is the nothing that distinguishes parallels. In other words, it is an empty space between, a void between, a division between, an *écart*, even an abyss that separates and joins (cf. VP 75/67). Maintaining an ontic identity, the relation is a duplication that is not a duplicity (VP 11/11).[6] *Différance is* a re-flection, a folding back over, and such a superposition defines doubling in Derrida. The nothing makes the relation called *différance* undecidable and not ambiguous; while, as we saw, ambiguity supposes the relative continuity of the two poles, undecidability supposes the relative discontinuity of the two poles. Finally, we can say that, because of the nothing, being, for Derrida, is not homogeneous. The nothing is the absolute nonsense, the absolute non-being, that makes the different senses of being possible. *Différance,* therefore, refers to nothing and, unlike Merleau-Ponty's flesh, not to something.

We can see how the nothing functions in Derrida by examining his analysis of auto-affection in *Voice and Phenomenon*'s Chapter 6," 'The Voice That Guards Silence." As Derrida says here, the necessity of auto-affection to bring about ideal meaning can be seen in Husserl's First Investigation move to interior monologue; in addition to these, Derrida relies on the *Ideas I,* #124, descriptions of the passage from experiential, and hence silent, sense to conceptual meaning, in short, the passage from experience to the *logos*. On the basis of the #124 descriptions, Derrida realizes that interior monologue, as a transition to ideality, must make use of a medium (*milieu*) or an element.[7] As Derrida says, "Husserl is unable to bracket what in glossamatics is called the 'substance of expression' without menacing his whole enterprise" (VP

86/76–77). Since Husserl is describing a monologue, this "substance" must be the voice. It seems that hearing oneself speak, which relies on the phonic carrier, allows meaning to be constituted as both an ideality, and thus opposed to me, and also as something absolutely close to me and thus still inside me (VP 83/75). Being diaphanous and alive, breath allows the meaning to be present—thus appears as an ideality and not to pass outside into the world—it is still animated by my intention (VP 87/77). In other words, auto-affection supposes "that a pure difference comes to divide self-presence" (VP 92/82). This difference is pure because, as constitutive of ideality, auto-affection "creates nothing"; ideality is neither a being nor a produced object, neither a natural thing nor a cultural thing (VP 93/84). Moreover, being constituted interiorly, ideality is engendered by nothing (in the world) (VP 93/83). Pure difference must be a difference, which is not a difference, that is, not a difference between beings.

Yet, what makes it a difference is that ideality cannot be itself unless it can be repeated indefinitely; the passage to ideality (or to an ideal object) is a "passage to the limit" or to infinity (VP 84/75; cf. LOG 146/134). The requirement of indefiniteness turns auto-affection into synthesis and pure difference into impure difference, in a word, into *différance*.[8] According to Derrida, Husserl (or Western metaphysics in general) privileges the voice because it is temporal (VP 93–96/83–86). As is well known from Derrida's own analyses of Husserlian temporalization in *Voice and Phenomenon,* Chapter 5, retention is the possibility of indefinite repetition in what appears now. As indefinite, retention always implies the absence, the destruction, indeed, the death of each unique now—this indefiniteness is why the experience of voice in Derrida is the experience of death[9]—indefiniteness implies that a space must be open between the now and the retention. The present in turn is a synthesis of the now and retention: a nothing that joins and divides. Moreover, as indefinite, this retentional trace implies the possibility of externalization, of the world, and of space. As Derrida says, "Taking auto-affection as the operation of the voice, auto-affection supposes a pure difference comes to divide self-presence. In this pure difference is rooted the possibility of everything we think we exclude from auto-affection: space, the outside, the world, the body, etc." (VP 92/82). *Différance* therefore makes impurity intrinsic to purity.

On the basis of this analysis of auto-affection, we can sharpen the comparison with the flesh's structure in Merleau-Ponty. Most importantly, the inclusion of indefiniteness within auto-affection implies that auto-affection is a sort of writing. The internality of writing leads to the structure of supplementarity. The structure of supplementarity cannot be understood in terms of a circle.[10] Everything, as we saw with Merleau-Ponty, is supposed to be understood in terms of the total situation; everything, even ideas made possible by writing, is supposed to return to or, better, turn within, being; being, for Merleau-Ponty, is first.

We see now, however, with Derrida, that the most basic characteristic of writing, absence or death, is internal to speech and therefore to thought (cf. VP 92/82). Writing's internality implies that what has traditionally been seen as second (or even third) is actually first, the *sine qua non* of thought. Writing even precedes being insofar as writing conditions history and all genesis. Thus writing is a supplement in two senses. On the one hand, it is a supplement in the sense of being superfluous, even in the sense of an accident; speech seems to be entirely and solely dependent on my animation. So writing is second (or even third, nothing more than a simulacrum). On the other hand, writing is a supplement in the sense of being essential, even in the sense of being necessary; there could be no speech without "signifying forms" (or codes) whose indefinite iterability implies death, absence, the nothing (cf. VP 13/13, 55–56/50; MP 378/318). So writing is first; it is what Derrida calls arche-writing.

How are we to understand this structure of the supplement? Unlike Merleau-Ponty, for whom everything turns on the notion of possibility, for Derrida everything turns on the notion of impossibility. Everything, for Derrida, turns on the notion of impossibility because Derrida's thought, starting from writing, is a thought of formalization. *And this formalization is really the ineradicable opposition between Merleau-Ponty and Derrida.* For Derrida, form is the only way to think the "beyond" of being; he says in "Form and Meaning: A Note on the Phenomenology of Language,"

> One might think then that the *sense of Being* has been limited by the
> imposition of the form which, in its most overt value and since the origin
> of philosophy, seems to have assigned to Being, along with the authority
> of the is, the closure of presence, the form-of-presence, presence-in-form,
> form-presence. One might think, on the other hand, that formality—or
> formalization—is limited by the sense of Being which, in fact, has never
> been separated from its determination as presence, beneath the excellent
> surveillance of the is: and henceforth the thinking of form has the power
> to extend itself beyond the thinking of Being. (MP 206–7/172, Derrida's
> emphasis; cf. also MP 206n14/172n16)

Writing is first of all defined by form, the letters. In order for writing to be itself, it must be separated from the one who draws it. The gap opened by formal repeatability, an iterability to infinity, implies that the same form can enter into different, even unforeseen, contexts and utilizations. The same form can be used either seriously or non-seriously. Unlike Merleau-Ponty, for Derrida these superfluous accidents—sarcasm, parody, etc.—must be conceived as "necessary accidents." *And this necessity of accidents as well defines an ineradicable difference between Derrida and Merleau-Ponty.* These "accidents" do not befall the forms; these impossibilities are of the forms. Thus the accidents that come to be associated with letters cannot be separated from the formality of the forms. And, as Derrida says often, the forms of writing are at once the condition for the possibility and the condition for the impossibility of communication (VP 113/101; LOG 84/87). Being the condition for the possibility and impossibility, forms suffocate the intention and yet they remain. Like rote learning, like what Merleau-Ponty calls the museum in "Indirect Language and the Voices of Silence" (S 79/63; cf. VI 203/154), a form is a remainder or remnant (*reste*), something dead and yet still moving; it survives, a spirit, a specter. Or, as Derrida also calls writing, it is a machine, which through its functioning can produce the impossible and thereby exceed all circularity (MP 126/105).

III. *Ousia* and *Gramme*

We can summarize the differences between Merleau-Ponty and Derrida in the following way. We started with the difference between interrogative elements (and this is probably not the most decisive difference): being versus writing. Within this difference, we were able to see that while for Merleau-Ponty being is homogeneous, relatively continuous, and undivided, writing for Derrida is heterogeneous, relatively discontinuous, and divided. On the basis of this difference, the different structures of the flesh and *différance* arose: circularity versus supplementarity. What organizes the structure of the flesh in Merleau-Ponty is the notion of possibility; in contrast, for Derrida the notion of impossibility organizes the structure of supplementarity. For Merleau-Ponty, the circular structure of being—content—accounts only for differences as possibilities of being. In contrast, for Derrida, the structure of supplementarity—formalization—accounts for alterities that are impossible. In fact, this difference between possibility and impossibility allows us to define Merleau-Ponty's and Derrida's respective uses of the word *écart*. Nevertheless, as we know from the working notes for *The Visible and the Invisible* and from "Indirect Language and the Voices of Silence," Merleau-Ponty was trying to appropriate the Saussurean notion of diacritical difference for his descriptions of experience itself (VI 267/213). Perhaps, if he had succeeded in transforming his descriptions of experience in terms of diacritics, he would have had to push the notion of ambiguity into undecidability. Indeed, what we can see from Merleau-Ponty's last lecture course on Husserl's "The Origin of Geometry" indicates that this may have been the direction of his final philosophy. We saw that Merleau-Ponty recognizes that the idealizations made possible by writing lead to impossibilities. Speaking of the generation of ideas, he says, almost at the very end of *The Visible and the Invisible*'s completed part, that "We shall have to follow more closely this transition from the mute world to the speaking world" (VI 202/154). Who knows what would have happened if Merleau-Ponty had had the time to follow this transition more closely? Perhaps, if he had had the time, he would have felt compelled to change the title of this book one more time; perhaps he would have even felt compelled to change it from *The Visible and the Invisible* to something like *Ousia and Gramme*.[11]

4　The Legacy of Husserl's "The Origin of Geometry"

The Limits of Phenomenology in Merleau-Ponty and Derrida

Nothing is more confusing than to examine, side by side, Merleau-Ponty's late writings with Derrida's early writing; it almost seems as though we are reading the same philosopher. Most obviously, the confusion arises because, in the decade from the late Fifties to the late Sixties, there is a massive terminological and thematic overlap between, say, Merleau-Ponty's 1961 *The Visible and the Invisible* and Derrida's 1967 *Voice and Phenomenon;*[1] indeed, most of this overlap centers around one word, the French word "écart." The confusion is exacerbated by the fact that this overlap occurs precisely when Merleau-Ponty's career comes to an end and Derrida's is just at its beginning. When, however, Derrida matures and becomes Derrida, the confusion seems to dissipate. No one would think, for example, that Merleau-Ponty had written this strange thing called *Glas.* Here at last, in 1974 (when *Glas* is published), one can say easily that there is no confusion between the philosophies of Merleau-Ponty and Derrida. But Derrida brings the confusion back in his 1990 *Memoirs of the Blind* when he himself suggests he is extending Merleau-Ponty:

> In order to be absolutely foreign to the visible, this invisibility would
> still inhabit the visible, or rather, it would come to haunt it to the point
> of being confused with it, in order to assure, from the specter of this
> very impossibility, its own proper resource. The visible *as such* would be
> invisible, not as visibility, the *phenomenality* or *essence* of the visible, but
> as the singular body of the visible itself, right on [*à même*] the visible—so
> that, by emanation, and as if it were secreting its own *medium* [*médium*],
> the visible would produce blindness. Whence a program for an entire
> rereading of the later Merleau-Ponty.[2]

Derrida continues by saying that, if he were to pursue this re-reading of Merleau-Ponty, he would follow the traces of "absolute invisibility," a "pure transcendence without an ontic face." This last phrase comes from a working note to *The Visible and the Invisible* dated January 1960, in which Merleau-Ponty also says, "Elaborate a phenomenology of 'the other world,' as the *limit of a phenomenology* of the imaginary and the hidden" (VI 283/229, my emphasis). This phrase—"the limit of a phenomenology"—refers to a lecture course Merleau-Ponty presented in 1959–60 called "Husserl at the Limits of Phenomenology" concerning Husserl's last writings but especially his "The Origin of Geometry."[3] The publication, in 1998, of the notes for this course makes the confusion between Merleau-Ponty and Derrida even more overwhelming, since here Merleau-Ponty stresses that the constitution of ideal objects takes place through writing, just as Derrida had stressed in his 1962 Introduction to his French translation of "The Origin of Geometry." In fact, while reading these two texts together, one has the experience that Merleau-Ponty sounds more like Derrida than Derrida does in the Introduction. The question now is obvious: are we supposed to think, now, in light of these "new" Notes, that Derrida's philosophy somehow continues that of Merleau-Ponty?

In light of these Notes, I think we have to answer this question with a "yes." Indeed, it seems to me that the confusion of the two philosophers is justified. Despite appearances—Merleau-Ponty as the philosopher of speech; Derrida as the philosopher of writing—this difference between speech and writing does not absolutely determine the relation between Merleau-Ponty and Derrida. In short, this difference is not decisive. At almost the exact same moment, in the late Fifties, Derrida and Merleau-Ponty have stumbled upon the same structure of experience, and, most generally, we can call this structure the structure of the experience of intersubjectivity.[4] What we call this structure—speech or writing—is not decisive. Both, of course, use other terms to designate it. From the *Phenomenology of Perception* on, it is called the *Fundierung* relation (PHP 147–48/127, 451–52/394); from *Voice and Phenomenon* on, it is called *différance*. But, in the Notes, Merleau-Ponty appropriates another Husserlian term besides *Fundierung* to designate this structure; *this* appropriation is decisive: he appropriates the exact term Derrida will appropriate in *Voice and Phenomenon: Verflechtung* (interweaving, *entrelacement*) (VP 20/20). Merleau-Ponty says, "True Husserlian thought: man, world, language are interwoven, *verflochten*. A thick identity exists there, which truly contains difference" (HL BN 25). Nothing could sound more Derridean.

So what this investigation aims to do, most basically, is to compare Merleau-Ponty's Notes and Derrida's Introduction in order to demonstrate the continuity between Merleau-Ponty and Derrida and thereby to justify the confusion that usually surrounds their relation. In fact, I hope to demonstrate that there is an exact point of continuity between them; this exact point of continuity, as we are going to see, lies in a certain concept of necessity. If there is this exact point of continuity, in a certain concept of necessity, then I think we can say that Merleau-Ponty's spirit lives on in Derrida, even in Derrida's most recent writings; perhaps we have to say that Merleau-Ponty *eventually* could have, would have, written a book like *Glas*. But we can go even farther. If this heritage that I am going to lay out between Merleau-Ponty and Derrida is correct, then one has to say, as well, that *Husserl's spirit* lives on in Merleau-Ponty's final writing and even in Derrida's most recent writings.[5] We have to say that Merleau-Ponty at the end of his career, when he is ontologizing phenomenology, is still faithful to Husserl, and we have to say that Derrida, even in his eschatological writings like the 1993 *Specters of Marx,* is still faithful to Husserl. But again, most basically, what I intend to do is work out a comparison of Merleau-Ponty's Notes on, and Derrida's Introduction to, Husserl's "The Origin of Geometry." The exact point of continuity comes from "The Origin of Geometry." So let us now turn to these two texts.

I. The Necessity of *Stiftung:* Writing

Both Merleau-Ponty's 1960 Notes and Derrida's 1962 Introduction concern what Husserl himself calls *Stiftung,* institution, establishment, or foundation (HUS 366/354; see n3). On the one hand, Derrida says in section 10 of his Introduction:

> This is how the motif of finitude has perhaps more affinity with the principle of a phenomenology which would be *stretched* between the *finitizing* consciousness of its principle [that is, the principle of all principles] and the *infinitizing* consciousness of its final *foundation* [that is, the Idea in the Kantian sense; *fondement*], the "Endstiftung" indefinitely deferred [*differée*] in its content, but always evident in its regulative value. (LOG 151/138, Derrida's emphasis)

Here, with *Stiftung,* we have Derrida's earliest use of the verb "differer." So we can say that the Husserlian problem of *Stiftung* is the context for Derrida developing his most famous concept, that of *différance.* But, on the other hand, Merleau-Ponty says in his Notes that

> Stiftung is not an enveloping thought, but open thought, not the intended and *Vorhabe* of the actual center, but the intended which is <u>off center</u> and which will be rectified, not the positing of an end, but the positing of a style, not frontal grasp, but lateral divergence, algae brought up from the depths. (HL BN 13, Merleau-Ponty's underlining)

Here, with *Stiftung,* Merleau-Ponty speaks of the divergence. So, again, we can say that the Husserlian problem of *Stiftung* is the context for Merleau-Ponty developing his most famous final concept: the *écart,* which is the basis for the chiasm. But, more importantly, the problem of *Stiftung* implies that both Merleau-Ponty and Derrida develop their basic concepts as concepts of writing. Merleau-Ponty in the Notes and Derrida in the Introduction recognize that writing is necessary for *Stiftung.*

Everyone knows that Husserl, in "The Origin of Geometry," discusses documentation and thus "writing-down" (*Niederschrift*); writing-down is the last step in the original institution of geometrical ideal objects. If we can speak of steps here, there are two prior steps: internal subjective iteration and then linguistic expression in the community of the inventor. Finally, there is documentation; this is what Husserl says, and for both Merleau-Ponty and Derrida, this is the most important thing Husserl says in "The Origin of Geometry":

> Now we must note that the objectivity of the ideal structure has not yet been fully constituted through such actual transferring of what has been originally produced in one to others who originally reproduce it. What is lacking is the *persisting existence* of the "ideal objects" even during periods in which the inventor and his fellows are no longer wakefully so connected or even are no longer alive. What is lacking is their continuing-to-be even when no one has realized them in self-evidence. The important function of written, documenting linguistic expression is that it makes communications possible without immediate or mediate personal address; it is, so to speak, communication become virtual. (HUS 371/360, my emphasis)

As both Merleau-Ponty and Derrida recognize, this comment means that writing is *necessary* in order for an ideal object to be fully constituted, in other words, to be what it is (HL BN 13; cf. PHP 206/177; LOG 86/89); Derrida in the Introduction calls it an "eidetic necessity" (LOG 17n1/36n21). Thus, for both Merleau-Ponty and Derrida, "the written"—Merleau-Ponty uses the word "l'écrit" (HL BN 12)—or "writing"—Derrida uses the word "l'écriture" (LOG 84/87)—is not a mere "substitute" for or a "degradation" of the sense (HL BN 13). It is not merely "congealed speech" (HL BN 43); it is not mere transmission or communication (HL BN 13, 43); nor is the writing-down mere "abbreviations," "codification," "signs," or "clothing" (HL BN 40; LOG 86/89). It is not a "defect" (HL BN 40), nor is it a merely "worldly and mnemotechnical aid" (LOG 86/89). The passage above—and I think this is crucial—implies all of these negative characterizations of writing because in it Husserl says "something is lacking" (*es fehlt*); the necessity of writing-down

comes from this lack in the "ideal structure"; the lack—here is the necessity—
needs to be filled in.

Husserl points to this need of filling in, when, in "The Origin of Geometry," he says, "the writing-down effects a transformation of the original mode
of being of the sense-structure" (HUS 371/361). Most obviously, and of
course both Merleau-Ponty and Derrida note this in their texts, the transformation of the ontological status of the sense-structure means that writing
endows the sense-structure with the characteristic of being "non-spatio-
temporal" (LOG 88/90) or "supratemporal" (HL BN 11); this supratemporality or omnitemporality is the persisting existence mentioned above, "their
continuing-to-be even when no one has realized them in self-evidence." Prior
to the achievement of omnitemporality, the sense-structure is too subjective (or transient) and not objective enough (or permanent). Merleau-Ponty,
for example, calls the sense-structure an "intra-psychic event" (HL BN 29).
However, just as prior to the transformation, the sense-structure is too subjective, after the transformation, when the sense-structure has achieved omnitemporality, it is too objective. As Merleau-Ponty says, it becomes a "monument" (HL BN 43), or, as Derrida says, it becomes a "lapidary inscription"
(LOG 85/88). But the transformation of the ontological status of the sense-
structure into omnitemporality does not mean, for Husserl, of course, that
the sense-structure, now ideal object, exists outside of time; as Derrida says,
quoting *Experience and Judgment*, " 'supratemporality implies omnitemporality,' and the latter itself [is] only 'a mode of temporality' " (LOG 165/148).
So when writing effects a transformation of the ontological mode of the
sense-structure, it also makes the ideal object "sensible" and "public," as
Merleau-Ponty says (HL BN 43); it comes "in the world" (HL BN 40); or, as
Derrida says, it is "incarnated," "localized and temporalized" (LOG 86/89).
So, as both Merleau-Ponty and Derrida see, the necessity of writing-down
must be "double" (HL BN 16)—this is Merleau-Ponty's word, sounding like
Derrida—or "ambiguous"—this is Derrida's word, sounding like Merleau-
Ponty (LOG 84/87). So far, then, we have seen that the necessity of writing is
based in a lack, which *needs*—this need is the source of the necessity—to be
filled in. And we have seen that this lack is double: sense lacks objectivity,
which produces a need to go beyond subjective experience; and sense lacks
subjectivity, which produces a need to go beyond ideal objectivity. In other
words, on the one hand, sense must be written down in order to be omnitem-
poral, in order to exceed subjective experience; on the other hand, sense must
be written down in order to be temporal, in order to make itself available to
subjective experience. In short, the writing-down turns the sense-structure
into sedimentation (HL BN 13; LOG 92/93). The mention of sedimentation,
of course, conjures up the image of survival. So let us examine this survival.

II. The Necessity of Writing: Survival

Merleau-Ponty characterizes the persisting existence that the written makes available to sense as "the Book" (HL BN 43 marginal note, 40). What one is supposed to imagine here is a book containing many leaves (HL BN 29), and on each page there are formulas, geometrical formulas, of course. These formulas on the page do not change. This image is why Merleau-Ponty says that the Book or the written gives us "the <u>exact</u> sense" (HL BN 43, Merleau-Ponty's underlining). Indeed, the *exact* sense is precisely what we have when we have memorized a formula: $C = A + B$. The image of the Book, therefore, is an image of memorization, of a memorandum, which amounts to a sort of forgetfulness of the kind of acts that produced the formula. Making an allusion to the body, Merleau-Ponty calls this "sclerosis" (HL BN 43). This is what Husserl himself, of course, called *Sinnentleerung* or the crisis. But we must not forget that, even with this emptying out of sense, the formulas have persisting existence, and thus the sense of geometry has a unity over and above its psychological institution; the persisting existence of the Book gives us the sense of "the," as Merleau-Ponty says, *the* one and only geometry (HL BN 8). There *must be* memorization. Memorization gives us the unity of geometry, that it is one thing with one voice, that it is, we might say, univocal.

In his Introduction, Derrida calls the persisting existence that writing makes available to sense "univocity" (LOG 103–4/101–2). Derrida focuses on the question of univocity because Husserl himself in "The Origin of Geometry" recommends to individual scientists that, when they write, they strive to form expressions that are univocal (HUS 372/362). Derrida calls this recommendation "the imperative of univocity" (LOG 101/100; cf. HL BN 13), and the word "imperative," of course, suggests that here we are dealing with a necessity. Derrida says, "Univocity only indicates the limpidity of the historical ether. . . . Husserl's demand for univocity . . . is therefore only the reduction of empirical history towards a pure history. Such a reduction must [the verb Derrida uses here is *devoir*] be recommended indefinitely" (LOG 104/102). In other words, for Derrida, there must be iteration even though, like Merleau-Ponty's Book, this iteration is forgetfulness and the emptying out of sense. There must be sameness if there is to be any communication. But Derrida also says—and here I continue the comment I just quoted, "Such a reduction must be recommended indefinitely, for language neither can nor must [again the verb here is *devoir*] maintain itself under the protection of univocity" (LOG 104/102). We are now confronted with the other necessity. For Derrida in the Introduction, univocal expression is smooth and thereby provides no "fold" into which a culture or a language, as it advances, could deposit "more or less virtual significations" (LOG 103/101). In other words, univocity would "sterilize or paralyze history in the poverty of an indefinite iteration" (LOG 104/102). So, there must be equivocity, for Derrida, as well if there is to be history or communication because communication itself requires that there be others and thus that the sense of the words be "other" (LOG 107/104).

Turning back to Merleau-Ponty's Notes, we find this necessity of equivocity under what he calls the "second power of sedimentation" (HL BN 43).[6] Although the Book endows sense with persisting existence, this persisting existence "sublimates"—this is Merleau-Ponty's word—what was only empirically accomplished (HL BN 43). This sublimation institutes the "pre-existence of the ideal" (HL BN 12–13, 43); here Merleau-Ponty relies on Husserl's comment that "what is lacking is their continuing-to-be even when no one has realized them in self-evidence" and that, in the written, "communication becomes virtual." What these comments mean for Merleau-Ponty is that there are "virtualities," that is, "virtual creations," which are not actual (HL BN 40); we can even say that the "sublimation" of the empirical institutes virtual idealities, which "have never been experienced by anyone and they have never been conceived with evidence" (HL BN 40). These virtual idealities are necessary so that there is progress in the science; without these virtual idealities what Husserl calls reactivation would be just the "reconquest of lost time," "of a certain forgetfulness"; because of the virtual idealities, reactivation, as Merleau-Ponty says, "consists in going farther in the same direction" (HL BN 43). In other words, without the sublimation, reactivation would be nothing more than a sterile iteration; if a culture or a tradition is "to advance," to use Derrida's words, "equivocity," or to use Merleau-Ponty's "virtuality," is necessary.

So what we have seen so far is a double or ambiguous necessity in both Merleau-Ponty and Derrida. The necessity of writing consists in the double movement of the communication and of virtuality, or in the ambiguity of iteration and of alterity. It seems to me that one image in Merleau-Ponty's Notes and one image in Derrida's Introduction crystallize this necessity, and here we start to see the profound implications of it. When Merleau-Ponty speaks of the Book, he calls it a *grimoire,* a book of spells or incantations (HL BN 40, 43). There is one obvious reason why Merleau-Ponty appeals to this image: at least since the time of the *Phenomenology of Perception,* he had been referring to perception as a "magical" relation (PHP 207/178). So, here in the Notes, Merleau-Ponty uses the word "grimoire" in order to intend a pre-scientific and therefore non-causal relation of institution by the written. The non-causal nature of tradition, as Husserl himself specifies it in "The Origin of Geometry" (HUS 366/354), is a continuous theme in the Notes; *Urstiftung,* as Husserl himself says, is "spiritual becoming" (HL BN 25; HUS 366/355). In fact, Merleau-Ponty entitles a section of his course notes "The General Problem of Spiritual Mutation" (see HL BN 2; cf. HL BN 46). The institution of ideal objects is, for Merleau-Ponty, this very problem of spiritual mutation. So the Book understood as a *grimoire* obviously is supposed to make us think of the "conjuring up" of spirits. In addition to this image of the *grimoire*, Merleau-Ponty in the Notes (but also in other texts from this period such as "The Philosopher and His Shadow" [S 27/180]) makes use of an idea from Valéry, that the author, the actual person such as a Camus—Camus is Merleau-Ponty's own example (HL BN 2)—is "the impostor of the writer" (HL BN 40, 4). Unlike the author, that is, the actual person Camus, the writer, Merleau-Ponty is implying, is at the level of the written as providing virtual idealities. So the conjuring up of spirits thanks to the incantations found in the book of spells does not bring back Camus the author but Camus the writer. In fact, the image of the *grimoire* implies that the author named Camus must die. The written for Merleau-Ponty, therefore, implies the necessity of death.

In order to understand this necessity of death in more detail, let us turn now to the crystallizing image in Derrida's Introduction. This is the image of "the silence of prehistoric arcana and buried civilizations, the entombment of lost intentions and guarded secrets, the illegibility of lapidary inscription" (LOG 85/88). This image of "the entombment of lost intentions" "unseals" what Derrida here calls "the transcendental sense of death."[7] We can understand this phrase, "the transcendental sense of death," only in light of Husserl's definition of the transcendental as being different from empirical or psychological subjectivity; Derrida realizes that, if the transcendental is not and cannot be restricted to actual subjects, then its institution requires the, in principle (the *en droit*), death of every actual subject (LOG 85/88). In "The Origin of Geometry, according to Derrida, we see that writing is the "agency" that implements this necessary death; writing is the agency that "unites" death, as Derrida says, "to the absolute of an intentional right"; without the agency of writing and therefore the death of the actual author, there would be no virtual *communication,* that is, there would be no ego common to us all, no communal ego. And yet, writing is also the agency that makes this communication fail, when writing becomes sterile iteration: this failure, we can say, is the very death of the *logos* (cf. LOG 165/149). So writing also requires the life of actual subjects to make the *logos* be *virtual* communication, that is, to make the common ego be individuated in each of us. In other words, the *logos,* for both Merleau-Ponty and Derrida, would not live unless the author died; there would be no omnitemporality of sense without this liberation from the spatio-temporal conditions of institution; there would be no communication. On the other hand, the *logos* would itself die unless there were humans to reactivate it; there would be no temporality of sense without this localization and temporalization of sense in the world; there would be no virtuality.

Of course, throughout his writings Derrida constantly talks about death, whereas Merleau-Ponty almost never mentions it. Yet, in these Notes, Merleau-Ponty mentions death in the context of Husserl's well-known comment that it is impossible to reactivate everything; this is what Merleau-Ponty says: "Is there coincidence with the totality of the *Urstiftung*, if the tradition is always forgetfulness? . . . Wouldn't coincidence be the death of the *logos* since forgetfulness makes tradition fruitful?" (HL BN 9).[8] Merleau-Ponty is suggesting here that the very life of the *logos* depends on the factual author being dead *and* on someone being alive here and now. So the *logos* itself, for Merleau-Ponty in the Notes and for Derrida in his Introduction, is a type of sur-vival; indeed, the double necessity of the lack of persisting existence is focused in this word "sur-vival." What this double necessity necessitates, what it commands, is that sense survive: sense must go beyond or over, "sur," life—that is, that it must die—and sense must be superlife, "sur" again, that is, it must go beyond or over death. Thus, since this prefix "sur" means death, it points to a very specific form of negativity, which we must now investigate.

III. The Necessity of Survival: Negativity

In the Notes, Merleau-Ponty specifies the lack of persisting existence as a "negativity" (HL BN 9); here, as in "Philosophie aujourd'hui" in the *Notes de Cours, 1959–61* (NC 102–3), Merleau-Ponty quotes Heidegger speaking of "the nothing that nothings" (HL BN 36). As Heidegger says in "What Is Metaphysics?" the nothing that nothings is not a "nullity."[9] If it were a nullity, it would only be the counter-concept to Being, and therefore itself would depend on negation. The Heideggerian nothing, however, is not derived from negation but is the origin of negation. Negation originates in the nothing insofar as it is an experience, the experience of anxiety, and, obviously, given what we know about Division 2 of *Being and Time*, we are still talking of death. Yet, since this experience of the nothing is an experience, we must say that the nothing is actually a sort of positivity, a something, an *Etwas*, as Heidegger says (cf. NC 102).[10] Thus, for Heidegger, the nothing is internal to Being; in fact, without this experience of anxiety we would, for Heidegger, have no access to the Being of beings. Clearly influenced by Heidegger, Merleau-Ponty engages in a similar discussion of negativity in *The Visible and the Invisible*, in particular in the chapter entitled "Interrogation and Dialectic" where Merleau-Ponty is engaging in a debate with Sartre. What is most clear in this chapter is that Merleau-Ponty is concerned to distinguish this negativity from a pure nothingness, from what Heidegger called a nullity: wholly positive being and pure nothingness are at least solidary if not indiscernible because they both revolve around a negation which makes them be counter-concepts (cf. S 30/21). As in Heidegger, therefore, Merleau-Ponty's negativity is a negativity that is within Being; it is the "true negative," and thus it is, as Merleau-Ponty says frequently in *The Visible and the Invisible,* "something" (e.g., VI 121/89).[11]

So Merleau-Ponty, in *The Visible and the Invisible* and in the Notes on "The Origin of Geometry," defines this lack as a "hollow" (HL BN 8; VI 196/281); unlike the well-known Sartrean "hole of being" that suggests a void over and against a fullness, which, in other words, suggests counter-concepts and opposition, the Merleau-Pontean hollow suggests an opening within something, in something which is not opposed to the hollow (VI 249–50/196). In the Notes and in *The Visible and the Invisible,* Merleau-Ponty defines the hollow as *Nichturpräsentierbarkeit,* "originary non-presentability" (HL BN 12; VI 292/238–39). Merleau-Ponty's "originary non-presentability" is referring to an essential aspect of intersubjective experience learned from Husserl, that is, that I can never have the interior life of another present for me. In the Notes, taking up what we see in "Indirect Language and the Voices of Silence," Merleau-Ponty adds to this essential aspect of intersubjective experience; for Merleau-Ponty, the non-presentability of the other to me is a kind of muteness, and this muteness does not mean that the other is not speaking because he or she is dumb. There is always, for Merleau-Ponty, a background of language, the ready-made or spoken language, within which the muteness lies. So, in the Notes, Merleau-Ponty says, "before language, a 'mute' experience and an experience which calls from itself for its 'expression,' but a 'pure' expression, i.e., foundation and not product of language. Therefore a *Vorsprache,* a down-side or 'other side' of language, an *Ur-sprung* of language" (HL BN 29). Here I think it is important to recall that Merleau-Ponty had defined expression in the *Phenomenology of Perception* in terms of the phrase "mettre en forme" (e.g., PHP 220/189). The Merleau-Pontean silence therefore is a thought, but one which is *gestaltlos,* as Merleau-Ponty says in the Notes (HL BN 32), "formless," and as formless, it is not nothing but rather something which needs—"which calls from itself"—expression.

With this formless content in mind, let us now turn to Derrida. As in Merleau-Ponty's later writings, in Derrida's Introduction, there is a continuous theme of negativity (LOG 17n1/36n21); the prefix "non" appears countless times (e.g., LOG 112/109). In the Introduction, there are only fleeting references to Heidegger and no reference to any specific Heidegger work; so we can conclude that in 1962 Derrida had not read Heidegger profoundly—in fact, his concern with negativity in the Introduction seems to be inspired by

Hyppolite's Hegel (cf. LOG 58n1/67n62). We can see the connection to Hegel clearly in Derrida's 1964 "Violence and Metaphysics"; there, Derrida says,

> As it was for Hegel, the "false infinity" for Levinas would be the indefinite, *negative* form of infinity. But, since Levinas conceives *true* alterity as non-negativity (nonnegative transcendence), he can make the other the true infinity, and make the same (in strange complicity with negativity) the false-infinity. Which would have been absolutely mad to Hegel . . . : how can alterity be separated from negativity, how can alterity be separated from the "false infinity"? (ED 175/119, Derrida's emphasis)

As this passage indicates, Derrida cannot imagine alterity without negativity. Thus, a certain concept of negativity will continue to be important for Derrida, and eventually, very quickly, it will be associated with Heidegger's nothing. For instance, in the Introduction to *Voice and Phenomenon,* echoing Heidegger, Derrida uses the word "rien" as a substantive, saying "this nothing which distinguishes the parallels," for example (VI 12/12). This substantive use of *rien* implies that, here in Derrida (as we saw in Merleau-Ponty), we do not have a pure nothingness. Derrida, in "Violence and Metaphysics," too refers to a "hollow" (ED 124/83); and, as have seen, Derrida in the Introduction speaks of "the *silence* of prehistoric arcana." And, of course, there is the title of Chapter 6 of *Voice and Phenomenon,* "The Voice That Guards Silence." All of these phrases make one think of Merleau-Ponty.

Nevertheless, in the Introduction, Derrida, *unlike Merleau-Ponty,*[12] determines the lack of persisting existence that necessitates survival, and thus determines this negativity, when he analyzes Husserl's discussion of idealization in "The Origin of Geometry" (HUS 375/365). What is important for Derrida is that, in "The Origin of Geometry," Husserl says that "The peculiar sort of self-evidence belonging to such idealizations will concern us later." Husserl, of course, never returns to it. So, for Derrida, the question is: Is there any evidence for such idealizations? The idealization of which Husserl is speaking is the breakthrough of a sense toward an "indefinite iteration," "a passage to the limit," "an Idea in the Kantian sense" (LOG 147/135). But, as soon as we understand that an Idea in the Kantian sense means infinity, we know that the sense cannot be given in an intuition or be given in evidence (LOG 147/134–35, 152/139). Intuition or evidence, being given in person, is always finite. So, for Derrida, this evidence, if we can still call it that, is formal; or perhaps better, this experience is the experience of formality. We can have evidence only of the form of infinity but not its content; we have no evidence of infinity itself (LOG 152–53/139). In other words, what is lacking and what then brings about a need for survival in Derrida is not formless content as in Merleau-Ponty but rather contentless form. In Derrida, the need for survival comes from a formalization without content. What we have is a finite form that needs indefinitely to become fulfilled.

Now, in the Introduction, Derrida speaks of the Idea in the Kantian sense as "its own original presence" (LOG 152/139); but, by the time of *Voice and Phenomenon* this "original presence" will be called "non-presence" (VP 5/6, 71/63). It is especially clear in *Voice and Phenomenon* that this Derridean *non-présence* derives from the experience of the other since Derrida claims that Husserl's "solitary life of the soul" in the First Investigation anticipates "the sphere of ownness" in the Fifth Cartesian Meditation; thus Derrida's "non-presence" resembles Merleau-Ponty's *Nichturpräsentierbarkeit,* insofar as both concepts derive from the essential aspect of the experience of the other, that the other's interior life is not directly present to me, but only appresented to me. Yet, what Derrida is implying both in the Introduction and in *Voice and Phenomenon* is that, when I have an appresentation of the other, what I have is the form of the other and not its content; this lack of content is what makes the other other for Derrida, and it also keeps the form of the other indefinitely open *to* fulfillment.

Before we turn to the fourth and last section, I am going to summarize what we have seen so far. On the basis of what Husserl says in "The Origin of Geometry" about the institution of ideal objects requiring writing because the sense structure "lacks" "persisting existence," both Merleau-Ponty and Derrida assert a double necessity, the necessity of going beyond subjective experience in order to be objective, and the necessity of going beyond ideal objectivity in order to be available to subjective experience. By focusing on the crystallizing images of the *grimoire* (in Merleau-Ponty) and the entombment of lost intentions in Derrida, we were able to see that this double necessity implies a certain concept of sur-vival, beyond life, that is, death; and beyond death, that is, life. Then we focused only on the first side of this concept of survival. Going beyond life implies a negativity. Here, in the discussion of negativity, we first discovered a similarity—Merleau-Ponty's "originary non-presentability" looks to be the same as Derrida's "non-presence"—then we discovered a difference—perhaps the difference between Derrida and Merleau-Ponty—for Merleau-Ponty, the negativity of writing is a formless content, whereas for Derrida, the negativity of writing is a contentless form. Nevertheless, we are still able to see the exact point of continuity between Merleau-Ponty and Derrida since, for both, the negativity of writing, that the author must die, is, as Merleau-Ponty says, "a call to reiteration" (HL BN 38) and, as Derrida says, "a first posting" (*un premier envoi*) (LOG 36/50). In other words, the negativity of writing implies that writing is always, for both Merleau-Ponty and Derrida, defined by the dative case: it is a sending to. But, with the dative, we turn now to the other side of the necessity, that the object must become subjective. We are going to start with Merleau-Ponty.

IV. The Necessity of Negativity: Faith

In the Notes, Merleau-Ponty indeed defines speech as "speaking to" (HL BN 40). He defines speech in this way because he is trying to understand language that is not "ready-made" but language "in the making." Here Merleau-Ponty, of course, is utilizing a distinction that he developed in earlier works, and I have already referred to it: the well-known distinction between "speaking speech" and "spoken speech" (PHP 229/197; also S 56/44–45).[13] In fact, he uses these exact terms in the Notes (HL BN 29). Whereas spoken speech is "ready-made" language—a language someone has *spoken*—speaking speech is language in the making (HL BN 38)—a language I *am speaking* (HL BN 25). Therefore, speaking speech is a *praxis;* Merleau-Ponty says, "Speech is a *praxis:* the only way to understand speech is to speak (to speak to . . . or be interpellated by . . .)" (HL BN 38). This being interpellated by—someone is interrogating "to" me—needs a response. Merleau-Ponty defines the response to interpellation in terms of what Husserl calls *Nachverstehen* in "The Origin of Geometry" (HUS 371/360; HL BN 12; cf. PHP 208n2/ 179n2). In the dative relation of hearing—when someone is questioning "to" me—I always encounter the *Nicthurpräsentierbarkeit* of the other. Because *Nachverstehen* encounters the limit of that which cannot be re-animated—the negativity of death—*Nachverstehen* is, for Merleau-Ponty, first a kind of passivity or a receptivity (HL BN 36). In the Notes, Merleau-Ponty says that geometrical ideality "calls me to" *Nachverstehen* (HL BN 15, 38). Thus, in order to hear this call, I must be quiet; obviously, if someone is interrogating (to) me, I must listen. So the passivity of *Nachverstehen* must be conceived as mute or silent. But again, this muteness does not, for Merleau-Ponty, mean a lack of language; it does not mean that I am dumb. In fact, I have the ready-made forms of spoken speech available to me.

Yet, it is precisely this specific silence of expression that makes *Nachverstehen* be active. Precisely because *Nachverstehen* encounters the limit of nonpresentability—precisely because it is passive and *lacks* activity—it *must* be active. In *Nach-verstehen,* there is an activity of repeating—the *Nach*—which makes that hearing is not mere "association" or "receptivity" (HL BN 30, 36); *Nachverstehen* works with passivity, Merleau-Ponty says. This working with passivity makes *Nachverstehen* be, for Merleau-Ponty, the experience of *Deckung, recouvrement,* coincidence (HL BN 37). But here, coincidence does not mean that all of a sudden I have access to your thoughts. Instead, when I listen and understand your question, *again, Nach,* what I am doing is actualizing virtualities: ideality, as Merleau-Ponty says, "appears at the edge of speech" (HL BN 31, 12). In other words,

> [Husserl places] openness to others and openness to ideality into the law
> of the praxical-perceptive, i.e., it consists in turning the others into
> the other side of my world and in turning ideality into the *Etwas* [the
> something] upon which these two sides are articulated, the pivot of the
> "speaking to . . . " a pivot, that is, to an invisible through which the visible
> holds. The vertical Being as the being of praxis, as the correlate of Speech.
> (HL BN 12, Merleau-Ponty's underlining)

This comment means that, when someone is interrogating (to) me, he or she is expressing an ideality in the ready-made forms of spoken speech. But, since I do not have access to the soul of the other—his or her soul is not-presentable, even, so to speak, dead—then the expressed ideality is separated from this person. It is at the "pivot"—Merleau-Ponty also uses the words "hinge" (HL BN 12, 13) and "jointure" (HL BN 43)[14]—between us. Thus, when I listen and then respond, I repeat the ideality. But also, since I have only the ideality and not its "soul," I must create an other "side" of the ideality. The silence of my listening must be put into a form, and this form will be derived from the ready-made forms. But when I put my silence into the lin-guistic form, this insertion re-creates it. For Merleau-Ponty, *Nachverstehen* is *Nacherzeugung.* In other words, with Merleau-Ponty, every time I under-stand again, I institute again; in other words, every re-understanding is a re-commencement; every re-understanding is another beginning.

In the Notes, Merleau-Ponty distinguishes what Husserl calls "Nachverste-hen" from what he (following Husserl) calls "reactivation"; reactivation, for Merleau-Ponty, aims at reactivating everything (HL BN 13). This comment means that reactivation aims at being entirely active; it does not work with the passivity. The passivity that defines *Nachverstehen* is why Merleau-Ponty says that *Nachverstehen* is not a "survey" (*survol*) (HL BN 29). In *The Visible and the Invisible,* to survey (*survoler*) is to soar over and thereby dominate (VI 109/177), and Merleau-Ponty even defines *survoler* in *The Visible and the Invisible,* as "reactivating all the sedimented thoughts" (VI 150/112). But, if *Nachverstehen* is not *une pensée en survol,* then we know that it is what Merleau-Ponty as early as the *Phenomenology of Perception* and as late as *The Visible and the Invisible* calls "originary faith." The word "faith" does not oc-cur in Merleau-Ponty's Notes on "The Origin of Geometry," but it seems to me that *Nachverstehen* substitutes for it. Indeed, in the Notes, Merleau-Ponty speaks of a "knowledge of non-knowledge" which suggests faith (HL BN 8, 11, 14). For Merleau-Ponty, when I respond to the interpellation, or, better, to the interrogation, I must have faith in the one who is speaking to me; I do not know what the person is asking of me, since I cannot soar over his or her thoughts; he or she is a ghostly presence. But also, I must have faith in myself; I do not know what I am going to say since it lies in silence, formless; I am a ghostly self-presence.[15]

This language of ghosts, of course, refers to Derrida, but it seems legitimate here because Derrida develops the concept of specter in conjunction with a concept of faith. Retrospectively, we can see that Derrida's early writings were going in the direction of faith even though they do not contain a theme of faith. It is possible to see now that, in the Introduction, when Derrida is speaking of the "strange presence" of the Idea in the Kantian sense, this strange presence implies a kind of faith. Moreover, at the conclusion of *Voice and Phenomenon,* when Derrida says, "As for what 'begins' then 'beyond' absolute knowledge, *unheard-of* thoughts are required" (VP 115/102, Derrida's emphasis), we now know that this "beyond absolute knowledge" is a kind of faith. Most basically, as in Merleau-Ponty, faith in Derrida is a dative relation. We can see this clearly in the title of Derrida's last Levinas book, *Adieu,* which means not only "good-bye," but also "to God." But, as we have already noted, in both the Introduction and *Voice and Phenomenon,* Derrida emphasizes the dative relation: in Husserl, language or the *logos* or form, as Derrida says, is always "relation to the object" (VP 110/98; LOG 153/139). Thus, as in Merleau-Ponty—and we are still on the second side of the necessity, making the object subjective—in Derrida the *logos* interrogates (to) me and "demands" a response (cf. LOG 162/146).

One of the most remarkable things about Derrida's Introduction is that it contains an explicit theme of responsibility. Given the necessity of death, we know that responsibility in Derrida must be defined by "bringing the sense to life" (LOG 100–101/99). But as soon as we recognize that responsibility is a kind of conjuring up of ghosts, then we have to see that responsibility is a kind of faith. When I hear a word or read a text, this *logos* always indicates a non-presence, which eliminates the possibility of absolute knowledge; as in Merleau-Ponty, responsibility in Derrida is not *une pensée en survol.* But, although responsibility is a kind of faith in the other that I have resurrected, responsibility is also a kind of faith in myself. I must be the one who can do this; as Derrida says, "I restore [the sense's] *dependence* in regard to my own act and reproduce it in me" (LOG 100–101/99, my emphasis). I am the one selected, on whom the sense depends. The dependence of sense on me is why Derrida in the last section of the Introduction defines responsibility in the following way: "To make oneself responsible is to concern oneself [*se charger*] with a heard speech; it is to take upon oneself the exchange of sense in order to stand guard over its progression" (LOG 166/149). Most generally, however, in the Introduction, Derrida defines responsibility as "fulfillment" (LOG

11/31). Clearly, this word means the completion, even the ending, of the sense in presence. But, since the sense is always infinite as an Idea in the Kantian sense, my response, which fulfills the question asked to me, does not and cannot ever completely fulfill it. The sense is always necessarily open to an indefinite number of fulfillments, completions, or ends. I must always fulfill this request over and over again. I have coined a word in order to speak about this structure in Derrida that faith always amounts to doing the end over an indefinite number of times; whereas Merleau-Ponty's faith is always a "recommencement" (HL BN 38), Derrida's faith is always a "refinition."

Conclusion: Husserl at the Limits of Phenomenology

Both the discourse of the end that we find in Derrida *and* the discourse of beginning that we find in Merleau-Ponty, of course, derive from Heidegger. Indeed, for both Merleau-Ponty and Derrida, the limit of Husserlian phenomenology lies in Heideggerian ontology. For both, this limit is the Heideggerian conception of negativity. For Merleau-Ponty, Heidegger's negativity is the limit of phenomenology, insofar as phenomenology seems to be a positivism (HL BN 31, 36). (It is here in the concept of negativity that Merleau-Ponty connects Heidegger to Bergson [NC 103, 114–15]; it seems to me that this connection may be the most original thing Merleau-Ponty ever did. If this were our project, we could establish, in light of this connection between Bergson and Heidegger, a different Merleau-Ponty than the one we are establishing now; we could establish a Merleau-Ponty that goes not in the direction of Derrida, but in the direction of Deleuze.)[16] So, as for Merleau-Ponty, for Derrida, the Heideggerian negativity is the limit of phenomenology. But, unlike Merleau-Ponty, for whom the negativity was a limit to phenomenology because phenomenology looks to be a positivism, Derrida sees a limit of phenomenology because phenomenology is a "a philosophy of seeing" (LOG 155/141), an "intuitionism" (VP 110/98). But, if the limit of phenomenology, for both Merleau-Ponty and Derrida, lies in Heidegger's negativity, then we must say that what is most important in Heidegger for both Merleau-Ponty and Derrida is the Heidegger's remembrance of the question of Being. In Heidegger's famous Introduction to *Being and Time,* Heidegger is defining being itself as a question: the question of being is the being of the question. Heidegger, of course, did not have in mind the kind of question that one finds in school, where the teacher, knowing the answer in advance, relinquishes the student of any responsibility for thinking. A genuine question in contrast is one whose answer we do not know; it is a question for which there is no response. This lack of an answer is why a question, a question's openness, can account for the universality of Being. Yet, a genuine question as well demands a response; a question must be a quest for an answer. This demand for an answer is why a question, the question's closure, can account for the determination of being. It is this conception of a question, as at once open and closed, at once irresponsible and responsible, that is the guiding idea for Merleau-Ponty's final philosophy. Without Heidegger's conception of Being as a question we would not have Merleau-Ponty's conception of Being as interrogation. But also, the Being of the question is the guiding idea for all of Derrida's texts from the Sixties. For instance, "Violence and Metaphysics" begins by speaking of "a community of the question" (ED 118/80). At this point, in the Sixties, the continuity between Derrida and Merleau-Ponty is remarkable. Yet, already in "Violence and Metaphysics," Derrida has the means for eliminating this confusion: when he speaks of the community of the question, Derrida also speaks of an "injunction" of the question (ED 119/80). This injunction implies that a command precedes the question. Eventually, because of this prior command, Derrida, in his 1987 *De l'esprit*, will question Heidegger's priority of the question. For Derrida now, prior to the question of Being is the command of a promise; it is a deathbed promise: "promise me that you will survive!"[17] The response to this command is faith, faith in the one making me promise and faith in me, the one who must keep the promise sometime in the future. It seems to me that even here, when Derrida departs from the Heideggerian question for the promise, Merleau-Ponty's spirit survives in him. Because Merleau-Ponty takes up the theme of writing in the Course Notes on "The Origin of Geometry," we can perhaps predict that Merleau-Ponty, following the logic of death that writing implies, would have eventually transformed the question into the promise. This prediction seems especially reliable if we recall that Merleau-Ponty ends his 1952 candidacy abstract for the Collège de France by speaking of the establishment of an ethics.[18]

But, if Merleau-Ponty's spirit survives in Derrida, then we must say that Husserl's spirit survives in both. If a limit as, in the limit of phenomenology, is a negativity, then we know that the limit of phenomenology could not establish ontology as a mere counter-concept. Indeed, both Merleau-Ponty in his Notes and Derrida in his Introduction point to a "convergence" of phenomenology and ontology (HL BN 37). Derrida says, for instance, that "for both Husserl and Heidegger, the complicity of appearing and dissimulation seems . . . primordial, essential, and definitive" (LOG 151n1/138n164), while Merleau-Ponty claims that by continuing beyond the fact of constituting-transcendental consciousness, Husserl "testifies to *Seyn*" spelt with a "y" and crossed-out (HL BN 37). Thus, it seems to me that both Derrida and Merleau-Ponty are incredibly faithful to Husserl. It is well known, of course, that Merleau-Ponty loves to quote this passage from Husserl's *Cartesian Medita-*

tions (section 16): "It is the experience . . . still mute which we are concerned with leading to the pure expression of its own meaning (VI 171/129, 203/155; cf. HL BN 2, 33). Similarly—however, this is not well known—Derrida's concept of non-presence (and thus his famous critique of the metaphysics of presence) derives from the fact that Husserl's conception of the Idea in the Kantian sense necessarily implies a lack of adequate intuitive fulfillment; in the Introduction, Derrida says, "The idea [in the Kantian sense] is the pole of a pure intention, empty of every determinate object. It alone reveals, then, the being of the intention: intentionality itself" (LOG 153/139). We can say that, even in their most non-phenomenological positions, Derrida and Merleau-Ponty are still trying to think through Husserl's discovery of intentionality. Merleau-Ponty is putting the silence of Husserl's thought into language, whereas Derrida is bringing Husserl's language into an intuition. We must conclude: Husserl's spirit is coming to presence in Derrida and Merleau-Ponty, and therefore Husserl could have no greater legacy.

5 The End of Phenomenology

Expressionism in Merleau-Ponty and Deleuze

> The divine things hidden since the beginning of the world are clearly perceived
> through the understanding of God's creatures.
>
> —Romans 1:20

Probably stimulated by Levinas's requirements for an ethics, the return to the subject has fueled a renewed interest in classical phenomenology. As Jean Greisch bluntly puts it, "after a period dominated by structuralism and critique of metaphysics, a new generation of contemporary philosophers has rediscovered phenomenology as a real possibility for thinking."[1] Given this *nouvelle vague phénoménologique*—Greisch includes many well-known Merleau-Ponty scholars among his list of philosophers involved in "the new phenomenological wave"—then what are we to make of the challenge to phenomenology made in the Sixties and Seventies in the name of structuralism and post-structuralism? Has phenomenology met the challenge by means of a more profound understanding of intersubjectivity, of the other?[2] Are we now simply supposed to abandon the challenge? The philosophy of Gilles Deleuze confronts phenomenology—of any ilk, from Hegel to Maldiney—with its most powerful challenge, a challenge that takes two forms.

On the one hand, there is the challenge of immanence. One can find this challenge in Deleuze's writings as late as *What Is Philosophy?* (1991) and as early as *Empiricism and Subjectivity* (1953). The challenge of immanence states that there is no two-world ontology, that being is said in only one way, that essence does not lie outside of appearance; in short, the challenge of immanence eliminates transcendence: God is dead. The challenge of immanence, however, appears to be nothing less than the challenge with which phenomenology confronts traditional metaphysics; the epoche is a process in which one switches off the belief in things in themselves in order to arrive at a plane of immanence: being is phenomenon. Despite this similarity, Deleuze argues that phenomenology reinstates a dative; it relates the plane of immanence back *to* a subject that constitutes the given. So in *What Is Philosophy?* Deleuze says, "Beginning with Descartes, and then with Kant and Husserl, the cogito makes it possible to treat the plane of immanence as a field of consciousness. Immanence is supposed to be immanent to a pure consciousness, to a thinking subject" (QPH 47–48/46). In *Empiricism and Subjectivity*, he says, "We embark upon a transcendental critique when, having situated ourselves on a methodologically reduced plane that provides an essential certainty . . . we ask: how can there be a given, how can something be given to a subject, and how can the subject give something to itself? . . . The critique is empirical when, having situated ourselves in a purely immanent point of view . . . we ask: how is the subject constituted in the given?"[3] The challenge of immanence then is the challenge of empiricism, and this is why in *What Is Philosophy?* Deleuze suggests that the plane of immanence is a "radical empiricism" (QPH 49/47). On the other hand, there is the challenge of difference, which finds its inspiration in Heidegger. In *Difference and Repetition* (1968), Deleuze says,

> According to Heidegger's ontological intuition, difference must be articulation and connection in itself; it must relate different to different without any mediation whatsoever by the identical, the similar, analogous or the opposed. There must be a differenciation of difference, an in-itself which is like a *differenciator*, a *Sich-unterscheidende*, by virtue of which the different is gathered all at once rather than represented on condition of a prior resemblance, identity, analogy or opposition. (DR 154/117, Deleuze's emphasis)[4]

The challenge then amounts to this: according to its very notion, a ground must never resemble that which it grounds. In other words, there must be a heterogeneity between ground and grounded, between condition and conditioned.[5] According to Deleuze, phenomenology does not meet the challenge of difference because the reduction moves the phenomenologist from natural attitude opinions or common sense back to *Urdoxa* or primal faith. In *What Is Philosophy?* Deleuze says,

> Phenomenology wanted to renew our concepts by giving us perceptions and affections that would make us give birth to the world, not as babies or hominids but as beings, by right, whose proto-opinions would be the foundations of this world. But we do not fight against perceptual and affective clichés if we do not fight against the machine that produces them. By invoking primordial lived-experience, by turning immanence into an immanence to a subject, phenomenology could not prevent the subject from forming no more than opinions that would already draw the cliché from new perceptions and promised affections. (QPH 142/149–50; DR 179/137)

The cliché would be a generality more eminent or primal than any particular (*Urdoxa*), but a generality nonetheless under which particulars could be subsumed; the machine is the subject drawing resemblances out of perceptions, listening to the sense murmured by things.

If we combine the two challenges, we must characterize Deleuze's philosophy, as he himself does in *Difference and Repetition,* with an oxymoronic expression: "transcendental empiricism" (DR 80/57).[6] Although this characterization suggests a contradiction, in fact it does not. It is nothing less than the paradox of expression. In *Expressionism in Philosophy: Spinoza* (1968), Deleuze says, "The paradox is that at once 'the expressed' *does not exist* outside of the expression and yet bears no resemblance to it, but is *essentially* related to what expresses itself as distinct from the expression itself" (SPE 310/333, Deleuze's emphasis). Expression is the plane of immanence, which implies that the expressed does not exist outside of it. But, having no resemblance to expression, the expressed, as the essence of what expresses itself, is distinct from expression itself. According to Deleuze, the expressed is "sense" (*sens*) (SPE 311/335). If sense is the key to Deleuze's double challenge to phenomenology, then we must privilege his 1969 *Logic of Sense.* In fact, Michel Foucault has already privileged this text, when he says, in "Theatrum Philosophicum," that "*The Logic of Sense* can be read as the most alien book imaginable from [Merleau-Ponty's] *The Phenomenology of Perception.*"[7] Foucault is undoubtedly correct. In *The Phenomenology of Perception,* Merleau-Ponty defines the phenomenology of *The Phenomenology of Perception* as "a study of the appearance of being to consciousness"; thereby, he introduces the dative and relates the plane of immanence back to consciousness. Moreover, Merleau-Ponty repeatedly appeals to a primordial faith in order to ground knowledge; for instance, he says in "Others and the Human World,"

> My consciousness of constructing an objective truth would never provide me with anything more than an objective truth for me, and my greatest attempt at impartiality would never enable me to overcome my subjectivity (as Descartes so well expresses it by the hypothesis of the evil genius), if I had not, below my judgments, the primordial certainty of being in contact with being itself, if, before any willful taking up of a position I were not already *situated* in an intersubjective world, and if science too were not supported by this originary *doxa.* (PHP 408/355, Merleau-Ponty's emphasis)

Nevertheless, *The Phenomenology of Perception* is the text in which Merleau-Ponty says,

> What we have discovered through the study of motility is a new sense for the word "sense." The great strength of intellectualist psychology and idealist philosophy comes from their having no difficulty in showing that perception and thought have an intrinsic sense. . . . The *Cogito* was the *prise de*

conscience of this interiority. But all meaning was thereby conceived as an act of thought, as the work of a pure I, and although rationalism easily refuted empiricism, it was itself unable to account for the variety of experiences, for the element of nonsense in, for the contingency of content. (PHP 171–72/146–47)

In order to determine how alien *The Logic of Sense* is from *The Phenomenology of Perception*, we must examine the relation of sense to nonsense in each. In other words, in order to determine whether phenomenology—taking *The Phenomenology of Perception* as an exemplary case—withstands the Deleuzian double challenge, we must examine expression.

I. The Transcendental Field in Deleuze

The title *The Logic of Sense* comes from Hyppolite's 1952 *Logic and Existence*, which is a study of Hegel's logic. In *Logic and Existence*, equating the Hegelian concept with sense, Hyppolite explicitly defines Hegel's logic as a logic of sense. Recognizing the dependence of Hegel's *Logic* on the earlier *Phenomenology of Spirit*, Hyppolite describes Hegel's phenomenology as the generation of sense from the sensible. And finally, trying to demonstrate the relevance of Hegel's thought to the then contemporary philosophy, Hyppolite describes the movement that leads to the logic of sense in Hegel as a "reduction" or as a process of "bracketing." This is an obvious allusion to Husserl. Given the influence that Hyppolite exerts on Deleuze—Deleuze, for instance, dedicates his first book on Hume to Hyppolite[8]—we can see that, although Deleuze does not call his philosophy a phenomenology (cf. LS 33/21), *The Logic of Sense* takes place entirely under the sign of the phenomenological reduction (cf. LS 123/101). Without the reduction, it would be impossible for Deleuze to return to the surface, in other words, to the sensible, to the appearances, to the phenomena, to the plane of immanence. As in all phenomenology, Deleuze's return to the surface does not imply the complete elimination of the difference between appearance and essence; instead, as Hyppolite would say, there is sense within the sensible. As Deleuze says, "sense is the characteristic discovery of transcendental philosophy . . . it replaces the old metaphysical Essences" (LS 128/105).[9] Deleuze's project therefore in *The Logic of Sense* is the determination of the donation of sense, Husserl's *Sinngebung* or sense-bestowal (LS 117/96, 87/69, 94/76; cf. DR 201/155). But unlike phenomenology, which turns the plane of immanence into an immanence to consciousness which consists in an *Urdoxa* or generalities through which the different kinds of belief are generated (LS 119/97), Deleuze's logic of sense is "inspired in its entirety by empiricism" (LS 32/20).

It is Sartre's notion of an impersonal transcendental field that, according to Deleuze, "restores the rights of immanence," frees immanence from being immanent to something other than itself, and turns phenomenology into "a radical empiricism" (QPH 49/47).[10] The transcendental field therefore, must correspond, Deleuze says, to the conditions that Sartre laid down in his "decisive" 1936 *The Transcendence of the Ego* (LS 120/98–99).[11] The transcendental ego, according to Sartre, is unnecessary for the unification of objects,[12] for the unification and individuation of consciousness,[13] and is itself moreover a constituted object.[14] Therefore the transcendental field must be conceived as an absolutely impersonal or non-personal consciousness;[15] it would be equivalent to what Hyppolite in 1957 would call a "subjectless transcendental field."[16] As impersonal and non-individuated, the transcendental field, for Deleuze, consists in the "they" or the "one" (*l'on*) (LS 178/152). But this *das Man* is not equivalent to what is expressed in common sense or in *doxa*. The phrase "everyone recognizes that," for example, does not express Deleuze's "they," because there is always, according to Deleuze, a "profound, sensitive conscience" who does not recognize what everyone else claims to recognize (DR 74/52). This sensitive conscience is a "sensitive point," a point of tears and joy, sickness and health, hope and anxiety, a turning point, a bottleneck, a boiling point. The transcendental field, therefore, consists in such sensitive points, in what Deleuze calls "singularities" or "anti-generalities" (LS 121/99).

Because of the connection to Merleau-Ponty, which we are trying to prepare, it is important here to note what Deleuze (and Guattari) say in *A Thousand Plateaus*: "It seems to us that Husserl brought thought a decisive step forward when he discovered a region of vague and material essences (in other words, essences that are vagabond, anexact and yet rigorous)."[17] Immediately after this comment Deleuze (and Guattari) connect Husserl's vague morphological essences to their own notion of singularities. This connection implies that what Deleuze calls singularities in *The Logic of Sense* are at least related to if not equivalent to what Husserl calls "eidetic singularities" in *Ideas I;* eidetic singularities are material essences, which have species and genera (and thus generality) over them, but have no particularizations under them (see *Ideas I,* #12). In other words, eidetic singularities are essences of, that is, generated from, facts. This connection between Deleuzian singularities and Husserlian eidetic singularities is significant for our purposes because Husserl utilizes the notion of an eidetic singularity in his late fragment "The Origin of Geometry," a text which Merleau-Ponty studied carefully.

The most precise definition of singularities, however for Deleuze, lies in the context of expression, which in *The Logic of Sense* refers to Husserl as well, Husserl's *Ideas I,* paragraph #124:[18] singularities are that which is expressed in an expression or that which is perceived in a perception, in a word, sense (LS 32/20). From Husserl's notion of sense, Deleuze extracts two characteristics: neutrality and sterility. A singularity is *sterile* because, as Husserl says, and Deleuze quotes this from paragraph 124, "the stratum of expression is not productive." Sterility then means that a singularity is nothing more than an incorporeal double of the expression or of what is perceived (LS 97–98/78–79, 146–51/122–25). Describing the existence of such idealities, Deleuze says that sense is an "extra-being" or a "phantasm" (LS 17/7). To define singularities in terms of sterility means not only that they are caused by bodies but also that they are nothing but "surface effects" or "ideal events." What is crucial to the logic of sense is that sense be conceived as an event (LS 34/22).

But as an event, sense also differs from bodies. We can see this difference by means of the characteristic of neutrality. A singularity is neutral—and neutrality is why a singularity is a singularity and not a mere duplicity—because Husserl, according to Deleuze, distinguishes a noema "from the physical object, from the psychological or 'lived,' from mental representations and from logical concepts" (LS 32/20). Singularities then are free from the modalities of the proposition as well as from the modalities of consciousness. A singularity therefore is indifferent to all the oppositions in which the modalities of the proposition and the modalities of consciousness consist; strictly speaking, a singularity is neither personal nor impersonal, neither individual nor collective, but a singularity, being indifferent to oppositions, is also a-conceptual, anti-general (LS 67/52), and unconscious (LS 128/105). Not determined by such oppositions, singularities, for Deleuze, form a sort of layer over the surface of bodies. Insofar as they are heterogeneous to the surface—caused by but independent of bodies—singularities themselves are generative.[19] Yet this generative power results neither in making sense originary nor in eliminating sense's event character. Sense, or more precisely singularities, "sort of cause" (LS 115/94) insofar as they participate in structures.[20]

To describe structures, Deleuze relies upon three well-known structural linguistic principles (LS 65–66/50–51). First, utilizing the distinction between signifier and signified, he says that a structure consists in two heterogeneous series (LS 65/50); roughly, these two heterogeneous series are always respectively equivalent to language and perception, words and things, phantasms and bodies. Second, appropriating the Saussurean notion of value, Deleuze says that the terms within the two series exist only through their relations with one another; singularities correspond to the value of these relations.[21] And third, he appropriates Levi-Strauss's notion of a floating signifier, which Deleuze calls the "paradoxical element" (LS 64–66/49–50, 120/98). The paradoxical element is what donates or bestows sense on the two series within the structure; it generates "the emission [or jet] of singularities" (LS 66/51).[22] For Deleuze, the paradoxical element donates sense precisely because it is non-sense (LS 83/66). Nonsense here has nothing to do with the philosophy of the absurd, which had defined nonsense simply as the absence of sense (LS 88/71). In contrast, Deleuzian nonsense is not in a simple oppositional relation to sense (LS 89/71); rather, sense and nonsense exist in "an original type of intrinsic relation, a mode of co-presence" (LS 85/68). The paradoxical element is this co-presence of sense and non-sense. In the signified series, referring to no sense, the paradoxical element appears as a lack. In the signifying series, referring to no sense, the paradoxical element appears as an excess; not imprisoned in a sense, the paradoxical element actually generates too much sense. The paradoxical element, therefore for Deleuze, is *the* Event through which all of the other events are distributed. Having no sense and producing too much sense, the paradoxical element is a repetition without original (cf. LS 44–45/31–32, 118/97).[23] Deleuze thinks about the paradoxical element in a number of ways, as a miming operation (LS 80/63), and as an irresolvable problem with an indefinite number of solutions. Yet, the clearest example of a paradoxical element, for Deleuze, comes from Proust: Combray in *In Search of Lost Time* (DR 115/85).

In *Difference and Repetition* (and in his 1963 *Proust and Signs*),[24] Deleuze discusses Proustian experiences (that is, the well-known experiences of involuntary memory, the taste of the madeleine, for example) in terms of the structuralism just outlined (DR 160n1/122). According to Deleuze, a Proustian experience consists in two series: that of the former present (Combray as it was lived)—this is the signified series—and that of a present present (the narrator's present)—this is the signifier series. In Proustian experience, there is clearly a similarity, even an identity, between the two series; the taste of the madeleine remains the same from the former present to the present present. But, according to Deleuze, the taste possesses "power" because it envelops the paradoxical element, "something that can no longer be defined by an identity"; the paradoxical element is "Combray as it is in itself, as a fragment of a pure past, in its double irreducibility to the present that it has been (perception) and to the present present in which it might reappear or be reconstituted (voluntary memory)" (DR 160n1/122). The madeleine's taste, therefore, brings Combray back not as it was present nor as it could be present. Combray comes back only insofar as we forget the former present and the present present; it comes back as immemorial or eternal, as Deleuze says, "in the form of a past that was never present" (*sous forme d'un passé qui ne fut jamais présent*) (DR 115/85; cf. DR 111–12/82). This phrase, "a past that was never present," indeed, Deleuze's entire discussion of Proust here in *Difference and Repetition* as well as in *Proust and Signs*, is dependent upon Deleuze's interpretation of Bergson. The importance of Bergson for Deleuze is well known. Based in Bergson's notion of pure memory, the notion of a past that was never present, for Deleuze, is a form freed from the present, from the former present and from the present present. Freed from the present, this form is empty, which, on the one hand, allows the two series to resonate or be given sense, and, on the other, allows the form to be repeated in a way which overflows the two series. The empty form of Combray issues forth then with something entirely new, an artwork, the work entitled *In Search of Lost Time* (DR 160n1/122). When this past which was never present issues forth with a work, the work, according to Deleuze, is autonomous or independent in regard to the pure past (DR 122/90). The work's independence implies, for Deleuze, therefore, that the pure past, what grounds or conditions, differs from that which it conditions or grounds, the future.

The work's independence from its conditions of production functions as the most basic principle for Deleuze in *The Logic of Sense* (cf. LS 117/96). Most generally, this principle says: "the foundation can never resemble what it founds" (LS 120/99; cf. DR 119/88). In other words, and this comment shows how much the problem of genesis animates Deleuze's thought, we cannot, he says, "go from the conditioned to the condition in order to think of the condition in the image of the conditioned as the simple form of possibility. The condition cannot have with its negative the same kind of relation that the conditioned has with its negative" (LS 85/68; cf. 128/105). Thus, in order to be one, a ground must never borrow its characteristics from what it grounds; it must presuppose nothing of what it engenders (LS 118/97). We must never, for Deleuze, conceive the generation of sense from bodies on the basis of homogeneity;[25] we must never conceive the generation of sense on the basis of resemblance. Indeed, the lack of resemblance is what defines expression for Deleuze; he says in *Expressionism in Philosophy: Spinoza,* "The significance of Spinozism seems to me this: it . . . frees expression from any subordination to emanative or exemplary causality. Expression itself no longer emanates, no longer resembles anything" (SPE 133/180).[26]

II. The Transcendental Field in Merleau-Ponty

There are two ways in which we can see that Merleau-Ponty respects Deleuze's principle of heterogeneity between the ground and grounded, and these two ways correspond to the two aspects of the transcendental field as described in the chapter of *The Phenomenology of Perception* entitled "The Phenomenal Field." These two aspects are the creative operation and the facticity of the unreflective (PHP 74/61). For Merleau-Ponty, every active process of sense-bestowal appears derivative and secondary in relation to the facticity of the unreflective (PHP 489–90/428–29; cf. PHP 498/436, 501/439, 513/450). Following Sartre's requirement, Merleau-Ponty calls this passive aspect of the transcendental field prepersonal and anonymous (PHP 250–51/216; see also PHP 98/82, 503/441). And like Deleuze, Merleau-Ponty designates this prepersonal aspect of the field with the pronoun "one" or "they" (PHP 277/240).[27] But unlike Deleuze, Merleau-Ponty speaks of this anonymity as generality. What Merleau-Ponty calls the "halo of generality" found around my individuality (PHP 511/448) must be distinguished from what Merleau-Ponty calls an "empty form" (PHP 193/165). Merleau-Ponty associates the empty form of generality with objective thought, with an idea in the Platonic sense of the term (PHP 85–86/71–72; cf. PHP 196/168). In other words, the empty form of generality is hypostatized into a thing separate from the sensible; it is turned into a rule, law, or concept. So we cannot associate what Merleau-Ponty calls an empty form with what Deleuze calls an empty form; such a Merleau-Pontean empty form is a transcendence having an existence separate from the plane of immanence. But there is another kind of generality in Merleau-Ponty; this is the generality of sense. Merleau-Ponty says, "Here [in the acquisition of language] we have an encounter of the human and the inhuman and, as it were, a behavior of the world, a certain inflexion of its style, and the generality of sense as well as that of the vocable is not that of a concept, but of the world as typic" (PHP 462/403). Merleau-Ponty's use of the Kantian term "typic" (as well as his use of the term "schema") implies throughout *The Phenomenology of Perception* a generality that cannot be reduced to a law or formula (cf. PHP 349/303, 358/310, 99/83, 377/326, 377/327); thus, it can never be entirely uprooted from the sensible. Moreover, the notion of style implies a universalization of what has occurred only once; indeed, we can say already that the notion of style implies singularity.[28] But even more importantly, Merleau-Ponty calls this second type of generality, which is not abstracted from experience but is internal to it, a trace (PHP 404/351–52; cf. 358/310, 399/347, 401/349, 406/354), a trace of an "originary past" (PHP 403/351).[29]

Merleau-Ponty's mention here, in the chapter on others, of an "originary past" refers us back to the famous passage at the very end of the "Sentir" chapter. As is well known, there Merleau-Ponty says that the unreflective "constitutes for [radical reflection] something like an original past, a past that has never been present" (*un passé qui n'a jamais été présent*) (PHP 280/242). In a discussion of Derrida and Merleau-Ponty, M. C. Dillon has provided an interpretation of this phrase; in order to interpret this phrase correctly, he insists that we put the phrase in context. For Dillon, putting the phrase in context means putting it in the context of the discussion at the end of the "Sentir" chapter. "In context," he says, "it is clear that the 'past that has never been present' has never been present to reflective consciousness which must draw upon that anonymous past in its appropriating reprise: never present to reflective consciousness, but fully present to pre-reflective consciousness."[30] Despite the apparent sense that Dillon's interpretation makes, his interpretation is, so to speak, upside down. We must not, as Dillon does, interpret the originary past on the basis of consciousness (either reflective or unreflective), on the basis of perception or bodily engagement with the world, but rather interpret the unreflective on the basis of the originary past. Indeed—and this is crucial for seeing whether *The Phenomenology of Perception* withstands the Deleuzian double challenge—we must interpret Merleau-Ponty's notion of "primordial *doxa*" by means of the originary past. We must interpret these notions on the basis of the originary past because of the constant privilege Merleau-Ponty gives to temporality throughout *The Phenomenology of Perception*. Thus, to put the phrase "a past that has never been present" in context means putting it in the context of the "Temporality" chapter.

Three comments are in order when we put this phrase within the context of the "Temporality" chapter. First, the notion of trace developed there depends on what Merleau-Ponty calls "the sense or significance of the past" (PHP 472/413). As elsewhere in *The Phenomenology* (PHP 203/174), the notion of the trace in the "Temporality" chapter is not that of a physiological trace in the brain nor that of a psychological trace in the psyche (PHP 472–73/415). Instead, Merleau-Ponty speaks of a trace like a carving in a wooden table. I would not be able to recognize such a carving as a trace of a past experience without the sense of the past. In other words, without the sense of the past, I would not be able to recognize something present as referring to the past; without the sense of the past, there would be no memories, no recollections. The sense of the past, for Merleau-Ponty, is what allows us to differentiate between a present that is the present and a present that refers to the past. Since what Merleau-Ponty is calling the sense of the past establishes the difference between the present and the past, it cannot be dependent on the present or on perception. Merleau-Ponty's sense of the past is what Bergson would call pure memory, and this brings us to the second comment.[31] In the "Temporality" chapter, Merleau-Ponty criticizes Bergson's notion of a pure memory, but, strangely, the position that he criticizes is not the one Bergson lays out in *Matter and Memory*. Merleau-Ponty says, "When [Bergson] says that the duration 'snowballs upon itself,' and when he postulates memories in themselves accumulating in the unconscious, he makes time out of the preserved present, evolution out of the evolved" (PHP 474n1/415n1). The position that Merleau-Ponty is ascribing to Bergson and *rejecting* is one that conceives the past as something caused by and dependent upon the present. This position, in other words, conceives the past as a "weakened perception," and this is how Merleau-Ponty, in the "Expression" chapter, interprets Bergson's notion of "pure memory" (PHP 210/180). Yet, in *Matter and Memory*, Bergson himself rejects the conception of pure memory as a "weakened perception."[32] Moreover, Bergson says, "philosophers insist on regarding the difference between actual sensations and pure memory as a mere difference in degree, and not in kind. In our view the difference is radical."[33] We must suppose that if Merleau-Ponty rejects the conception that he incorrectly attributes to Bergson, then he actually supports Bergson's position. We must say therefore that Merleau-Ponty conceives the originary past or the sense of the past as a pure past, a past different in kind from the present perception and therefore as a past that was never present. Third, there is textual evidence in the "Temporality" chapter to support this claim. There Merleau-Ponty says that "the present . . . enjoys a privilege because it is the zone in which being and consciousness coincide" (PHP 484–85/424). This comment seems to eliminate the very possibility of a past that has never been present; if the present holds such a privilege, then it seems that the past must not only be caused by a present but also must depend upon it. Yet, Merleau-Ponty says later on the same page that

> In the present and in perception, my being and my consciousness are unified, not that my being is reducible to the knowledge I have of it or that it is clearly set out before me—on the contrary perception is opaque, for it brings into play, beneath what I know, my sensory fields which are my primitive complicities with the world. (PHP 485/424)

This comment implies that the present perception is always dependent upon the sensory fields, upon the primitive complicities with world, in other words, upon the facticity of the unreflective. It turns out then that the past is not dependent on a present; as Merleau-Ponty also says here, "no one of time's dimensions can be deduced from the rest" (PHP 484/424). Instead, it seem that the present itself is dependent on a past, on the "original or originary past." Being caused by a present but not dependent upon it, this type of past amounts to a repetition without original. Thus the "Temporality" chapter implies a type of past that is, as Deleuze would say, "impassible," eternal, immemorial. In fact, only this interpretation, the interpretation that allies Merleau-Ponty's "a past that has never been present" with Deleuze's "a past that was never present," can explain why Merleau-Ponty uses the phrase "un passé originel" in the "Sentir" chapter. If it is the case that "to be fully present to prereflective consciousness" means to be dependent on prereflective consciousness's present, then it is impossible to explain why Merleau-Ponty would use the adjective "originel" to modify the word "passé." If the past is dependent on the prereflective consciousness's present, then it is derivative from that present and is not itself original, is not itself a sort of "origin."

But, for Merleau-Ponty, the "original past," the unreflective, is something like an "origin," or more precisely, a "cause," on the basis of which expression creates.[34] For Deleuze, as we have seen, expression is not defined in terms of resemblance; instead of resemblance, expression for Deleuze is the actualization of the virtual (DR 273/211). Similarly, Merleau-Ponty defines expression as effectuation (PHP 213/183).[35] Explicitly, Merleau-Ponty separates effectuation from translation and reproduction; he also distinguishes it from what he calls "objective resemblance," that is, from the process of onomatopoeia (PHP 218/187). But that Merleau-Ponty calls expression a process that extracts from objects their "emotional essence" (PHP 218/187) does not imply that expression is *subjective* resemblance. There is no subjective resemblance between the object and the expression because the object has no emotional charge until our bodies and our world are put into an emotional form (PHP 220/189). Therefore, it seems that one must say that expression in Merleau-Ponty does not at all consist in natural resemblance.[36] Instead of resemblance, the *mise en forme* defines expression. Although the phrase "mise en forme" is common throughout *The Phenomenology of Perception* (e.g., PHP 89/75, 354/306), in the expression chapter Merleau-Ponty also uses the word "mimique" to describe the expressive operation (PHP 212/182, 218/187; cf. PHP 191/163, 191/164). *Mimique,* of course, refers to the mime's activities, which, while clearly recognizable as a repetition of an object (cf. PHP 218/187), do not merely resemble the object. The mime's activities have the power to generate something that in turn can be put into words, to generate sense; in other words, the mime's activities are able to generate what both Merleau-Ponty and Deleuze would call a work of art, because the mime's activities have the power to stylize,[37] or, better, the power to exaggerate the object. The mime's activities are dependent not on the real object but on what is virtual in the object, on what was never real in the object. In other words, while caused by the present, the mime's effectuations are not dependent on the present. Not dependent on the real, the Merleau-Pontean mime is able to carry the virtual to the nth power. This excess based in a lack is why Merleau-Ponty says that "We cannot economize on this power which creates significations and which communicates them" (PHP 221/189). Therefore, perhaps we can say about Merleau-Ponty's *mimique* what Mallarmé says about his Pierrot: "Here advancing, there remembering, to the future, to the past, under the false appearance of the present—in such a manner the Mime proceeds, whose game is limited to a perpetual allusion, without breaking the mirror."[38]

This interpretation of Merleau-Ponty's notion of expression implies that sense-bestowal in Merleau-Ponty happens; sense is an event. Sense is an event because it is generated out of that which lacks sense, the general. What is general lacks sense because it is freed from the present. And being freed from the present, the general in Merleau-Ponty is identical to what Deleuze calls a singularity. Merleau-Ponty's "original past" functions therefore exactly like Deleuze's "paradoxical element"; it donates too much sense because it has no sense. If Merleau-Ponty's original past functions like a Deleuzian paradoxical element, then it will be necessary to reinterpret all of Merleau-Ponty's comments in *The Phenomenology of Perception* concerning sense and nonsense. For instance, writing in 1945, Merleau-Ponty associates, in the chapter on space, the notion of sense with rationalism and the notion of nonsense with a philosophy of the absurd (PHP 341/295); Deleuze, as we already noted, rejects this absurdist notion of nonsense. Yet, in the same chapter, Merleau-Ponty says, "Rationalism and skepticism draw their sustenance from an actual life of consciousness which they both hypocritically take for granted, without which they can neither be conceived nor even experienced, and in which it is impossible to say that *everything has a sense* or that *everything is nonsense,* but only that *there is sense* [*il y a du sens*]" (PHP 342/296, Merleau-Ponty's emphasis). If we must equate "nonsense" in this quote with the absurdist absence of sense, then it is dependent on sense as sense's mere negation. If this negative relation is correct, however, then we must confront the fact that the *il y a* in the passage refers to a type of nonsense different from the absurdist notion. We would have to conceive *il y a* in terms of what Deleuze calls "an original type of intrinsic relation, a mode of co-presence" of sense and nonsense. And, finally, if this interpretation of the *il y a* is correct, then we must say that Merleau-Ponty, in *The Phenomenology of Perception,* precisely respects Deleuze's principle of heterogeneity between the ground and grounded.

III. The Danger of Immanence

Nevertheless, *The Phenomenology of Perception* cannot by itself decide whether phenomenology withstands the Deleuzian double challenge. The decisive question is this: can phenomenology be anything other than a phenomenology of subjectivity (as the general form of all subjects)? According to Deleuze, as soon as a philosopher turns immanence into immanence to consciousness, the difference between ground and grounded collapses. Generality, resemblance, and analogy determine all relations. Even when phenomenology tries to show that consciousness is constituted, that it involves a moment of passivity, responds to the call of the other, it reinstates transcendence. According to Deleuze, the "modern moment" is defined by a reversal: "we are no longer satisfied with thinking immanence as immanent to a transcendent; we want to think transcendence within the immanent, and it is from transcendence that a breach is expected" (QPH 48/47). When phenomenology makes immanence be immanent to a transcendental subjectivity, it finds at the heart of this field a "cipher" which refers to another consciousness; Deleuze says, "This is what happens in Husserl and many of his successors who discover in the Other [*l'Autre*] or in the Flesh, the mole of the transcendent within immanence itself" (QPH 48/46). Instead of immanence being ascribed to something other, God, immanence itself is made to disgorge the transcendent everywhere; in the modern moment we think that immanence is a prison—solipsism—from which the transcendent will save us (QPH 49/47). Merleau-Ponty's *The Phenomenology of Perception* illustrates this modern moment. In the chapter "Others and the Human World," trying to establish the basis of a common human cultural world over and above a natural world, Merleau-Ponty says, "When I turn towards perception, and pass from direct perception to thinking about that perception, I reenact it, and find at work in my organs of perception a thought older than myself of which those organs are merely the trace. In the same way, I understand the existence of others [*autrui*]" (PHP 404/351–52). That Merleau-Ponty uses the word "la pensée" here means that the habits of my perceptual organs have resulted from a thinking subject (although a thinking subject somewhere in the past) like mine just as the movements of another living body result from a thinking subject like mine; these traces are nothing more than sediments of past lived or subjective experiences like mine. That Merleau-Ponty uses the phrase "de la même manière" implies that my bodily mimicries are based in a resemblance; and immediately after this phrase (echoing Husserl's Fifth Cartesian Meditation) Merleau-Ponty discusses analogy, stressing that the process just described is not analogical reasoning but a sort of immediate analogy. No matter how hard one tries to reinterpret *The Phenomenology of Perception*, one cannot do away with the fact that subjectivity is at the center: "Things and instants link up with one another to form a world only across that ambiguous being known as subjectivity" (PHP 384/333). Merleau-Ponty, of course, knew this (cf. VI 253/200).[39]

That *The Phenomenology of Perception* does not free itself from subjectivity is why only *The Visible and the Invisible* can decide whether phenomenology withstands the Deleuzian double challenge. In *The Visible and the Invisible* (and in other later texts), Merleau-Ponty conceives being not as subject but as infinity (VI 223/169). Perhaps the greatest thing that Merleau-Ponty has ever written is the following:

The extraordinary harmony of external and internal is possible only through the mediation of a *positive infinite* or (since every restriction to a certain kind of infinity would be a seed of negation) an infinite infinite. It is in this positive infinite that the actual existence of things *partes extra partes* and extension as we think of it (which on the contrary is continuous and infinite) communicate or are joined together. If, at the center and so to speak in the kernel of Being, there is an infinite infinite, every partial being directly or indirectly presupposes it, and is in return really or eminently contained in it. (S 187/148–49, Merleau-Ponty's emphasis)[40]

A positive infinite, conceived without the seed of negation, is a pure plane of immanence. An infinite infinite expresses itself without end; there is no interruption of its movement. Therefore transcendence cannot enter and limit it, establish another world, an Other, a second meaning of Being (QPH 49/47).[41] In an infinite infinite, there can be no *analogia entis*. Being conceived as an infinite infinite is why Merleau-Ponty can say in "Philosophy and Non-philosophy since Hegel" (1961) that "Ambiguity is not a lack of univocity. Ambiguity is 'good.'"[42] And as early as 1951–52, Merleau-Ponty had connected the notion of good ambiguity with that of expression.[43] Although we cannot say for certain, it looks as though Merleau-Ponty was going to utilize in *The Visible and the Invisible* the notion of expression to decipher the chiasm; he says, "And henceforth movement, touch, vision, applying themselves to the other and to themselves, return towards their source and, in the patient and silent labor of desire, begin the paradox of expression" (VI 189/ 144). But was phenomenology going to be the way through which Merleau-Ponty would explicate the paradox of expression? Can there be a phenomenology of expression? Or is it the case that phenomenology always, necessarily, associates expression with emanation and creation? Can phenomenology accept pantheism, which Deleuze calls the "danger of immanence" (SPE 309/ 333)? We do not know the answer to these questions because Merleau-Ponty never had the chance to raise and answer this one: "Raise the question: the invisible life, the invisible community, the invisible other, the invisible culture. Elaborate a phenomenology of the 'other world,' as the limit of a phenomenology of the imaginary and the 'hidden'" (VI 283/229).[44]

6 The End of Ontology

Interrogation in Merleau-Ponty and Deleuze

Today the phenomenological philosophy of Edmund Husserl is at an end.[1] But we must never forget the basic problem with which it began: the return to the things themselves. For Husserl, of course, we return to the things themselves by enacting the phenomenological reduction. Without question, the reduction is Husserl's greatest discovery. As it is described, for instance, in *Ideas I,* the reduction requires that the phenomenologist bracket the existence of transcendency.[2] By doing so, the phenomenologist makes immanence be complete. In effect, therefore, with the reduction Husserl is announcing that God is dead. Nevertheless, after this announcement, Husserl ends up relating immanence *to* the transcendental subject as the constitutive source of all things given immanently. This dative is phenomenology's first failure to reach the things themselves because it takes transcendental subjectivity as the thing itself. But phenomenology fails to reach the things themselves in a second way. In order for a ground to be what it is—a ground—it must presuppose nothing of what it grounds. In other words, the ground must never resemble, indeed, it must be heterogeneous to that which it grounds. In phenomenology, the reduction moves the phenomenologist from everyday opinions back to *Urdoxa,* from natural beliefs to primal faith. As the ground of the natural attitude, the doxic modalities of transcendental consciousness, however, are copied from everyday opinions. Therefore, despite proclaiming itself presuppositionless, phenomenology ends by doing nothing more than justifying what everyone believes; moving in this circle, phenomenology is never anything but a subjectivism.

Heidegger seems to correct the subjectivistic failures of phenomenology when he reopens the question of Being. The question of Being in *Being and Time*[3] does not simply transform phenomenology into ontology; rather, it turns interrogation into the very "intentionality" of being itself. In Heideggerian ontology, therefore, being questions itself; but, questioning itself, Being does not become for Heidegger an empty generality separated from individual beings. Questioning itself, being questions the beings, which means that Being is the Being *of* beings. Therefore, Heidegger maintains the remarkable discovery of the phenomenological reduction: immanence is complete. However, while it is the Being of beings, Being, for Heidegger, differs from all beings. In the early "What Is Metaphysics?" Heidegger emphasizes the difference between Being and beings by defining Being as "the nothing."[4] Defined as "the nothing," the ground of the phenomena—Being—becomes an *Abgrund*. Because Being is an abyss, the ground in Heidegger seems not to be copied from what it grounds. Indeed, when Heidegger finally puts Being under the sign of the cross, he simultaneously announces that God is dead, thereby making immanence complete, *and* differentiates the ground from the grounded thereby making Being heterogeneous to the beings.[5] Heidegger's transformation of phenomenology into ontology, therefore, seems to reach the thing itself: Being.

Under Heidegger's influence, twentieth-century ontology has appropriated interrogation in order to define being itself. In the second half of the twentieth century, we can see the appropriation of interrogation to define Being in Merleau-Ponty and in Deleuze. Everyone knows that, under Heidegger's influence, Merleau-Ponty moves from a phenomenology of perception to an ontology of the visible and the invisible, an ontology that revolves around interrogation or the question. But, when we turn to Deleuze, no one seems to recognize that, like Merleau-Ponty, Deleuze too develops an ontology that revolves around the question.[6] For Deleuze, Being is interrogation (DR 89/64). Moreover, the first philosopher that Deleuze mentions in *Difference and Repetition* is neither Bergson nor Nietzsche nor Spinoza as one would expect; rather, it is Heidegger (DR 1/xix). Indeed, what Deleuze calls "Heidegger's ontological intuition" (DR 154/117)—that difference must relate different to different without any mediation whatsoever by the identical—entirely guides Deleuze in *Difference and Repetition*. Therefore, I think that it is no exaggeration to say that *Difference and Repetition* is Deleuze's *Being and Time*. I even think that it is no exaggeration to say that the publication of Deleuze's *Difference and Repetition* in 1968 is as important as the publication of *Being and Time* in 1927. I think this because, when Deleuze in *Difference and Repetition* defines what he calls "the three powers" of the question (DR 251–69/195–208), he sets a new standard for ontology. Deleuze's three powers of the question finally puts an end to the subjectivizing tendency of ontology, a tendency, I believe, that one can still find in both Heidegger's ontology and Merleau-Ponty's ontology. In fact, here I intend to argue that the ontology Merleau-Ponty develops in *The Visible and the Invisible* does not really correct phenomenology's subjectivistic failures. Although it is probably impossible to demonstrate this claim with certainty—*The Visible and the Invisible*, of course, remains incomplete—by trying to demonstrate it, I hope to show that one very big difference distinguishes the ontology of Merleau-Ponty from that of Deleuze. The difference between them lies in where each begins, with Being or with the beings. This beginning determines the role of the negative in one's ontology. The role of the negative in one's ontology in turn determines whether one's ontology subjectivizes Being; negating is always a subjective, even humanistic, practice. So the big difference that I would like to determine is the difference between Being and beings. Which one— Being or beings—is the thing itself or the things themselves? This question of "which one" leads us to a point of diffraction, a diffraction into faith and knowledge, religion and epistemology.[7]

I. Heidegger

To approach this point of diffraction, we must begin by determining both Deleuze's and Merleau-Ponty's relations to Heidegger. Nietzsche's doctrine of eternal return entirely determines Deleuze's relation with Heidegger. In *Difference and Repetition,* Deleuze asks, "does [Heidegger] effectuate the conversion after which . . . Being [*l'être*] is said only of difference and, in this sense, revolves around the being [*l'étant*]? Does [Heidegger] conceive the being [*l'étant*] in such a manner that it will be truly disengaged from any subordination in relation to the identity of representation? It would seem not," Deleuze continues, "given [Heidegger's] critique of the Nietzschean eternal return" (DR 91/66).[8] According to Heidegger in his lectures, Nietzsche's eternal recurrence combines both fundamental determinations of being found at the beginning of Western metaphysics: becoming and permanence.[9] Nietzsche's thinking, for Heidegger, indeed stretches back to the beginning; but it does not reach the beginning *as* beginning, what Heidegger calls the *anfänglichen Anfang.* In other words, Nietzsche's thinking in the eternal recurrence does not reach back to the experience that generated all beings and all ontological determinations based in beings. Nietzsche's thinking does not reach back to being *as such.* Therefore, in Heidegger's eyes, beings still determine Nietzsche's fundamental metaphysical position; the most basic principle of Nietzsche's thinking—the will to power—still revolves around the being. Such a beginning in the being implies that his thinking remains firmly entrenched in Platonism. Nietzsche's thinking may reverse the Platonic schema of the sensible and the supersensible, but it does not "twist free," as Heidegger says.[10] Reversing but not twisting free, Nietzsche's thinking for Heidegger brings metaphysics to an end.

From Heidegger, Deleuze appropriates the notion of a reversal of Platonism. In *Difference and Repetition,* he says, "The task of modern philosophy has been defined: to reverse Platonism" (DR 82/59). Also from Heidegger, Deleuze accepts the interpretation that Platonism begins with the being. Deleuze accepts this interpretation because he abandons Heidegger's requirement that thinking begin with Being. To require that thinking begin with being, as Heidegger requires, means that we can conceive of being only negatively; with this beginning, we say Being cannot be conceived as a being. For Deleuze, to conceive Being as this "not a being" maintains the negative as the motor of Being. In contrast therefore to Heidegger, Deleuze starts with the beings. To start with the beings means that each and every being is a beginning;[11] there is no *anfänglichen Anfang* because each and every being is affirmed. For Deleuze, affirmation, not negation, is the motor of Being (DR 74/52). Affirmed, each being is free to repeat itself, to realize what is virtual in itself, and thereby to become what it *is*. We must stress the word "is" here; through repetition a being is selected to be, it becomes Being. As Deleuze says, "If 'the being' is above all difference and beginning, Being is itself repetition, the re-beginning [*recommencement*] of the being" (DR 261/202). The repetition of difference is how Deleuze interprets Nietzsche's eternal return doctrine. Beginning with the affirmation of beings, Deleuze turns Nietzsche's doctrine of eternal return into a "labyrinth" (DR 77/55) more "torturous" (DR 122/91, 76/54) than a circle (NP 52/46, 55/49, 225/197). This image of Being as a more torturous labyrinth is why, for Deleuze, as he himself has often said, the issue has never been the overcoming of philosophy or the death of metaphysics (NP 223/195; QPH 14/9). Deleuze's reversal of Platonism "conserves" elements of Platonism (DR 82/59).[12]

For Deleuze, the beginning in Being is what is most controversial in Heidegger's reading of Nietzsche, perhaps in Heidegger's entire philosophy; this beginning is controversial because for Deleuze the beings are the things themselves. Heidegger's beginning in Being, however, is not controversial for Merleau-Ponty. In fact, in the Course Notes from 1959 to 1961, Merleau-Ponty seems to be using Heidegger's later ontology as a model for his own "indirect ontology" (NC 147–48).[13] Here, for instance, Merleau-Ponty describes the ontology found in *Being and Time* as a "direct philosophy" and describes Heidegger's later meditation on the truth of essence as a "turning towards an analysis which is no longer direct" (NC 94–95). Moreover, here in the Course Notes, Merleau-Ponty seems to be using Heidegger in order to justify starting his own ontology in a consideration of nature. So the 1959–61 Course Notes imply that Merleau-Ponty is reading Heidegger's later essays as if they were precisely what he would call "indirect language" (S 54/43).[14] Only Heidegger's procedure of trying to express directly what cannot be expressed directly allows silence to break through. Therefore, for Merleau-Ponty, ontology must be indirect in this exact sense: Being must be methodologically mediated by beings and expressed in the language of beings.[15] Undoubtedly, indirectness is a "law of ontology" for Merleau-Ponty (RC 125/156). Nevertheless, that ontology must be indirect for Merleau-Ponty does not mean that Being is not the beginning. In regard to the beginning in Being, Heidegger and

Merleau-Ponty are indistinguishable; for Merleau-Ponty, Being is the thing itself.

Therefore, what is more important than whether Merleau-Ponty and Heidegger differ over the question of direct and indirect ontology is that for both Being is the beginning and not the beings. For Merleau-Ponty, beings mediate our access to Being, but the indirect ontologist can go up to being through a series of "reductions" of the beings. Merleau-Ponty describes this process of reductions in a famous published working note from February 1959; he says,

> I will finally be able to take a position in ontology . . . only after the series of reductions the book develops and which are all in the first one, but also are really accomplished only in the last one. This reversal itself—*circulus vitiosus deus*—is not hesitation, bad faith and bad dialectic, but return to *Sigè*, the abyss. *One cannot make a direct ontology.* My "indirect" method (Being in the beings) is alone conformed with Being—"negative philosophy" like "negative theology." (VI 233/179, Merleau-Ponty's emphasis)

On the basis of this passage, we can see that Merleau-Ponty is conceiving the reductions as a series of negations; hence Merleau-Ponty's phrase " 'negative philosophy' like 'negative theology.' " The 1960–61 course "Philosophy and Non-philosophy since Hegel," however, shows that, despite these negations, the Being that we reach is not "positive" (NC 275/9). Neither is it purely negative (VI 96/67).[16] Instead, the Being that we reach is *Sigè*, the abyss, in other words, the *Abgrund*.[17] In order to understand this *Abgrund*, we must take into account that, in the middle of this working note, Merleau-Ponty cites Nietzsche's *Beyond Good and Evil*: "circulus vitiosus deus." In his lectures on Nietzsche's doctrine of eternal return, Heidegger comments on this Latin statement.[18] He stresses that this statement is not a statement at all, but a question: "circulus vitiosus deus?" No matter how we end up translating this question, we must investigate the nature of a question. Thus, we must turn to Deleuze's determination of the three powers of the question.

II. The Three Powers of the Question in Deleuze

For Deleuze in *Difference and Repetition*, modern ontology "suffers from failures," because it does not recognize the objective power of the question (DR 253/196). Modern ontology continues to conceive the question either in terms of a provisional vagueness in a human subject, which an answer comes to fulfill, or in terms of an interiority which can never be fulfilled (DR 141/106). In the second case, Deleuze refers to the concept of a beautiful soul (DR 253/196; also DR 2/xx, 74–75/52–53, 267/207)—from Goethe's *Wilhelm Meister's Apprenticeship*: the beautiful soul keeps her thoughts on the inside and thereby does not let her beauty be destroyed; she is silent, her interiority ineffable.[19] Although Deleuze does not say whom he has in mind in this description of the failures of contemporary ontology, it is hard not to think of Merleau-Ponty here. No matter what, Deleuze is intending the three powers of the question to compensate for these subjective "failures" of contemporary ontology. For Deleuze, the three powers are powers over the subject, not powers of the subject.

The first power of the question is "to silence every . . . response which would claim to suppress the question in order to force the one response which always continues and maintains it" (DR 252/195, 142/107).[20] This first power refers to the question's most essential characteristic, which is that the question accepts no response that would terminate it. An "openness" defines the question. We also find this same characteristic in Merleau-Ponty (cf. VI 162/121).[21] But, in Deleuze's formulation of the first power the most important word is the verb "forcer." What Deleuze sees in the question is the power of an imperative. With a question, for Deleuze, it is not the case that I can say, "under these conditions, I must ask and must find an answer for the question." Rather, the imperative is categorical: "Answer the question!" In fact, I am not the one asking the question; the question is being asked of me. So I experience the question as an event that happens to me. In all of its cruelty, forcing an answer out of me, the question makes me aware of my powerlessness. For Deleuze, because the question is an event, the categorical imperative is not moral; it is aleatory. Yet, although the imperative has its source in chance, it is not arbitrary. The arbitrariness of the command disappears if I affirm the question enough (DR 256/198). This, for Deleuze, cannot be stressed enough: the whole of chance must be affirmed. In other words, the openness of the question necessarily requires that I say "yes," "yes, I'm the one"; every answer in which I say "no" closes the question. Indeed, for Deleuze, any question to which I can answer "no" is not a genuine question. If I say "yes" enough to the question, if I say "yes" to the whole of chance, then "the roll of the dice" is not fragmented into good and evil parts. The dice throw is thereby transformed into destiny (DR 113/83); the imperative of the question is the imperative of an adventure.

The idea of an adventure opens the second power of the question. The question, according to Deleuze, "[puts] into play the questioner as much as that which is questioned and [puts the question] itself into question" (DR 253/195). If the answer forced from me is the one that affirms the question and thereby keeps it open, the answer appears as a paradox, an enigma, or a problem. Every question, for Deleuze, must be led back to the problem from which it emanates (DR 253/196, 115/85). Affirming the question means that the questioner as well as the one questioned are forced to act, are forced to solve the problem. One has been selected; one is going to be tested (*éprouvé*); one has been put into play. This "putting into play" refers back again to the dice throw. The dice, which have been thrown "in the sky" (this is Deleuze's expression), are chance. But, when they "roll out on earth," an event happens which establishes the necessity of an imperative. "The imperative," as Deleuze says, "is to throw" (DR 255/198). The second throw is the attempt to solve the problem, to be never done with it. Thus the second throw requires that the questioner as much as the questioned put themselves at risk. This second throw is the power of decision (DR 255/197). One decides to do what one can to solve a problem. The second power of the question therefore is the "transmutation" of our powerlessness into power (*'l'impouvoir' se transmue en puissance*) (DR 258/199).

The decision to do what one can to solve the problem opens the question's third power. When a problem is solved, it brings about, as Deleuze himself says, "the revelation of Being as corresponding to the question" (DR 253/196). Despite the Heideggerian tone of this comment, Deleuze is not speaking of *aletheia*; truth implies that the questioning is terminated. To say that the solution to the problem is the revelation of truth means that the question and the problem on which it is based were errors, errors which the solution corrects (cf. DR 193/148). The revelation of Being as truth means that the adventure was a straying off course. For Deleuze, however, Being distributes itself in beings in an "errant" manner (DR 54/36). Therefore, what the question reveals is not *aletheia*, but errancy (DR 80/57, 149/112); the revelation of Being continues "to err." Indeed, it is errancy itself, for Deleuze, which keeps the question open (cf. DR 142/107).

To separate Being from truth is also to separate Being from subjectivity. To say, however, that the revelation of Being is not truth and therefore not subjective does not imply that the revelation of Being is non-epistemic. In fact, errancy for Deleuze is knowledge. In *Difference and Repetition,* Deleuze uses the word "knowledge" (*connaissance*) in the sense of learning (DR 89/63–64). To learn something is not to represent it to oneself; it is to take something into one's being that one did not have before (DR 118/87). What is taken into one's being that one did not have before is what Deleuze calls an "idea" (DR 89/64). An idea "is an objective entity, but one of which we cannot say that it exists in itself: it insists or subsists, possessing a quasi-being or an extra-being, that minimum of being common to real, possible, or even impossible objects" (DR 202/156). If the idea does not have existence in itself, it is not a Platonic idea. Moreover, since the idea is learned, it is not an innate idea. Although the idea in Deleuze must be conceived as engendered, the idea's existence is not relative to the individual who has it. Ideas, for Deleuze, have virtual existence (DR 269/208). An actual thing has an existence, which is completely and entirely determined (DR 270/209). What an idea can do, however, is not entirely determined. Therefore, for Deleuze, an idea is not clear and distinct, but distinct and obscure. Because they are obscure, ideas engender more questions and problems, more differences (DR 192/147).

Because ideas are not actual, Deleuze says that ideas must be defined as "non-being" (DR 253/196, 246–47/191). For Deleuze, however, this non-being is not the negative; the negative is an illusion (DR 89/63). It looks as though the negative generates change, but in fact what it does is negate a "pre-established identity" (DR 73/51). The result is that, when one negates the negation in order to generate an affirmation, one merely arrives back where one started. As Deleuze says, from the negative, "nothing follows" (DR 74/52); the negative produces a false movement and involves "a terrifying conservatism" (DR 75/53). In contrast, negation follows from affirmation as a genuine consequence, which means that something really happens, the transmutation of powerlessness into power. Because negation really follows from affirmation, Deleuze insists on writing non-being with the "non" between parentheses. When Deleuze insists on this convention of parenthesizing the "non," he is appropriating the concept of the phenomenological reduction. In Husserl's reduction, however, one brackets "being." Bracketing the being of the things that exist—the beings, in other words—mediates the phenomenologist's access to absolute being, which is transcendental consciousness. But the phenomenological bracketing then opens the problem of how to characterize the absolute being of transcendental consciousness. The only solution seems to be a negative characterization, which implies that the phenomenological reduction itself is a negative process. That it is a negative process can be seen clearly in Fink's analysis of it in the *Sixth Cartesian Meditation,* where he conceives absolute subjectivity as *mē on.*[22] Insofar as it parenthesizes being, the phenomenological reduction is still mystified by the negative. But this mystification by the negative can also be found in Heidegger's practice of crossing out the word "Being" (cf. DR 91/66). Placing the sign of the cross over Being implies that God as the Supreme Being and as the traditional conception of Being is dead. This *chiasm* placed over Being, however, also implies God's resurrection as *me on,* the Being that is conceivable only in negative determinations. Deleuze's practice of parenthesizing the "non" of "non-being" in no way follows the path of such a negative theology.

III. Perceptual Faith in Merleau-Ponty

Merleau-Ponty does not parenthesize the "non" of "non-being." In fact, as we have seen, in the working notes he accepts the model of negative theology for his indirect ontology. Merleau-Ponty accepts this model because, like Heidegger, Being is the beginning. Thus, like Heidegger, Merleau-Ponty must attempt—and we can see this attempt in the Course Notes from 1959 to 1961—to find, as the generative source of beings, something other than *Seiende*, especially something other than the beings that science determines (NC 102, 109). But, there is an additional problem for Merleau-Ponty; by trying to find something that is not a being, one can end up characterizing this "abyss" or "nothing" as absolute nothingness. The critique of Sartre in *The Visible and the Invisible* shows clearly that Merleau-Ponty realizes that wholly positive being and absolute nothingness are at least solidary if not indiscernible. This solidarity is why, as Merleau-Ponty tells us in the Introduction to *Signs,* it is "better to speak of the visible and the invisible . . . than to speak of being and nothingness" (S 30/21). According to Merleau-Ponty in the last Course Notes, Heidegger's later practice of crossing out the word "Being" does not fall into this trap of a negativism, which is inseparable from a positivism; Merleau-Ponty says, "what [Heidegger] calls *Seyn* or *S̶e̶y̶n* is *not nothing;* it is the 'es gibt,' the 'il y a,' the open 'etwas' to which we are open in the truth which we are" (NC 102, Merleau-Ponty's emphasis).

According to Merleau-Ponty in *The Visible and the Invisible,* this *etwas* or "something" encompasses our negations as well as our affirmations (VI 147/109). It glides beneath our "yes" and our "no" (VI 138/102) and "is silently behind all our affirmations, negations, and even behind all formulated questions" (VI 171/129). The "something" is, according to Merleau-Ponty, "an unknown intelligible place where the facts, the examples, ideas I lack should be found" (VI 171/129). The "something" is what is interrogated or what interrogates itself. For Merleau-Ponty, the "something" implies that interrogation cannot be conceived as it is in Sartre, where the one who questions himself about being discovers himself to be nothing (VI 95/67). Sartrean interrogation implies that the questioner is a subjective emptiness, which an essence or a fact comes to fulfill; it implies that "being and the world are unknowns" (VI 137/101). In contrast, Merleau-Ponty recognizes the essence of the question: a question can never be terminated or, as Merleau-Ponty himself says, "the lacuna will never be filled in" (VI 138/101, 142/105, 171/129). Although, for Merleau-Ponty, interrogation cannot be conceived as an epistemological question about essences or about facts (VI 168–69/127) or as an epistemological question about the nature of the world or about whether the world exists (VI 131/96), it is nevertheless a question about a "secret knowledge" (VI 162/121). Although Merleau-Ponty distinguishes interrogation from skepticism (VI 160/120), he defines it in terms of the question "que sais-je?" (VI 170/128). This "what do I know?'" pushes the epistemological question down into an examination of the very idea of knowledge (VI 171/129; cf. NC 356). As in Deleuze—and, indeed, the similarity between Merleau-Ponty and Deleuze in this regard is striking—in Merleau-Ponty, ideas define the negativity of Being (VI 198/151). In the final incomplete chapter, however, where Merleau-Ponty discusses ideas, he says an idea "is therefore not a *de facto* invisible, like one object hidden behind another, and not an absolute invisible which would have nothing to do with the visible. Rather, it is the invisible *of* this world, that which inhabits this world, sustains it, renders it visible, its own and interior possibility, the Being of this being" (VI 198/151, Merleau-Ponty's emphasis). Nothing in this comment implies that ideas can be made visible or present *as such;* thus they always remain absolutely invisible or absolutely absent or absolutely other, even as they become visible or come into presence or come into the same.[23] Ideas for Merleau-Ponty are as much an unconcealment as a concealment. We should notice, therefore, the Heideggerian formula in the comment "the Being of this being"; when Merleau-Ponty discusses the question "what do I know?" there are other Heideggerian formulas, for instance, "letting beings be" (VI 138/102; RC 179/199)[24] and "the unconcealment of Being" (VI 171/129). These Heideggerian formulas suggest that ideas are *aletheia.* And, of course, one of the titles Merleau-Ponty considered for the book we now call *The Visible and the Invisible* was "The Origin of Truth."

But to associate *ideas* with the unconcealment and concealment of Being is un-Heideggerian. In fact, Merleau-Ponty is very un-Heideggerian when he describes ideas in the following ways. He says, ideas "people" the great unpenetrated and discouraging night of our soul; ideas have a "presence, [the soul] feels like the presence of someone in the dark" (VI 197/198). These formulas are why I think that it is more significant, than his utilization of Heideggerian formulas, that Merleau-Ponty quotes the following passage from Husserl's *Cartesian Meditations;*[25] the passage comes from paragraph 16: "It is the experience . . . still mute which we are concerned with leading to the pure expression of its own meaning" (VI 171/129; cf. also VI 203/155; also NC 373).[26] That ideas "people" the visible is why the question "what do I know?" turns out to be a question of perceptual faith; we believe in ideas just as we believe in other people.

Like any faith, perceptual faith, for Merleau-Ponty, must be interrogated. Despite the fact that perceptual faith must be interrogated, perceptual faith is not primarily doubt; instead, it is "a first positivity" (VI 76/51). Therefore, it is not, as Merleau-Ponty says, "a beginning in negation and a maybe put in place of being" (VI 18–19/4). It is belief in the world, in the world as others perceive it, in the world as a collection of things (VI 84/57). As this naive belief, perceptual faith is beyond proofs (VI 48/28) and reasons for belief (VI 75/50). But also, as this belief, perceptual faith is "interwoven with incredulity, at each instance menaced by non-faith" (VI 48/28; cf. VI 140/103). This tissue of faith and non-faith Merleau-Ponty calls our "openness upon being" (VI 122/88). But once again, it seems to me, the Heideggerian language is not decisive for understanding perceptual faith in Merleau-Ponty; rather, it is the Husserlian language. In the appendix to *The Visible and the Invisible*, Merleau-Ponty says that "the 'perceptual faith includes everything that is given to the natural man in the original in a source-experience, with the force of what is inaugural and present in person" (VI 209/158). This description of perceptual faith refers to Husserl's "principle of all principles" which is found in *Ideas I*, paragraph 24: evidence is that which is present *in person.*

The "in person" to which Merleau-Ponty is leading us is a carnal experience; the flesh is *Urpräsentierbarkeit* (VI 178n/135n; cf. S 222/176). But, just as perceptual faith involves non-faith, the flesh involves *Nichturpräsentbarkeit*, an in principle, originary non-presentability (VI 308/254, 272/218–19). It is this originary non-presentability which is, for Merleau-Ponty, "the true negative," the true negative inside the positive, the true nothing inside the something, the true non-being inside Being. Merleau-Ponty determines this true negative in the working notes as the originary non-presentability of the alter ego, as the "other side" of the other's aesthesiological body, in short, the other's soul (VI 286/223, 257/203). The originary unpresentability of the other's ideas refers in particular to Husserl's description of *Fremderfahrung* in the Fifth Cartesian Meditation.[27] The Husserlian reference implies that, if the true negative in the flesh is for Merleau-Ponty the in principle inaccessibility of the other's soul, then it is the case that the flesh is *Einfühlung* (VI 231–32/178, 234/180, 235/182, 302/248);[28] the flesh, for Merleau-Ponty, like *Fremderfahrung* is sympathy.[29] It is the feeling of sympathy, therefore, that leads Merleau-Ponty in all of his last writings to speak of flesh as "indivision" (VI 262/208), as "anonymity" (VI 254/201), as the *Ineinander* (VI 234/180), and, of course, as the chiasm (VI 252/199)—instead of speaking of consciousness and subjectivity. But, all of these ways of speaking, including the flesh, describe inter-subjectivity. So, while the chiasm leads Merleau-Ponty to speak of "rejecting . . . the notion of the subject" (VI 292/239), it is precisely the chiasm of sympathy that brings about the resurrection of the subject. This resurrection of the subject is why Merleau-Ponty says in *The Visible and the Invisible* that what someone receives in the interrogation of perceptual faith is not an answer but "a confirmation of his astonishment" that there is a world. In other words, in Merleau-Pontean interrogation, what one receives by having pity on the other is a confirmation of one's faith.

IV. The Point of Diffraction in the *Personne*

Undoubtedly, under Heidegger's influence, both Merleau-Ponty and Deleuze turn to ontology in order to escape from the subjectivizing tendency that always plagues phenomenology. The attempt to go beyond subjectivism is why both Deleuze and Merleau-Ponty use the word "personne" to designate the subject (VI 254/201, 299/246; DR 253/196).[30] But, this word takes on different senses depending on whether one takes Being or the beings as the beginning. When one begins with Being, one must bracket the beings in order to have access to what they are not; this procedure makes negation primary, and since negating is always a subjective, even humanistic, process, the bracketing of the beings reinstates subjectivity at the beginning. In contrast, when one begins with the beings, one must bracket the "non" of non-being in order to have access to what they are; this procedure makes affirmation primary, and this bracketing does not allow subjectivity to be reinstated. Both ways of bracketing reduce the beings; both ways of bracketing dissolve the self. But in the negative bracketing, the beings are reduced to intersubjectivity; in this case the word "personne" means the anonymity of everyone, everyone because unified as specters. In contrast, in the affirmative bracketing, the beings are reduced to what we might call "interobjectivity";[31] in this case, the word "personne" also means anonymity, but the anonymity of "no one" at all, no one because differentiated as forces. For both Merleau-Ponty and Deleuze, the word "personne," of course, alludes to Ulysses's answer to the question "who is there?"; "personne" is the answer of the other.[32] Thus, the big difference between Being and beings leads to a difference in how one conceives the experience of the other.

When one conceives the *personne* as dissolving into intersubjectivity, one's experience of others is *Einfühlung*. Curiously, when Levinas translates Husserl's *Cartesian Meditations* into French, he refuses to translate *Einfühlung* when it occurs for the first time.[33] Nevertheless, I think the word must be translated into English (at least) as "sympathy," because, like *Einfühlung*, sympathy—more than the English word "empathy"—captures the sense of feeling together as one. Sympathy, as Husserl shows in the Fifth Cartesian Meditation, is a feeling of harmony with one another. In fact, one might compare the feeling of sympathy with the Kantian feeling of the beautiful.[34] What the feeling of the beautiful, like sympathy, responds to is the body. Following Husserl's descriptions of the body in terms of both *Körper* and *Leib*, Merleau-Ponty defines the flesh by the reversibility of the double sensation. One must always recall that the experience of the double sensation—one hand touching the other—can take many forms, one of which is the hands folded together for prayer.[35] The realization that hands folded together with thumbs crossed can define chiasmatic reversibility leads us to say that praying is interrogation in Merleau-Ponty. From one's solitude—indeed, from one's "radical separation"[36]—one implores the other to be there; one believes in the other, and the other confirms your belief when a person, when someone, reaches down and offers you a hand. Hands reaching out for hands establishes the peace (cf. VI 192/146).[37] The handshake is always, in Merleau-Ponty, a symbol of salvation. Through sympathy, everyone is saved, even the weak. Therefore, sympathy is a conservative feeling; the flesh is the mystery of the incarnation (cf. QPH 169/178); and the chiasm is the sign of the cross turning into the vicious circle in which God is resurrected.

In *Nietzsche and Philosophy,* Deleuze states that Nietzsche has no faith in the death of God because someone always finds a way of resurrecting Him (NP 180/156; cf. DR 117/86–87). How different an experience of the other we have in Deleuze, when we begin with the beings. Instead of the conservative feeling of pity,[38] we have the destructive feeling of cruelty (DR 43–44/28–29). Rather than a prayer, we have a police interrogation (DR 255/197). In a police interrogation, someone has selected you for questioning; the person needs to learn something from you. But, if you ask, "Who are you to ask the questions?" the person who is interrogating responds, "Shut up! I'm the one asking the questions here, not you. Answer the question!" This person is not beautiful; there is neither harmony nor peace here. This person is nothing but the sublime presence of force; this person is about to crack you wide open, violate you, and force an answer from you. Indeed, the force of this imperative—the question must be answered!—signifies, Deleuze says, "our greatest powerlessness" (*impuissance*) (DR 257/199). When you are forced to respond and say, "Yes, I'm the one!" then your powerlessness is transmuted into power. The transmutation of the fiat affects equally everyone who says "yes"; however, the affirmation is not salvation for all. In *Difference and Repetition,* Deleuze stresses that the transmutation of powerlessness into power can even take weakness itself as an object (DR 258/200). Imagine that the dice have rolled out so you really experience laziness as a problem. The solution to this problem lies precisely in not being lazy about laziness; the categorical imperative for you is that you persevere in your laziness: "Be lazy if you wish! However, be lazy all the way!" To be lazy in such a superior way would make you look like you were "descended from the gods" (DR 255/197), but it would also have a devastating consequence for you. For Deleuze, there is no return from this consequence, nor is there any resurrection; in other words, there is no thread to lead you out of the labyrinth.

The labyrinth and the circle are both symbols of Nietzsche's doctrine of eternal return. Heidegger claimed that this doctrine brings metaphysics to an end because Nietzsche's doctrine of eternal return remains within the two traditional determinations of presence, as permanence and becoming; Nietzsche's thinking did not reach back to the process of presencing. Presence allows us to make the difference between Merleau-Ponty and Deleuze as sharp as possible. Merleau-Ponty's ontology is led back through negation to God and thus to subjectivity in order to conceive the process of presencing, a process which is not present. This attempt to go beyond the metaphysics of presence is why Merleau-Ponty in the working notes comes back to something that in principle can never be presented. We have already noted that Deleuze never concerned himself with the overcoming of metaphysics. Indeed, one of the most striking things about *Difference and Repetition*—especially since it appears one year after Derrida's *Voice and Phenomenon*—is Deleuze's use of the word "presence" (e.g., DR 61/42). Deleuze's use of "presence" is why, I think, he claims, strangely, that Foucault's "major conversion" is the conversion of phenomenology into epistemology (F 117/109). This difference between presence and non-presence means that an extremely difficult question confronts us: which one is the thing itself or the things themselves? Is it the one flesh, which can never be present, or the multiple forces, which are too present? Undoubtedly, this question amounts to a diffraction between faith and knowledge. It seems to me that this is the position in which philosophy finds itself today: we are being forced to follow the diffraction of ontology to the point where it ends and turns into something else, into either religion or epistemology.

7 The Beginnings of Post-modernism

Phenomenology and Bergsonism, Derrida and Deleuze

For Fred Evans

Despite its abuse, the term "post-modernism" suggests two ideas. On the one hand, "post-modernism" suggests the idea that there is no transcendent truth for human life; there is some sort of lack. On the other, and as a direct consequence of the first, post-modernism suggests the idea that all things consist in a sort of fiction, and this fiction is excessive. If this is what the term "post-modernism" really means, then we can trace its sense back to two philosophical movements located at the beginning of this century: phenomenology and Bergsonism. Phenomenology and Bergsonism each establish four concepts that are the foundation of what we call post-modernism today. First, according to Husserl, there can be no phenomenology without the phenomenological reduction;[1] in "Philosophy as a Rigorous Science," Husserl describes the reduction in this way: in order to return to an "actual beginning," "all expressions that imply thetic existential positings of things in the framework of space, time, causality, etc. . . . must in principle be excluded."[2] In Bergsonism, the concept parallel to the reduction is "the turn of experience"; in *Matter and Memory*, Bergson says, philosophy must return to "experience at its source . . . above that decisive turn where . . . it becomes properly human experience."[3] Both the phenomenological reduction and the turn of experience imply the reduction of transcendence to immanence. If transcendence traditionally means atemporal truth, then the return to immanence means a return to temporal experience. Thus, in phenomenology we have the living present as the absolute form of all experience,[4] and in Bergsonism we have duration as what is absolute in life.[5] If duration and the living present insofar as absolute are the transcendental (but not transcendent) conditions of all experience, they cannot be identical to the experiences they condition. So we have the third concept. In his lectures on phenomenological psychology, Husserl differentiates between psychological experience and transcendental experience in terms of what he calls a "parallelism," but this parallelism is such that there is a perfect "concealment" of the transcendental in the psychological.[6] The Bergsonian concept equivalent to this is difference in nature; in *Time and Free Will,* Bergson establishes a difference in nature between psychological life and matter, but psychological life itself differs in nature with itself to the point where it evolves into matter.[7] Compared to the philosophical tradition, the concepts of parallelism and difference in nature are new kinds of differences. So if transcendental conditions can only be differentiated from the experiences they condition in these new ways, then the conditions themselves must be characterized in new ways. This brings us to the fourth pair of concepts. In *Ideas I,* paragraph 70, Husserl says that essences are clarified through "free phantasies"; indeed, he says, "fiction makes up the vital element of phenomenology."[8] In Bergson, the virtual is not the possible;[9] it is defined by being "real without being actual, ideal without being abstract,"[10] which means that the virtual too can be called a sort of fiction.

Over the first half of this century, these four pairs of concepts flowed into one term: "simulacrum."[11] Over the second half of this century, however, this term has suffered as much abuse as "post-modernism." The abuse of these terms has resulted in the fact that "post-modernism" no longer defines a philosophical movement, and "simulacrum" has lost all power to transform our most important contemporary philosophical debates.[12] Indeed, this dissipation of power is forcing us to reconsider the philosophical tradition of this century. We need to find the source from which the power of "post-modernism" and the "simulacrum" flowed. At the source, that is, at the point of diffraction, we might then be able to invent new terms that can lead us to think otherwise and to create new concepts.[13] Here I am going to argue that the source of post-modernism is life-philosophy and that the term that needs to be invented is "lifeism," and that "lifeism" will lead us to the new concept of a "creative tension of voices."

So what I am going to do is return to the apex of "post-modernism": the great French philosophy of the Sixties. At this moment, Derrida and Deleuze publish books on Husserl and Bergson within one year of each other: Derrida's 1967 *Voice and Phenomenon* and Deleuze's 1966 *Bergsonism.* In *Voice and Phenomenon,* on the basis of Husserl's phenomenology, Derrida develops the concept of the trace, which he associates with the simulacrum; in *Bergsonism,* on the basis of Bergson's evolutionism, Deleuze develops the concept of the virtual image, which he also associates with the simulacrum. Although my primary focus is going to be these two concepts, the trace and the virtual image, I am going to examine both of these seminal books by following four trajectories: destruction versus deconstruction; purity versus contamination; fiction understood as the virtual image versus fiction understood as the trace; and intuition versus language.

I. Deconstruction and Destruction

Both "deconstruction" and "destruction" come from Heidegger. "Deconstruction," however, has become synonymous with Derrida (MP 161–64/ 134–36). In contrast, Deleuze never uses the term "deconstruction," but he uses occasionally the term "destruction" (DR 91/66; LS 307/266). The issue between Derridean deconstruction and Deleuzian destruction lies in the target of these practices. When Deleuze speaks of destruction, he never uses Derrida's phrase "the metaphysics of presence"; instead, he speaks of "the destruction of Platonism." These two terms—"the metaphysics of presence" and "Platonism"—coincide in that both terms refer to the traditional philosophical conception of the origin of the world, ideas, for example, as atemporal; "the destruction of Platonism" or "the deconstruction of the metaphysics of presence" then would be a critique of this conception of ideas, a critique that places the ideas back into temporal experience. But the coincidence between the terms does not extend beyond this temporal critique.[14] On the one hand, Derrida defines presence as proximity (VP 83–84/75); this definition of presence as proximity implies that the deconstruction of the metaphysics of presence places the origin of presence in a distancing which makes the origin absent; in other words, ideas originate in a non-presencing. This distancing and non-presencing Derrida calls the trace. On the other hand, Deleuze defines Platonism in terms of its motivation "to repress" what Plato himself calls in *Republic* X calls "phantasma," that is, simulacra, copies of copies.[15] Platonism wants to repress simulacra "as deeply as possible, to shut [them] up in a cavern at the bottom of the Ocean" (LS 298/259), because the ideas in fact originate in the simulacra. This definition of Platonism's motivation as a distancing of the simulacra as far as to the bottom of the ocean implies that the destruction of Platonism brings up to the surface what had been distanced; in other words, the simulacra become proximate and present. In contrast, therefore, to traces that are non-presences and distant, the Deleuzian simulacra are presences, and they come too close. We can see already that the trace, which Derrida explicitly associates with the simulacrum in his 1972 essay on Nietzsche, *Spurs*,[16] does not really coincide with what Deleuze calls a simulacrum, which is related to the virtual image. Already they seem to form a sort of opposition, or better, a diffraction, because Derrida's deconstruction *contaminates* the metaphysics of presence with the non-presence of the trace, whereas Deleuze's destruction *purifies* Platonism with the presence of the virtual image.[17]

II. Contamination and Purity

This diffraction between contamination and purity is the second trajectory I would like to follow. When Deleuze qualifies certain terms as "pure"
(DR 83/59; LS 32/21), he is using the word "pure" in a sense that derives from
Bergson. Deleuze explains Bergson's well-known "obsession" with the pure
(BER 12/22) in terms of Bergson's appropriation of Plato's method of division (BER 11/22).[18] For Bergson, it is the job of philosophy to divide the badly
composed mixtures with which experience presents us *in fact* (BER 11–12/
22). We divide a factual mixture *badly,* for Bergson, if we make a quantitative
difference between time and space, which thereby turns time into a difference of degree of space. Here we have "an impure . . . mixed" idea measuring
the mixture. When we analyze mixtures into mediating ideas such as this, we
have, as Deleuze says, "lost the reason for the mixtures" (BER 12/22). For
Bergson, we analyze this mixture *well,* when we divide time and space into a
difference in nature between duration and extensity.[19] These two qualities become then, as Deleuze says, "two pure presences" (BER 12/22).[20] The two pure
presences are the *in principle* conditions of factual experience; here Deleuze
uses the *Quid facti–Quid juris* distinction, which in French is the *en fait–en
droit* opposition. These in principle conditions are the true sufficient reason
for the mixture (BER 20/28–29). Through the method of division, we have
ascended above the "turn of experience" at which experience becomes human
experience. So purity, first of all, means for Deleuze *en droit.*

But, as Deleuze stresses, the difficulty that plagued Plato's method of division disappears in Bergson (BER 24/32). Plato's method of division lacked a
middle term, a mediation in order to recognize the good side versus the bad
side in all mixtures. Plato had to resort to "inspiration," that is, to a myth in
order to make the selection (BER 24/32; DR 86/61; LS 294/254–55). So, in
Bergson, it seems as though we must have a mediating idea of difference of
nature—the, so to speak, *good* (*le Bien*), in order to know how to divide *well*
(*diviser bien*). But, according to Deleuze, Bergson makes the division immediately.[21] For Bergson, differences in nature occur only on the side of duration; duration itself "presents the way in which a thing varies qualitatively in
time" (BER 24/32); and duration is first of all our duration, human, psychological inner life. Duration is the "good side," the "true"[22] side, the side of
"essence," as Deleuze says (BER 24/32), whereas extensity is the bad side, the
false side, the side of appearance. It is our duration, therefore, that allows us
to "affirm and *immediately* recognize other durations above or below us,"
other differences in nature (BER 25/33, my emphasis). So purity in Deleuze
secondly means immediacy.

If we rely on Bergson's early writings, it looks as though duration and extensity were related as pure to impure, good to bad. But Bergson, as Deleuze insists (BER 27/34), progresses beyond this early view and realizes that extensity is one "side" of the Absolute and that the other "side" is duration. Duration is the contraction of all successive past events into a point in the present, whereas extensity is the relaxation of this point into the spatial coexistence of these events (BER 56–57/60–61). On either side of this point, we have two sides, as in two divergent lines. Because of relaxation, extensity is a multiplicity infinitely divisible in terms of numbers, whereas, because of contraction, duration is a multiplicity that cannot be divided in terms of numbers. Since extensity is arithmetically divisible, extensity is the side of differences in degree; since duration is arithmetically indivisible, duration is the side of qualitative differences (BER 24/32). Making extensity one side of the Absolute means, for Bergson, that science is not an artificial knowledge but a natural knowledge, since it is based in a difference in nature. Nevertheless, as we shall see, the illusions that overwhelm us (like Plato's myths) still come from the side of extensity and science; these illusions we will have to distinguish from the "true" side of duration since Deleuze suggests that essence too is a sort of fiction.

But, no matter what, when Bergson makes extensity and duration the two sides of the Absolute, he is in accordance with how Deleuze describes "Heidegger's ontological intuition": "difference must relate different to different without any mediation whatsoever by the identical" (DR 154/117). Deleuze interprets Heidegger's ontological difference as a thought of immediacy, because Deleuze's thought is anti-Hegelian.[23] In contrast, Derrida's thought is Hegelian.[24] We find the Hegelian source of Derrida's concept of contamination in his crucial 1964 essay on Levinas, "Violence and Metaphysics"; here Derrida says, "Pure difference is not absolutely different (from nondifference). Hegel's critique of the concept of pure difference is for us here, doubtless, the most uncircumventable theme. Hegel thought absolute difference, and showed that it can be pure only by being impure" (ED 227n1/320n91). This "Hegelianism" determines Derrida's interpretation of Heidegger's ontological difference as mediation.

In the Introduction to *Voice and Phenomenon*, Derrida uses Heidegger's ontological difference to interpret Husserl's phenomenological reduction.[25] Derrida recognizes that Husserl's phenomenological reduction attempts to divide life in general into transcendental life and psychological life (VP 10/ 11). But Derrida stresses that the phenomenological reduction does not make an "ontological duplication" (VP 10–11/11). Here Derrida is using the word "ontological" in a Husserlian sense, but what he is referring to is what Heidegger would call the ontic.[26] In Husserl, according to Derrida, the transcendental ego and the psychological ego are not two things separate from one another;[27] they are *ontically* identical but *ontologically* differentiated. Because, however, there is no ontic difference, because there is "nothing"—here Derrida follows Heidegger's use of "nothing" (VP 11/12; also ED 245/164)—because, we might say, there is the "nothing" between the transcendental and the empirical, Derrida argues that every time Husserl tries to define the transcendental without the empirical he fails, necessarily, to be rigorous. The transcendental is contaminated by the empirical and vice versa. So, unlike Deleuze who is concerned with dividing mixtures into pure differences in nature (into a duality), Derrida is concerned with a "unity" (VP 9/10) that mixes the transcendental and the empirical together.

The argument based on the lack of ontic difference organizes Derrida's entire consideration, in *Voice and Phenomenon,* of the problem of the sign in Husserl's phenomenology (VP 32/30). According to Husserl in the First Logical Investigation, signs can be divided essentially between two functions, expression and indication. The important word for Derrida is "function" because function implies that the difference between expression and indication is not a substantial distinction (VP 20/20). In other words, we are always dealing with one substantial term, the sign, which undergoes two different functions; but, since we do not have two separate signs, the two functions are always "interwoven" in any given sign. For Husserl, expression is interwoven with indication only *in fact; in principle,* expression and indication can be distinguished. Throughout *Voice and Phenomenon,* Derrida uses the *en fait–en droit* distinction. But, unlike Deleuze, for Derrida, this distinction is not rigorous. Lacking a substantial separation, whatever one distinguishes in principle must be the same, that is, mediated.

Mediation even defines, for Derrida, Husserl's living present. In *Voice and Phenomenon,* Derrida turns to Husserl's lectures on internal time consciousness, because Husserl's descriptions in the First Investigation suggest that in "the solitary life of the soul" there is no need for indication; psychic life is present to me immediately. In these lectures Husserl seems to prioritize the primal impression of the now point of the living present as an origin, but Husserl also stresses that the living present consists in a spreading out that includes necessarily not only the primal impression but also the retention of the recent past and the protention of the near future. For Derrida, what is at stake in these descriptions is that primal impression cannot be isolated from retention. So, if retention involves anything like a signifying relation, then the "radical difference" Husserl wants between indication and expression, indeed, between perception and recollection, or even between presentation and representation, is threatened (VP 73/65). Clearly, Derrida stresses that Husserl, in section 16 of the lectures, describes retention as a "non-perception" (VP 73/65), which immediately proves Derrida's point: the living present involves something like a sign, since retention "indicates" the recent past which must be absent; there is no pure expression in the solitary life of the soul. But one would mistakenly interpret what Derrida is doing here if one did not recognize that Derrida is following all the subtleties of Husserl's descriptions. Husserl calls retention "non-perception" because it is a type of mediation, like a sign, of non-presence. But also, Husserl calls retention "perception" because it "presences" immediately what has elapsed. Retention is at once both a presence and a non-presence, and this "at once" is why Derrida calls retention a trace. As we already noted, soon after *Voice and Phenomenon*, Derrida will call the trace the simulacrum, which implies that the trace can be characterized as a sort of fiction.

III. Fictions

So the trace brings us to the third trajectory, which goes in the direction of fiction and therefore truth. Heidegger, of course, had displaced the concept of truth, from the correspondence between a proposition and a state of affairs to an experience called *aletheia*. For Deleuze, Bergson enacts a similar displacement. Bergson places truth no longer in the solutions to problems but in the problems themselves (BER 3/15). This displacement allows Bergson to speak of true and false problems. False problems and the illusions that cause them come from a disregard for true differences in nature (BER 13/23). Since science is primarily concerned with differences in degree, science itself invites us to see the entire world in its terms. In other words, science invites us to "project" this side of the absolute onto the other, onto duration. Deleuze stresses that, since the differences in degree determined by science are, for Bergson, the other side of the Absolute and therefore natural, the illusions and false problems that arise from them are immanent to the absolute (BER 26–27/34–35). Here Bergson follows a Kantian inspiration (BER 10/20–21).[28] Being immanent, these illusions, therefore, can only be "repressed" by the differences in nature given to us by duration (BER 27–28/35); they can never be entirely eliminated (BER 10/21).

Bergson himself calls the projection of differences of degree onto duration "the retrograde movement of the true" (BER 7/18). For example, the traditional metaphysical problem contained in the question "Why is there something rather than nothing?" brings forth this answer. In order to explain why we have the particular reality in front of us, we assume there was a set of possibilities that contained every imaginable possibility. This set of possibilities is larger than the real, like an ill-fitting set of clothes; it implies that "the whole is already given" (BER 101/98). Because the whole set of possibilities is not yet realized, it is called nothingness. The realization of the not yet realized possibilities occurs through the limitation of the set down to the particular reality in front of us. So realization would be nothing more than the endowment of certain possibilities with reality. Reality then would not be different from the possibilities but would rather resemble them. What has happened to produce this problem, according to Deleuze, is that the particular reality in front of us is conceived as a difference in degree of all possible reality in general (BER 101/98). Then an image of this particular reality is taken and projected backwards in time as one of the not yet realized possibilities. But this "retrojection" means that it is not the real that resembles the non-real possibilities; it is the image of non-real possibilities that has been copied off the real. The image "has been abstracted from the real once made" (BER 101/98). Therefore, this image is an illusion, a myth, a fiction. And the traditional metaphysical problem of why there is something rather than nothing is a false problem.

For Deleuze, following Bergson, every false problem and its illusion is generated from this combination of possibility and negation (BER 100/98). In contrast, true problems derive from genuine differences in nature. Genuine differences in nature are conditions of experience, lying beyond the "turn" in experience. As conditions of experience, they are ideal, *en droit* (BER 13/23), but, for Deleuze, *en droit* means virtual (BER 111/106). The virtual must not be confused with the possible. The possible is a term defined in opposition to the real; the possible therefore always lacks reality. In contrast, the virtual is a term defined in opposition to the actual; insofar as the virtual is defined in opposition to the actual it is real and positive (BER 99/96). As real and positive, these conditions are virtual images: "pure presences."[29] A virtual image, for Deleuze, is a point that must be "tailored to the thing itself, which only suits that thing, and which, in this sense, is no broader than what it must account for" (BER 19/28; QPH 25/20). That these conditions do not contain more than reality is why they are conditions of real experience; they are not Kantian conditions of possible experience (BER 13/23).[30] That they correspond precisely to particular realities is why these virtual images are true. Therefore, for Deleuze, as well as for Bergson, the true problems concern these true conditions. The question is: "How do these differences in nature relate to one another?"

The solution to this problem is where we encounter the fictional character of the virtual image. These pure presences are tendencies; thus they are, as Deleuze stresses, *sens* (BER 91/88), directions, divergent lines that can be developed into a convergent "virtual image" (BER 20/28). This virtual image that returns from the turn in which we made a difference in nature is the "original point" of convergence. This original point is the true sufficient reason of the thing (BER 20/28–29). Unlike conditions of possibility, with this sufficient reason (BER 35–36/42), "the whole is not given" (BER 108/104).[31] That the whole is not given—it is in default—means that the virtual image has "the power" (*la puissance*) of being divided (BER 116/110), of being divided even into arithmetical units. The original point of convergence "possesses number *en puissance*," as Deleuze says (BER 36/42, 40/45, 95/93, 103/100). The original point of convergence has, therefore, the power of being "explicated" (BER 98/95) into two different divergent lines. Because the original point of convergence is simple or continuous, its explication follows the model of alteration (BER 23/32, 42/47), not that of alterity.[32] The alteration makes a difference, because what it creates does not correspond to or resemble reality. This disparity with the real is why the virtual image is fictional or false. Although the virtual image is an image and therefore a repetition, it is not a re-presentation, that is, a presentation of the same reality again. Rather, the virtual image is what Deleuze in "Reversing Platonism" calls the simulacrum; it has "the power of the false" (LS 303/263). Repetition in Deleuze is the power to extend a sense as far as the nth power, where it is transformed into something different, something that has never been present before, the new. Calling the solution to the problem the new and not *aletheia* means that, for Deleuze, the solution never closes off the problem.

When describing the creation of the new, Deleuze always speaks of "tracing" a line (QPH 36/38);[33] so one could speak of a concept of the trace in Deleuze. In addition, whenever Derrida describes the trace throughout his writings, it sounds like what Deleuze calls the virtual image. This similarity is especially striking in Chapter 4 of *Voice and Phenomenon*, where Derrida says that "the sign is originally worked by fiction" (VP 63/56). Derrida makes this comment in reference not to indication, but in reference to expression insofar as expression must in a sense be fictional since expression is defined by the presentation, not of a real thing, but of an ideal meaning. Derrida, of course, recalls Husserl's comment in *Ideas I* about fiction. Fiction is the vital element of phenomenology because fiction can neutralize the existence of the thing in order to give us its eidetic determinations (VP 4/6, 55/49; LOG 29/45). Since indication, however, is defined by its reference to factual things and therefore can be distant and absent, indication too is in a sense fictional; as Derrida says, "The indicative sign falls outside the content of absolutely ideal objectivity, that is, outside truth" (VP 31/30). Therefore, for Derrida, because indication and expression share the same signifying form, it is impossible to distinguish the two senses of fiction rigorously (VP 55–56/49–50). Because of this role of fiction, Derrida's concept of trace remains very close to what Deleuze calls the virtual image.[34] But three characteristics separate Derrida's trace from Deleuze's virtual image.

First, Derrida's concept of trace is formalistic.[35] Derrida says in his 1967 essay "Form and Meaning: A Note on the Phenomenology of Language" that "form would be already in itself the trace . . . of a certain non-presence" (MP 206n14/172n16). Derrida makes this comment because, in his 1962 Introduction to Husserl's "The Origin of Geometry," he discovered that no ideality could be constituted without being embodied in a repeatable form such as a sign (LOG 86n3/89n92). In other words, signification conditions the movement and concept of truth (VP 26/25). For Deleuze in contrast, the virtual image is a tendency, not a form (BER 91/88). Second, Derrida does not use the word "virtual" to qualify the trace; instead, he uses "possibility" and "conditions of possibility." So in Derrida we seem to have a combination of possibility and negation; he speaks, as we have seen, of non-presence and the "nothing." But actually this combination does not resemble what Bergson calls "the retrograde movement of the true" because the Derridean conditions are also "conditions of impossibility" (VP 113/101). The trace is at once the condition for the possibility and the condition for the impossibility of presence. For Derrida, the phrase "condition of impossibility" means a lack of power,[36] an *impuissance* (LOG 171/153). It is impossible that presence not be formed, which implies that presence is always contaminated. For Derrida, however, impossibility also means necessity: the French idiom *il faut* is a technical term in Derrida.[37] It is not only impossible that presence not be formed, but also necessary that presence be formed. The necessity of this formation or tracing, however, implies a power, the power of form (MP 201–2/168–69). A form, for Derrida, is defined by iterability, the power to be repeated as far as possible, beyond any given presence into non-presence, beyond any given sense into nonsense, and, so it seems, beyond truth into illusion (cf. VP 64–65/58). But this power of repetition, unlike the power of the virtual, does not make a difference in the sense of a difference of nature; every repetition is contaminated with the same form. Third, the model of repetition in the trace for Derrida is alterity, not alteration as in the virtuality of the virtual image for Deleuze. What is most striking about *Voice and Phenomenon* in comparison to Derrida's earlier books on Husserl[38] is his association of the First Investigation's descriptions of "the solitary life of the soul" with the Fifth Cartesian Meditation's descriptions of "the sphere of ownness" (VP 42/39). Derrida is led to this association undoubtedly because of his encounter with Levinas in "Violence and Metaphysics." Derrida's emphasis of the relation with the other implies that the trace is defined by representation (*Vergegenwärtigung*) (VP 49n1/45n4). The term "Vergegenwärtigung" suggests that the representation of the trace is the presentation (*Gegenwärtigung*) again of the same thing. But, in *Voice and Phenomenon* as in "Violence and Metaphysics," Derrida (again following the subtleties of Husserl's descriptions) points out that *Appräsentation*, which is essentially connected to *Vergegenwärtigung*

(VP 5/7), consists in an "*irreducibly mediate . . .* intentionality aiming at the other as other" (ED 182/123, Derrida's emphasis); "the other's ownness, . . . the self-presence of the other, . . . its primordial presentation is closed to me" (VP 42/39). If there is any Husserlian concept that anticipates the Derridean concept of the trace, it is appresentation as described in paragraph 50 of the *Cartesian Meditations.*[39] Appresentation implies "the necessity of mediation" and the impossibility of an intuition of the other as other. But, unlike Husserlian appresentation, which is analogical, the Derridean trace is not defined by resemblance since the trace is always a trace of an interiority that is forever closed to me. In short, the interiority of the other is not a presence that a re-presentation could resemble. The trace therefore is a form that iterates an other who has never been present; it is like a missive whose author has always already been concealed, "lethic," a specter.[40]

IV. Language and Intuition

The impossibility of an intuition of the other due to the mediation of the trace brings us to the last trajectory: intuition versus language. It is not insignificant that Deleuze begins *Bergsonism* with a discussion of Bergsonian intuition; in his earlier essay on Bergson, Deleuze had already characterized Bergson's thought as a "superior empiricism."[41] But also, in this early essay, Deleuze says that "intuition is the *jouissance* of difference."[42] The word "jouissance" immediately implies that intuition is based on life; Bergsonian intuition is primarily affective. Thus, in *Bergsonism,* Deleuze insists that intuition has its genesis in what Bergson calls "creative emotion" (BER 115–117/110). Many emotions arise as a result of a representation of a thing, but a creative emotion, according to Deleuze, precedes any representation and disrupts them (BER 116/110; cf. BER 16/26); it is a paradox (DR 250/194). A creative emotion, therefore, for Deleuze is a feeling that is unrecognizable and too close. Being too close, it is a power, a power of such force that, when I feel it, I say, "I have no choice" (BER 116/110). If creative emotion gives me no choice me but to act, then Bergsonian intuition is a "volitional intuition" (LS 175/149). As Bergson himself says, intuition is not contemplation, but a "leap." Insofar as intuition is a leap forced upon me by creative emotion, it is a leap into immediacy, into pure presence. A leap into pure presence, for Bergson as for Deleuze, does not mean that the whole is suddenly given to me. Instead, it means that the whole is not given; intuition then in Deleuze as in Bergson is perspectival. But Bergsonian perspectivism does not circle around an object taking up viewpoints, seeking the privileged view from nowhere. Instead, Bergsonian perspectivism lacks the center point. Not being a sort of circling, intuition in Deleuze is a leaping right into the object so that the object is not central, but itself consists in *glances* (LS 303/262).[43] Deleuze explains Bergson's perspectivism by means of the example of color.[44] On the one hand, one can eliminate from a color what makes it that particular color, take away, for example, what makes red red; this "bleaching out" allows all the colors to resemble each other and be subsumed under the general idea of color; here the general idea of color is abstract since it is different from the particular colors. In contrast, as Deleuze says, one can make "the colors pass through a convergent lens which condenses them into one point: in this case, we obtain 'the pure white light,' the light that 'made the differences between the tints re-emerge.'" This "pure white light" is what Deleuze calls the virtual image; here, being itself a color, white light is not different from the colors that it defines; it is concrete. The virtual image allows us to understand the particular colors because it is at the limit of a particular color, the last nuance of white. The intuition of this "pure white light" extends the colors to the nth power, as far as they can go, in order to converge and become something else, a new color. The intuition of this point where the colors converge is a becoming of color.[45]

It is not insignificant that Derrida begins his 1967 *Of Grammatology* by saying "the problem of language will never [be] simply one problem among others" (DLG 15/6).[46] Unlike Deleuze, Derrida is not an empiricist. Indeed, in "Violence and Metaphysics" Derrida criticizes Levinas's "superior empiricism" because all experience, even the experience of the other, necessarily requires speech, if it is to make a claim on you, if it is, for example, to make you promise to do something (ED 225–26/151–52, 225n2/320n90). The necessity of speech derives, as we have already noted, from the fact that the constitution of presence necessarily requires being embodied in indefinitely iterable signifying forms; for Derrida, that it must be possible for presence to be embodied in iterable forms means that it must be possible for presence to be written down (LOG 87–88/90). The possibility of being graphic in turn implies the death of the one who writes as soon as he writes. What Derrida calls *écriture* remains, necessarily, beyond the death of the author. In fact, Derrida stresses in *Voice and Phenomenon* that writing is defined by the necessity of remaining beyond the death of any given subject (VP 104/93). Because of the mortality they necessarily imply, the iterable forms are incommensurate with intuition. When I speak about something I intuit right now, the forms I use still function and must function even when I no longer have an intuition of the thing (VP 101/90–91). Because the form, or, more precisely, the trace, does not require intuition to function, intuition does not limit it. As unlimited, the trace contains the possibility of an unlimited number of "genres,"[47] that is, of genera, genres, or genders; the trace contains a "+R," "plus r," *plusieurs*, as Derrida says, several genders.[48] But, for Derrida, this dissemination of "genders" is not equivalent to indefinite perspectives on a central sex (DIS 281–82/249–50). Because the forms necessarily lack intuition, there can be no center; there can be only *glances*.[49] Being nothing but glances, the trace, therefore, for Derrida is always aporetical.[50] But the Derridean aporia is not the same as the Deleuzian paradox. The Derridean aporia is signification and *results* in an experience (cf. VP 111/99),[51] whereas the Deleuzian paradox is an experience that *precedes* any linguistic representation. Even though here we are at the precise point of diffraction between Derrida and Deleuze—at the point of a doubling between experience and language, between silence and voice—this difference in the priority—results, precedes—is why the Derridean trace is not *totally in affinity* with the Deleuzian virtual image.

V. A Nearly Total Affinity

Derrida has said that he always found himself "flustered" when he read Deleuze's work, because the "philosophical content" of Deleuze's work displayed "a nearly total affinity" to the philosophical content of his own.[52] What we have seen here is that the affinity is only "nearly total." Derrida's initial inspiration in Husserl led him to a prioritization of language and form, whereas Deleuze's initial inspiration in Bergson led him to the prioritization of intuition and tendency (the formless). But if there is a "nearly total affinity" between Derrida and Deleuze, this affinity is due to Heidegger. In *Being and Time,* Heidegger renewed ontology not simply by raising once again the question of Being, but also by determining being itself as a question. Both Derrida and Deleuze (like Merleau-Ponty) appropriate Heidegger's ontology of the question. For Deleuze, every question has to be led back to the problem from which it arose. More basic than the question, the problem in Deleuze is the problem of intuition. The paradox of presence presents an obstacle to life (BER 5/16); in other words, being too close, presence is always life threatening. I leap into the ocean whose engulfing presence makes me say, "I have no choice but to swim; otherwise I am going to die"; therefore I must learn how to swim, how to make myself be a convergent point through which the ocean's divergent forces flow. This solution is not true, but creative of something new, of a new life. For Deleuze therefore, we have an epistemological experience in which life, which is one life (univocal), is re-begun in the moment of death; death is the recommencement of life: life in death. But Derrida appropriates Heidegger's ontology of the question differently. For Derrida, every question has to be led back to the promise from which it arose. More basic than the question, the promise is the promise of language. For Derrida, language makes all promises,[53] because all promises must be based in indefinitely iterable forms. Therefore, all promises are necessarily deathbed promises, traces of someone not present. The ghost of my dead father demands of me to avenge his unjust murder; this demand can only be an aporia: how can I avenge my father's murder? I must have faith. But having nothing but faith, I can never know when I have completely finished with the keeping of the promise; I must keep on living for the promise. For Derrida, therefore, we have a religious experience in which death is "refinished" in the moment of life, which is more than one life (equivocal); life is the refinition of death: death in life.

Death in life; life in death. Perhaps this difference between Derrida and Deleuze is too small to make any difference. But, at least, this little difference allows us to see the source from which what we call "post-modernism" flowed; it flowed from the philosophy of life.[54] As soon as one says *Lebensphilosophie*, however, one is confronted with the problems of racism and sexism. Problems such as these are why Heidegger, in his Nietzsche lectures, says that he mistrusts the term "biologism." The term "biologism" cannot be dissociated from the biological sciences, which, like all sciences, rest on an already decided interpretation of Being, Being understood as an object mastered by technology. Heidegger is right: we need to "leap" into a "different kind of thinking," other than scientific, in order to break through this decision and understand Being.[55] But, perhaps today, we need, just as much, to leap back into the thinking that dominates the biological sciences. The term "post-modernism" has suffered so much abuse because the movements this term has designated have remained too far removed from the sciences. Therefore, we must invent a term that not only flows out of the most powerful concepts of this different kind of thinking but also leaps back into the domain of science. Perhaps the old Anglo-Saxon word "life" can make this leap. In philosophy it makes one think of Bergson's duration, and, because it is etymologically connected to the German word "Leib," it makes one think of Husserl's appresentation. This term, however, not only flows out from the beginnings of post-modernism; it also can take their power into scientific domains such as reproductive technology where the metaphysics of reproduction—either the metaphysics of presence or Platonism—can be deconstructed or destroyed, contaminated by nonpresence or purified into presences. Reproduction can be reinterpreted then in terms of the trace or the virtual image, form or tendency, in order to disseminate genders or create new colors. Perhaps this "lifeism" is already being done when a philosopher makes an unheard of conjunction like "psychology and nihilism," when a philosopher engages in "a genealogical critique of the computational model of mind" that traces this model back to its source in exhausted life, when he or she forces us finally to think about a "creative tension of voices" in order to establish new communities.[56]

8   The Beginnings of Thought

The Fundamental Experience in Derrida and Deleuze

Two systems of thought still determine what we think, especially as Continental philosophers. On the one hand, the system of thought that arose in Germany in the Twenties and Thirties, and, on the other, the French philosophy of the Sixties. What connects the two systems is the question of thinking. Thus despite appearances, French philosophy of the Sixties did not aim ultimately at destroying the subject or at overcoming humanism.[1] Its ultimate aim was a renewal of thinking. In the 1968 *Difference and Repetition,* quoting Heidegger's *What Is Called Thinking?* Deleuze says, "thought thinks only when it is constrained and forced, in the presence of what 'gives thinking,' in the presence of what is to be thought—and what is to be thought is really the unthinkable or the non-thought, that is, the perpetual *fact* that 'we have not yet thought'" (DR 188/144, Deleuze's emphasis).[2] In the 1966 *Les Mots et les choses,* Foucault says, "In our day it is no longer possible to think but in the void left by man's disappearance. . . . [This void] is nothing more and nothing less than the unfolding of a space in which it is once more possible to *think*" (MC 353/342, my emphasis). And in the 1967 *De la grammatologie,* Derrida says, "*thought* is here for us a perfectly neutral name, a textual blank space, the necessarily indeterminate index of an epoch to come of différance. *In a certain way, 'thought' means nothing*" (DLG 142/93, Derrida's emphasis). All three—Deleuze, Foucault, and Derrida—recognized that thought had become immobile. Thought could not move because "Platonism"—that is, any metaphysics of the transcendent—conceived thought as returning at the end to an idea that had already been present at the origin. Thought was caught between a beginning and an end. Thus in the Sixties a need is felt to liberate thought by re-conceiving history without end and without origin.[3]

This need to liberate thought results in the conceptual system that defines the great French philosophy of the Sixties. What follows is the system presented in its most schematic form. The need to liberate thought motivates a convergence between phenomenology and structuralism.[4] The convergence consists first in a reduction to sense, meaning the transformation of the metaphysical concept of essence (the transcendent) into the concept of sense (see LS 128/105). Unlike essence, sense is immanent to subjectivity. Immanence, however, must be made complete (see LE 230/176). Thus sense or subjectivity itself must be reduced, since sense still implies directionality (transcendence) and thus end and origin. Sense is reduced down to something non-subjective or non-sensical, that is, to a structure whose elements themselves do not signify (see MP 161–62/134). The reduction to a non-signifying structure prioritizes spatiality over temporality, that is, it prioritizes a non-mundane space, a profound space, a rarefied space. This is the space of memory. And what is discovered in this memorial space is *un défaut, un manque,*[5] a defect or a lack. This lack is experienced as a question insofar as every question, in order to be what it is, lacks an answer. The voice posing the question is asking the question of being, of existence, and thus of death. The great French philosophy of the Sixties depends fundamentally on an experience of death. But just as a question lacks an answer, it also demands an answer. Thus the question opens out onto an excess of answers and thus an excess of life. The question implies: life in death; death in life. The doubling of life in death and of death in life is a paradox. The paradox of the double is what finally enables the genuine movement of thought.

This chapter attempts to investigate the "point of diffraction" in this system of thought. It seems to me that the point is at its finest between Derrida and Deleuze. In his short memorial essay for Deleuze, Derrida said that there was "a nearly total affinity" between the philosophical content of his own work and that of Deleuze.[6] Derrida is right. Any cursory examination of their works, especially those from the Sixties, shows a remarkable similarity in themes and concepts. This "nearly total affinity" constantly threatens to absorb the diffraction back into its point. It is not the case that Derrida is the philosopher of pure transcendence and Deleuze the philosopher of pure immanence. Rather, and here we can see the diffraction disappear, both are philosophers of immanence. In order to keep the diffraction therefore from disappearing, we are going to insert four oppositions into it. First, Derrida is the true philosopher of unity, whereas Deleuze is the true philosopher of duality. Second Deleuze is the true philosopher of positivity, whereas Derrida is the true philosopher of negativity. Third, Deleuze is true philosopher of the "non-lieu," the non-place, whereas Derrida is the true philosopher of the "milieu," the halfway place. And lastly, Deleuze is the true philosopher of self-interrogation, whereas Derrida is the true philosopher of interrogation by another. We are saying "true" here because appearances do not always support the divisions we are going to make. But regardless of whether we say unity or duality, positivity or negativity, non-place or halfway place, self-interrogation or other-interrogation, the entire thinking of both Derrida and Deleuze flows from one point. Indeed, Derrida and Deleuze diffract at the precise point where thought begins, in paradox.

I. The Point of Diffraction

Throughout their careers, Derrida and Deleuze have continuously written about Artaud.[7] Artaud is important for them (and for Foucault) because he had always complained of "a central collapse of the mind, . . . a kind of erosion, both essential and fleeting, of my thinking."[8] Thinking begins with this collapse. There is an "impuissance" or "impouvoir" within thinking itself, which nevertheless "enables" (*pouvoir*) or "empowers" (*puissance*) me to think (DR 44/29, 192/147, 282/219; LS 184/157; ED 263/176, 238–39/350). In other words, there is something that cannot be thought, something that I am impotent and unable to think, which nevertheless—precisely because I cannot think it—forces me to think. For both Derrida and Deleuze, this *impuissance* that forces me to think is what Artaud calls cruelty. "Cruelty," Artaud says, "is . . . the submission to necessity."[9] As is well known, cruelty, for Artaud, was to be the basis of all theater. The "double" of this theater—as in Artaud's famous work *Le Théâtre et son double*—would be the plague.[10] A plague does not follow a previously given script or text; it is nothing but the expression of deadly forces, forces that express themselves in yells and cries: "the theater of cruelty." The theater of cruelty, whose actions cannot be thought, but which must be thought, would have to be experienced as a paradox.

In the Sixties there is one paradox that is common throughout French thought:[11] the paradox of *répétition*.[12] In order to understand it, we must first think about technological production, or, better, technological reproduction, or, better still, technological re-presentation. In technological re-presentation, there is always a determinate model. This model always comes first. Then, on the basis of this model, the products are produced; they always come second. In fact, we have such agencies as "quality control departments" in factories in order to ensure that the products repeat the model as closely as possible— without any making any difference. As is well known, the French word "répétition" means not only "repetition" but also "rehearsal." We can see the paradox if we ask the question "What is repeated in the rehearsal?" There are two possible answers to this question. We can say that what is repeated is the performance. But the performance comes after the repetition; indeed, the repetition produces the performance. So, what is first, the premiere is actually second. Or we can say that the rehearsal repeats the idea the playwright expressed in the script. This answer, of course, is true. Yet we would not say that the idea is actual until after the rehearsal. Again, what looks to be first is actually second. The idea must be actualized by the repetition. This unstoppable reversal of the first and the second is the paradox of *répétition*. It consists in a double or undecidable sense or direction (*sens*): at once a repetition (second) and a novelty (first). Here we have a repetition that repeats nothing, although it is a re-petition. And, insofar as it has no determinate origin, the repetition makes a difference, an endless difference. Unlike technological re-presentation, *répétition* lacks a model on the basis of which we could make each performance perfectly identical. This lack defines the space of the theater, and it is undoubtedly why it is interesting to see more than one performance of the same play. Both Derrida and Deleuze would call this original-less repetition a simulacrum. The paradox of *répétition* is the paradox of the simulacrum.

Following Klossowski and Foucault,[13] Deleuze made the concept of the simulacrum famous in *Difference and Repetition* and in *The Logic of Sense.* Yet, he had already introduced the term in his 1966 essay "Renverser le platonisme."[14] When he appended this essay in 1969 to *The Logic of Sense* (as "Plato and the Simulacrum"), he added a footnote to Derrida's 1968 "La Pharmacie de Platon" (LS 296n2/257n2).[15] In this note he says,

> Jacques Derrida has rediscovered this Platonic figure [i.e., the unpartici-
> pated, the participated, and the participant] by analyzing the relation
> between writing and the logos: the father of the logos, the logos itself,
> and writing. Writing is a simulacrum, a false suitor, insofar as it claims to
> take hold of the logos by violence and by ruse, or even to supplant it with-
> out passing through the father.

It is well known that, in "Plato and the Simulacrum," Deleuze uses the Neo-Platonic distinction between the unparticipated, the participated, and the participant, for example, the idea of justice, the quality of justice, and the just, in order to explain Platonism (LS 294/255; see also DR 87/62). Deleuze calls these three components the father, the daughter or fiancée, and the claimants or suitors. The simulacrum is a false suitor, as Deleuze says in the quotation above. Indeed, in "Plato's Pharmacy," Derrida calls *écriture* the simulacrum (DIS 146/127), the errant son in relation to the father, a false suitor. The simulacrum is the point of diffraction between Derrida and Deleuze.[16]

II. Simulacra

In the 1968 *Difference and Repetition,* Deleuze announced that "the task of modern philosophy" is the "reversal of Platonism" (DR 82/59; cf. also LS 306/265). Although in "Plato's Pharmacy" Derrida does not speak of "the task of modernity," as Deleuze does, he speaks of "today": "In many ways . . . we are *today* on the eve of Platonism" (DIS 122–23/107, my emphasis; see also DIS 187–88/158).[17] In *Difference and Repetition* as in "Plato and the Simulacrum," Deleuze attempts to understand Platonism through its "true secret" (DR 83–84/59–60), that is, through its "motivation" (LS 292/253) or its "philosophical decision" (DR 166/127). Derrida does the same (DIS 126/111, 111–12/98–99; cf. also DIS 133/117). Deleuze defines the decision in the following way. It consists in "subordinating difference to the powers of the Same and of the Similar, in declaring difference unthinkable in itself, and in sending difference and the simulacra back to the bottomless ocean" (DR 166/127; cf. LS 17/7). Now Derrida: it consists in being "intolerant in relation to [the] passage between the two contrary senses of the same word" (DIS 112/99). Here Derrida is referring to the word that Plato uses in the *Phaedrus* to describe writing, *pharmakon,* which contains the two contrary senses of remedy and poison. As we have already seen in Deleuze's note to "Plato's Pharmacy," the *pharmakon* is the simulacrum. In both *Difference and Repetition* and in "Plato and the Simulacrum" (the appendix to *The Logic of Sense*), Deleuze explains the simulacrum through the catechism, that is, God created man in His image, but through sin man has lost the resemblance and is yet an image (LS 297/257; DR 167/127). Although Derrida, in "Plato's Pharmacy," does not refer to the catechism as Deleuze does, his description of the simulacrum as an orphan, as a father-less son (DIS 86/76), suggests man after sin.[18] Thus, for Derrida as for Deleuze, the simulacrum is an original-less or model-less image. It is precisely the lack of the model that allows the simulacrum to be excessive. Thus for both to reverse Platonism is to do away with hierarchies, the first, the second, etc. As Deleuze says, to reverse Platonism means "to deny the primacy of an original over the copy, of a model over the image. It is to glorify the simulacra and reflections" (DR 92/66; cf. DR 165/126; LS 303/262). Obviously, with this description of reversing Platonism, we are still at the point of diffraction between Derrida and Deleuze.

In order to start to see the diffraction, we must pay careful attention to the respective definitions of Platonism. For Deleuze, the Platonic decision is one that subordinates *difference in itself* to the same. To return to the Neo-Platonic terms that Deleuze uses, the father (the unparticipated) is the same, whereas the false suitor, the simulacrum, is difference in itself.[19] This "in itself" means that difference is conceived without any mediation whatsoever. This *unmediated difference* is why Deleuze insists on a "difference in nature" between the simulacrum and the copy (LS 297/257). Copies or icons are "good images," according to Deleuze, because they are endowed with resemblance to an idea, a Platonic idea (LS 296/257). The copies therefore have only one sense, the good sense coming from the idea. "The simulacrum," in contrast, as Deleuze says in *The Logic of Sense,* "is an image without resemblance" (LS 297/257). In *Difference and Repetition,* he says, "in contrast to *icônes,* [the simulacra] have put resemblance on the outside and live on the basis of difference" (DR 167/128; cf. DR 87/62). Here we must assemble the specific characteristics of the Deleuzian simulacrum. First, since the simulacrum "lives from difference" or since it is not based in resemblance, it has "internalized a dissimilarity" (LS 297/258). It is what Deleuze calls a "singularity" (LS 69/53; cf. LS 299–300/260). To put this as simply as possible, a singularity, for Deleuze, is not a general form; it is an event. Thus the Deleuzian simulacrum is always based in the abyss, in the formless, in chaos (LS 192/164). As Deleuze says, "everything begins with the abyss" (LS 219/188). Yet, since the simulacrum is an image, it is formal and repeatable. Thus, second, the Deleuzian simulacrum—singularity—is defined by the "in-formal." "In-formality" means that since the simulacrum begins from the formless (chaos), its repetition is always unformable (different), subject to events. Since the Deleuzian simulacrum is always subject to events, it is always becoming more and less. The "simul" of the simul-acrum is always double. Simulacra go in two directions (*sens*) at once. In *The Logic of Sense*, Deleuze says that the simulacrum "*is* not more and less at the same time [*en même temps*] but *becomes* more and less at the same time" (LS 9/1, my emphasis). This difference between the "is" and the "becomes" means that the simulacrum is not defined by being but by *becoming*. Becoming is the third characteristic, and becoming for Deleuze only takes place at the surface. Thus, because Deleuze defines Platonism as the subordination of difference in itself to the same, reversing Platonism for Deleuze in fact means to make the simulacra rise to the surface (LS 302/262).[20]

Now, let us return to Derrida's definition of Platonism. As we saw, he says that the Platonic decision consists in being "intolerant in relation to [the] passage between the two contrary senses of the same word" (DIS 112/99). The two contrary senses of the same word of course suggests that the "simul" of the simulacrum, as in Deleuze, is double, the two senses or direction of the *pharmakon*. Yet, for Derrida, the Platonic intolerance means an intolerance to "a blend [*mélange*] of two pure, heterogeneous terms," to "a blend [*mélange*] and an impurity" (DIS 146/128). Using the Neo-Platonic terms again, we must say that, for Derrida, the father (the unparticipated) is not the same but pure heterogeneity, and the false suitor, the simulacrum, is not difference in itself but the same—but here understood as contamination. We must keep in mind that in *Voice and Phenomenon*, Derrida defines contamination by means of *la prise* (VP 20/21). Thus we must always be sensitive to Derrida's use of any word involving the verb "prendre" such as "comprendre," which means not only "to understand," but also and more importantly "to include." Because Derrida defines Platonism as the subordination of contamination to pure heterogeneity, the Derridean simulacrum has a different set of characteristics. Unlike the Deleuzian simulacrum, the Derridean one has put resemblance on the inside, in "the purity of the inside" (DIS 147/128). In "Plato's Pharmacy," Derrida maintains Plato's definition of the simulacrum (or writing, the *pharmakon*) as a copy of a copy (DIS 159/138). Moreover, Derrida defines the simulacrum through *mimesis* or imitation (DIS 157/137). As Derrida says, "everything begins with re-presentation" (VP 49n1/45n4). Thus first, the Derridean simulacrum is not defined by singularity but by generality (cf. MP 201/168). It is not defined by an event or by the formless; rather, it is defined by formality. To understand Derrida's formalism here, we have to recognize that Derrida is defining the simulacrum by the repetition of the word: two contrary senses *"in the same word"* (DIS 111/98, Derrida's emphasis). The word is "self-identical" (DIS 130/114), "is at once [*à la fois*] enough the same and enough other" (DIS 195/168). There is a minimal unity to any word, its phonic or graphic form, that must be imitated or repeated if it is to function. In "Plato's Pharmacy," Derrida calls this minimal form a "type" (*typos*) (DIS 119/104). It is this repeatable or iterable form that allows for the doubling of the sense. In fact, the Derridean simulacrum is doubled between presence and non-presence (DIS 194/168). The non-presence of the Derridean simulacrum (or of writing, the *pharmakon*), we might say, is singular and formless.[21] Therefore, second, the Derridean simulacrum is also defined by "in-formality." But the simulacrum's non-presence implies that the Derridean simulacrum is defined *neither by being nor by becoming*. As Derrida says, "writing (is) *epekeina tes ousias*" (DIS 194/168).[22] This "beyond being or presence," this non-presence or non-being—the third characteristic—is why Derrida also calls the simulacrum a trace (DIS 119/105, 176/152). That Derrida, however, must put the "is" between parentheses indicates that Derridean doubling consists in a kind of mediation: the wholly other than being takes (*pris*) being *and* is taken by being. Thus, because Derrida defines Platonism as the subordination of contamination (the same or mediation) to heterogeneity, the reversal of Platonism for him does not mean to make the simulacra rise to the surface; rather, it consists in "displacing" them into the "a wholly other field" in which being and the beyond being mutually contaminate one another (DIS 123/108).

We must make this diffraction more precise before it disappears back into the point. We were able to see that the simulacrum in both Derrida and Deleuze could be defined by in-formality. The simulacrum (in either Derrida or Deleuze) can never solely be defined by form, and thus it is singular; but also it can never be defined as formless since it is a repeatable image. The diffraction therefore must occur in the *relation* between formlessness and formality. Their respective definitions of Platonism allow us to see how they are conceiving the relation. For Derrida, the relation cannot be one of heterogeneity; it must be a relation of contamination (another name for Derrida's famous *différance*). For Deleuze, the relation cannot be one of homogeneity; it must be a relation of difference in itself. With contamination, Derrida is trying to conceive difference with mediation, whereas, with difference in itself, Deleuze is trying to conceive difference without mediation. Because Derrida is trying to conceive difference with mediation, he defines the simulacrum by resemblance. Because Deleuze is trying to conceive difference without mediation, he defines the simulacrum by dissimilarity. Moreover, because Deleuze is trying to conceive the difference between form and formless as immediacy, he conceives the relation between—this place—as the surface. Because Derrida is trying to conceive the difference between form and formless as mediation, he conceives the relation as a field. The surface implies a duality (dissimilarity), while the field implies a unity (resemblance). For Deleuze, the surface implies an immediate duality within becoming; for Derrida, the field implies a mediate unity to the "beyond being." Here, therefore, is the most precise formula of the diffraction: Deleuze is the true philosopher of duality; Derrida is the true philosopher of unity. In *The Logic of Sense*, Deleuze says, "This new duality of bodies or states of affairs and effects or incorporeal events [found in Stoic philosophy, which "dissociates" the effect from the cause] entails an upheaval in philosophy" (LS 16/6). In *Voice and Phenomenon*, Derrida says, "But the strange *unity* of these two parallels [that is, the parallel in Husserl between the empirical life and transcendental life], which relates one to the other, does not let itself be distributed by them and dividing itself *solders* [*soude*] finally the transcendental to its other" (VP 14/14, my emphasis). No matter what, however, whether we speak of a duality or a unity of form and the formless, for both Derrida and Deleuze, this question of the relation refers us to language (LS 16/6; VP 14/15).

III. Immediate Duality, Mediated Unity

When Derrida and Deleuze speak about language, they both use Husserl's concept of the noema to define sense. For both, what is important is that Husserl distinguishes the noema simultaneously from the physical object and from psychological lived experiences (LS 32/20; VP 4–5/6). To use Husserl's terminology, the noema is neither *real* nor *reell*, but *irreell*. For both, this non-regional existential status implies that the noema is a kind of an-archic repetition (ED 243/163; LS 55/41, 118/97). Derrida and Deleuze also both refer to paragraph 124 of Husserl's *Ideas I* (VP 19–20; LS 32/20).[23] As is well known, in paragraph 124 Husserl describes the passage from intuitive sense to conceptual meaning. Although here we have Husserl's distinction between *Sinn* and *Bedeutung*, we must recognize that sense is the broader term equivalent to the noema. There can be intuitive or perceptual sense and an expressive sense and a linguistic meaning that expresses the sense. Now, when Derrida looks at Husserl's description of the passage from intuition to meaning, what he focuses on is that, for Husserl, the passage is a "coincidence" (*Deckung*, *recouvrement*), which is not a "confusion" (MP 199–200/167). Thus for Derrida the passage is a repetition of the intuitive sense in a conceptual meaning which is formal. But the very repetition of the intuitive sense in the conceptual form, "the very formality without which expression would not be what it is," "displaces" the intuitive sense (MP 201/168). Because of the formality (the *typos* of "Plato's Pharmacy"), every expression is incomplete in relation to intuition or presence. To use the terminology of Husserl's First Logical Investigation, because every expression repeats the sense in the absence of intuition, every expression is therefore an index; it points to something absent. Thus we have *Derrida's* critique of Husserl in *Voice and Phenomenon*, which consists in showing the indivision, thus the unity, of expression and indication (the index). For Derrida, Husserl does not recognize that expression and indication use the same form; he does not recognize the resemblance between them. As Derrida says, "*One and the same* phenomenon can be apprehended as expression or as index, as discursive or non-discursive sign. That depends on the intentional lived experience that animates it. The functional character of the description immediately presents us with the full extent of the difficulty" (VP 20/20, my emphasis). Derrida therefore is taking up Husserl's concept of indication, which is always defined by a pointing relation (VP 24/23). In contrast, Deleuze is taking up Husserl's concept of expression, calling sense or the noema "the expressed." What Derrida sees in indication is mediation (VP 41/38), whereas what Deleuze sees in expression is immediacy (LS 162/137). Or, to put this another way—and we could see this already in the discussion of the simulacrum—for Derrida, the iterable ideality of the noema is more important than its event character (VP 55/50). Yet, for Deleuze, although "dry reiteration" defines the noema, the event character is more important: sense, a repeatable form, is always an effect (LS 87–88/70). Thus we have *Deleuze's* critique of Husserl in *The Logic of Sense*, which consists in showing the division, thus the duality, of expression from what causes it to be produced as an effect. Deleuze rejects Husserl's phenomenology as "the rigorous science of surface effects" (LS 33/21) because Husserl does not recognize that sense is based in the formless; he does not recognize the dissimilarity between the cause of sense and sense as an effect (LS 119/97–98). The expression is not a mere "shadow" that has the same "thesis" as what generates it (LS 147/122). As Deleuze says, "The foundation can never *resemble* what it founds" (LS 120/99, my emphasis; cf. LS 149/123). This Deleuzian principle, which is perhaps *the* defining principle of all of Deleuze's philosophy, implies that the foundation of sense is nonsense. Similarly, when Derrida adopts the functional status of the difference between expression and indication, he is implying that the foundation of sense is nonsense. Given what we have seen so far, we can immediately construct two formulas: for Deleuze, nonsense is immediately sense, and yet is divided from sense; for Derrida, nonsense is mediately sense and yet is united with sense.

The problem of the relation between sense and nonsense leads both Derrida and Deleuze to make Husserl's noema converge with what Lévi-Strauss called a "floating signifier" (LS 64/49; cf. ED 423/289). The floating signifier is always at once in default or is lacking and in excess in relation to the signified. In other words, it is at once sense (too much sense) and nonsense (not enough sense). For both Derrida and Deleuze, this relation is "out of joint,"[24] "disjoined," "out of correspondence," "unequal," "inadequate," or "violent" (LS 54/39; DR 119/88; VP 13/13; DIS 124/109). Thus the relation is defined by what Deleuze calls a "paradoxical instance" (or "element") (LS 68/53; DR 157/119)[25] or by what Derrida calls the "supplement" (VP 98/88; DIS 193/167).[26] Yet, for Deleuze, this specific relation between sense and nonsense must be non-exclusionary or internal (LS 89/71, 99/81). For Deleuze, what must be internal to sense is not logical absurdity (square circle), but rather the chaos and formlessness of the body, of the depth, of passions (LS 114/93, 92/74). Deleuze is careful to distinguish nonsense from what he calls "a-sense" or "sub-sense" (LS 111/90). With a-sense, the body, passion, has absorbed all activity, all sense, all formality. Whereas a-sense demolishes sense, nonsense grants sense, activity, what Deleuze calls "superior forms" (LS 131/107). Nonsense is defined for Deleuze as being devoid of sense (formless), but he is clear that this defect (*défaut*) does not mean that nonsense is the *absence* of sense. He says, "Nonsense is that which has no sense, and that which, as it enacts the donation of sense, is opposed to the absence of sense" (LS 89/71). Because nonsense "is opposed to the *absence* of sense," we must conceive Deleuzian nonsense as presence; indeed, he speaks of a "co-presence" of sense and nonsense (LS 85/68, 87/70). Although Deleuze uses a negation in the passage just quoted—"nonsense is that which has *no* sense"—"this negation no longer expresses anything negative, but rather releases the purely expressible with its two uneven halves" (LS 161–62/136, 148/123). Deleuzian nonsense is not only presence but also a positivity. Without a negation in the middle, we must on the one hand see the paradoxical instance as consisting in an immediate relation between sense and nonsense. Yet, since both are positivities, sense and nonsense do not resemble one another; there is a division between them: the in-formal. This double positivity—nonsense and sense are both positive, both presences—is why Deleuze defines the paradoxical instance as the "aliquid," the something (LS 84/49).

In contrast, when Derrida in *Voice and Phenomenon* speaks of the parallelism between any of the oppositions that organize Husserl's discourse, he says that the "nothing" (*rien*) is what separates the parallels (VP 12/12). Derrida's use of the "nothing" to designate the same relation as Deleuze designates with a positive term implies that Derrida conceives nonsense by means of negation. Like Deleuze, Derrida does not define nonsense as logical absurdity (square circle) (VP 110/98). A proposition like "the circle is square," while lacking any possible object to which it could refer, nevertheless is meaningful. It is meaningful because its grammatical form tolerates "a relation to an object" (VP 110–11/99). As Derrida says, "Here this aim [at an object] will always be disappointed, yet this proposition makes sense only because another content, put in this form (S is P), *would be able* to let us know and see an object" (VP 110/99, Derrida's emphasis). Thus nonsense for Derrida is defined by "non-presence," the lack of a presence of an object. Sense in turn would be constituted by its formal repeatability, but this very formal repeatability would always imply non-presence. Sense can and must be able to be repeated without an intuition of the object, in non-plentitude or non-fulfillment (VP 100/90). If nonsense for Derrida is defined by the lack of intuitive presence, then sense is always necessarily taken (*pris*) by nonsense. This being taken by nonsense for Derrida means being taken by everything that is "alien to expression" (VP 36/34), that is, by indication: "the effectivity of what is pronounced, the physical incarnation of the *Bedeutung* [meaning], the *body* of speech" (VP 36/34, my emphasis). As with Deleuze, here in Derrida, the reference to the body means a kind of involuntariness or passivity (VP 37/34). However, Derrida does not here understand the body (*Körper*) as divided from *Leib* or *Geist* (VP 37/35). For Derrida, there is always a modicum of formality. Being repeatable, the form of the body always exceeds intuitive presence; the interiority of the body always remains non-present. The supplement makes up for—supplements—the lack of intuitive presence of the interior of the body. Like the index finger, it points to the missing presence. Thus what Derrida calls the "supplement" (VP 98–99/88–89) consists in a relation different from what we just saw in Deleuze's paradoxical instance. Whereas the paradoxical instance unequally joins two presences, two positivities, the supplement unequally joins presence and non-presence. Whereas the Deleuzian paradoxical instance is defined by an immediate division between sense and nonsense, the Derridean supplement is defined by a mediate unity between sense and nonsense. Despite this difference between

the paradoxical instance and the supplement, we are still talking about a relation defined by the "simul," the "at the same time." Thus, as Derrida says,
"sense [has] a temporal nature" (VP 95/85).

When, in *Voice and Phenomenon,* Derrida examines Husserl's description
of temporalization, that is, of the living present, Derrida emphasizes a tension.[27] On the one hand, Husserl's "whole description is incomparably well
adapted to [an] original spreading-out" (VP 69/61). In fact, for Husserl, as
Derrida stresses, no now point can be separated from the "thick slice of time."
On the other hand, "this spreading out is . . . thought and described on the
basis of the self-identity of the now as a 'source-point'" (VP 69/61). Derrida's
analysis depends on the fact that Husserl makes the retention of the immediate past an irreducible component of the thick slice of time. No now point
can be separated from retention. Husserl says, at one point in the descriptions,
that retention is a "non-perception." For Derrida, that Husserl calls retention
"non-perception" implies that Husserl recognizes that "the eye closes," that
is, that retention consists in a non-presence. For Derrida, re-tention has always already re-peated something that is no longer present. As Derrida says,
"the ideality of the form [*Form*] of presence itself implies that it can be infinitely re-peatable, that its re-turn, as a return of the same, is necessary to
infinity and is inscribed in presence itself" (VP 75/67). The repetition of retention, "repetition in its most general form," is, for Derrida, the "constitution of a trace in the most universal sense" (VP 75/67). Thus, for Derrida,
since the trace is necessarily inscribed in presence, there is not a "radical difference," as Husserl wanted, between evidence and non-evidence, perception
and non-perception, between presence and that which is given mediately
through signs (VP 73/65). Rather, there is "a difference between two modifications of nonperception" (VP 75/65). This non-radical difference is what
Derrida calls "the same."

The non-radical difference between the trace's non-presence and presence
implies, for Derrida, that the living present is not simple in the literal sense
(VP 68/61, 74/66); it is not "folded once." As Derrida says, "the presence of
the present is thought of arising from the fold [*le pli*] of a return, from the
movement of repetition, not the reverse" (VP 76/68). Because the difference
between the trace and presence is the same, we must see that Derrida's fold is
a folding-in. The trace's non-presence has included (*a com-pris,* that is, has
contaminated) presence. Non-presence is implied (*im-pli-qué*) (VP 96/86) in
presence, and thus the fold is always "du-pli-cated" (VP 11/11). We can describe Derrida's fold therefore as a knot twisted together around a point that
is never fully present, a knot therefore always still loose, interwoven (VP
20/20), sewn together so that one cannot determine one side from the other,
so that one side mixes with the other. Derrida's fold is what we earlier calling

the displaced field (as opposed to the surface). In a later essay Derrida calls this field a "non-lieu," a "non-place."[28] But, because Derrida always emphasizes the "medium" (VP 85/76), we must characterize his "non-lieu" as a "milieu" (DIS 144/126), a halfway place, which never quite but almost gathers presence and non-presence into a unity: the same.[29] As is well known, Deleuze too uses the image of the fold and characterizes it as both a "milieu" and a "non-lieu" (LS 194–95/166). But Deleuze's fold is not the same but divided. It is not chiasmatic,[30] it is un-folded (*deplié*) (LS 31–32/20). Deleuze says, "Only by breaking open the circle, as in the case of the Möbius strip [the French word here is *anneau*, ring], by unfolding [*dépliant*] it lengthwise, by untwisting it, does the dimension of sense itself appear" (LS 31/20). In fact, Deleuze compares this "unfolding" operation to making a purse out of handkerchiefs sewn "in the wrong way" so that the outside surface and the inside surface are "continuous" (LS 21/11). "In the wrong way" means that they are not sewn into one another in order to form a medium. Rather, they face one another continuously, immediately, "unanimously,"[31] and nevertheless, the two surfaces are du-pli-cated, divided. This unfolding, for Deleuze, defines time.

Like Derrida, Deleuze is trying to conceive time not in terms of the present. As he says in his 1966 *Bergsonism,* "We are too accustomed to think in terms of the present" (BER 53/58). In *The Logic of Sense,* therefore, Deleuze speaks of "side-stepping" (*esquiver*) the present. This "side-stepping" can occur in two ways, what Deleuze calls "Chronos" and what he calls "Aion." Chronos, according to Deleuze, "sidesteps" the present in the now, in a "vast and thick" present that "absorbs" or "includes" (*comprend*) the past and future (LS 190/162, 193/164). Chronos therefore sidesteps the present by "mixing" (*mélanger*) the past and future together. We cannot fail to recognize the similarity of Chronos to Husserl's living present and even to Derrida's analysis of it, and, indeed, when Deleuze describes Chronos, he uses the phrase "living present" (LS 192/164). Aion, however, sidesteps the present in a different way. According to Deleuze, instead of the now, the instant "without thickness" defines Aion: "Instead of a present that absorbs the past and future, a future and a past divide the present at every instant, which subdivides it into past and future to infinity, in the two directions at once [*dans les deux sens à la fois*]" (LS 192–93/164). Because of this infinite division of the present, the instant cannot be identified with any "assignable present" (LS 193/165). Literally, the instant is nowhere or everywhere; as we have already noted, it is "atopon," the non-place, not the mi-lieu (LS 195/166). Aion breaks open the Möbius "ring" and changes it into "a straight line, limitless in both directions" (LS 194/165). This straight line is the Deleuzian surface. And Aion, for Deleuze, gives us a "lengthened, unfolded experience" (LS 32/20).

IV. The Experience of the Voice is the Experience of Death

These different places—the mi-lieu and the non-lieu—have different ontological statuses. The non-lieu in Deleuze is becoming, whereas the mi-lieu in Derrida is beyond being. Thus, as they themselves have done, we can return to the old scholastic ontological designations of univocity and equivocity. Indeed, Deleuze says that the Aion is the pure infinitive, the Verb (LS 216/184–85). When Deleuze speaks of "the univocity of being" (DR 57–61/39–42; LS 208–11/177–80), the "uni" here, the oneness, refers to immediacy. There is an immediate relation between the two sides of the surface, between nonsense and sense, between past and future. This immediate relation is literally the "verb," the voice. The verb for Deleuze is always the infinitive, which implies that the verb is the place of becoming. Thus the phrase "the univocity of being" means "the becoming of being," or, better, "the immediate becoming of being." Now, the "uni" of the two sides is accomplished by the voice, but the voice cannot be a vocal medium for Deleuze. Such a mediation would introduce equivocity. Therefore, according to Deleuze, only silence allows for an "immediate communication" between the two sides (LS 162/137). Thus, as strange as this sounds, in *The Logic of Sense*, Deleuze says that the "verb," literally, the voice, is silent (LS 281/241). To use the terminology of *Difference and Repetition*, the verb is the "loquendum," that is, what is language and silence at the same time (DR 186–87/143). In *The Logic of Sense*, the *loquendum* is what Deleuze (appropriating Lewis Carroll) calls a "portmanteau word," that is, a word that unifies two other words without a copula, in other words, unifies them with a silent verb, for example, "slithy" (= lithe-slimy-active) and "mimsy" (= flimsy-miserable) (LS 61/45). A portmanteau word is the paradoxical instance. Thus, in *The Logic of Sense*, Deleuze calls the silent verb "the paradox of the voice": "[the voice] has the dimensions of a language without having its conditions; it awaits the event that will make it a language. It is no longer noise but not yet language" (LS 226/194).

As we saw, the paradoxical instance functions, for Deleuze, between two presences or positivities. We can see now that it functions between two sounds: noise and language. Noise, for Deleuze, is the noise of singularities, of the abyss, of the body, of passions (LS 130/106–7). It is "the full voice of intoxication and anger" (LS 130/107). This noise is "clamor" (cf. DR 52/35, 114/83–84, 389/304). This noise is the "noisy events" of death (DR 212/163). As Deleuze says, "sickness and death are the event itself" (LS 131/108), or "every event [is] a kind of plague, war, wound, or death" (LS 177/151). Following Blanchot, Deleuze distinguishes between two kinds of death; death is double (LS 177–78/151–52, 182–83/156, 258–59/222; DR 148–49/112–13). On the one hand, death is personal: I am dying. It attacks my body in the present, causing me to cry and yell, forcing noise out of me. This noise is not yet language. On the other hand, death is impersonal: they (*on*) are dying. This death of them (*l'on*) is incorporeal since it is not grounded in my body. But this impersonal death also "sidesteps" the present. This death is the infinitive death of them in which *one* (*on*) never finishes dying. This second death is silent, or this silence is a dead space, in which nothing noisy happens, the non-lieu. Yet, for Deleuze, the silent death of them is the genuine event in which "death turns against death" in order to produce an excess of life. This "strangely impersonal death," Deleuze says, is "always to come, the source of an incessant multiple adventure in a persistent *question*" (DR 148/112, my emphasis).

Thus, by stressing this question, we can provide an example of the experience of the voice. It comes from *Difference and Repetition:* the police interrogation (DR 255/197). In a police interrogation, the detectives ask the questions. I am *powerless* in relation to them. I do not know the answer (cf. LS 220/194). And if I say, "Who are you to ask the questions?" the detectives reply by inflicting pain on me, on my own body. I am dying. Even though I am innocent, they impose an imperative: "Answer the question!" When I asked, "Who are you to ask the questions?" that was stupid. It relies on the voice of others: "My father has lots of money. Who are you to ask the questions?" (cf. LS 219–20/193–94). But if there is "simply a silence with only the noise of my own breathing" (cf. LS 180/154), then thinking begins. Thinking begins in silence, when no longer relying on the voice of others—they are silenced—one begins to respond in one voice, the voice of everyone or no one: *On*. Then the transmutation of powerlessness into power occurs: one invents a response to the question. The experience of the voice in Deleuze therefore is the experience of being "demolished" (LS 180–89/154–61). The police interrogation, for Deleuze, is an experience, a test, an ordeal, *une épreuve.*

Whereas the Deleuzian voice is the voice of one, the Derridean voice is the voice of the other. The title of Derrida's 1967 study of Husserl, *La Voix et le phénomène,* refers back to his earlier 1962 Introduction to his French translation of Husserl's "The Origin of Geometry." There (LOG 104/102), Derrida realizes that language consists in a double necessity or imperative. Simultaneously, language must be equivocal and univocal. We were able to anticipate this duplicity in Derrida, when we noted that for him indication, the relation of pointing to, defines language. A "relation to" always defines language for Derrida. By means of its repeatability, language must always be the same, univocal, and sent *to* an other who is not present, who is beyond being (beyond presence), equivocal. Although, for both Derrida and Deleuze, the verb defines language, for Derrida, the verb is always in the dative case; it always has an indirect object. Thus the "verb," in Derrida, literally the voice, is always an address *to* me from the other. This necessary equivocity of the other organizes Chapter 7 of *Voice and Phenomenon:* "The Voice That Keeps Silence." Here Derrida is examining what Husserl says about the pre-expressive stratum of sense, "the absolute silence of the self relation" (VP 77/69). Derrida therefore is examining the experience of auto-affection, of the fold. Inside myself when I speak to myself, I make no actual vocalization. Thus auto-affection consists in a voice that keeps silence. In this experience, according to Derrida, I must hear myself speak at the very moment I speak. It is the same me speaking as hearing: uni-vocal. Yet, given that I am not the one speaking when I am the one hearing and vice versa, it is not the same me speaking as hearing: equi-vocal. Because there is always a retention inseparable from the now, from the very moment in which I am hearing, there is always an other in me, in the same, speaking to me or right on me (VP 92–93/82–83). Earlier we encountered the fundamental principle of Deleuze's entire thinking (immediate duality), that the ground can never resemble what it grounds. Now we encounter the fundamental principle of Derrida's entire thinking (mediate unity): I can never have a presentation of the interior life of an other, but only ever a re-presentation (never *Gegenwärtigung* but only ever *Vergegenwärtigung*). Derrida has taken this phenomenological insight from Husserl's Fifth Cartesian Meditation and generalized it to all experience, even my own internal experience. Even though this other is in me, is the same as me, I can only have a re-presentation of that other. Thus, while this other speaks to me, inside me, this other hides silence in the voice (*Ver-gegenwärtigung*). This other me is always already non-present, beyond being, thus dead.

For Derrida, too, the experience of the voice is the experience of death. Again in the earlier Introduction to Husserl's "The Origin of Geometry," Derrida had realized that if sense is defined as indefinite re-iteration, then it required necessarily to be embodied in language, vocalized, and ultimately written down (LOG 88/90). Yet, if linguistic embodiment implied indefinite re-iteration, then whenever I speak, my disappearance in general is implied (VP 60–61/54–55). My death is implied even when I use an indexical such as "me" (VP 108/96–97); the very fact that it points to me across a distance implies that it does not require me to be present, up close to it; the indexical is right on me yet not identical to me. I am already other and absent from it. For Derrida, as for Deleuze, the experience of death is double. On the one hand, it is the death of me. Whenever I speak, when, for example, I say, "I am dead," this speaking constitutes a repeatable form that necessarily survives without me. On the other hand, for Derrida, death is also the death of an other. Whenever I speak, when, for example, I say, "I am alive," this speaking fills a repeatable form with presence, a repeatable form that has survived the death of countless others. Quoting the Biblical definition of Yahweh as "I am He who is," Derrida says that this sentence is "the *confession* [*l'aveu*] of a mortal" (VP 61/54, my emphasis).[32]

Thus, by stressing this confession, we can provide an example in Derrida of the experience of the voice. It comes from *Voice and Phenomenon* (VP 78–79/70–71). Instead of a police interrogation, as with Deleuze, we have, with Derrida, a self-interrogation. The experience of the voice in Derrida is not just any internal soliloquy. It occurs when I have wronged another. Thus the experience consists in me "addressing myself to myself as to a second person whom I blame, exhort, call to a decision or a remorse" (cf. VP 79/71). When I say to myself, "You have gone wrong, you can't go on like that!" (cf. VP 78/70), I become other. As an other, as other no longer here, as an other speaking from the grave, wronged, I put myself in question. Again as in the police interrogation, the other asks the questions: "Why did you act that way?" Again, I am *powerless* in relation to the other. I am caught (*pris*). When I ask this ghost who troubles me "What am I to do?" he remains silent. Must I risk my life for the other who haunts me? I do not know what to do or say; I cannot decide. I do not know how to right this wrong, and, in fact, nothing can ever right it. But, if I believe in the voice of the other, then thinking begins. Then the transmutation of powerlessness into power occurs: even though it is impossible, one decides. The experience of the voice in Derrida therefore is the experience of bad conscience. The self-interrogation, for Derrida, is also an experience, a test, an ordeal, *une épreuve* (cf. VP 111/99).

V. Conclusion: The Beginnings of Thought

The point of diffraction in the great French philosophy of the Sixties is at its finest between Derrida and Deleuze. As we have seen, the *point* is the simulacrum understood through in-formality. If we can speak this way, the *diffraction* consists in Derrida emphasizing the "form" (repetition) and in Deleuze emphasizing the "in" (event). This slight difference of emphasis between difference in itself and contamination allowed us to insert oppositions into the diffraction. For Deleuze, the relation between form and formless, that is, the "simul" of the simulacrum, is a relation of immediate duality (dissimilarity). For Derrida, the same relation is a relation of mediate unity (resemblance). Two presences or two positivities (sense and nonsense) constitute the Deleuzian immediate duality. Presence and non-presence, a positive and a negative (sense and nonsense), constitute the Derridean mediate unity.[33] Thus going across the convergence between phenomenology and structuralism, between the noema and the floating signifier, we had the opposition between the Deleuzian paradoxical instance and the Derridean supplement. And this opposition led us to time—the "simul" again—in which we were able to see that Derrida conceives the place between form and formless as a chiasmic fold, the mi-lieu (the displaced field) and Deleuze conceives this place as an untied fold, the non-lieu (the surface). The idea of the fold finally led us to the experience of the voice. Here the opposition becomes the opposition between interrogation by another, the police interrogation in Deleuze, and self-interrogation, the confession in Derrida. But as we just saw, this characterization actually means that, in Deleuze, the interrogation by another is an interrogation by the self understood as the "one," the "dissolved self," as Deleuze would say. In Derrida, the characterization actually means that the self-interrogation is an interrogation by an other. But here we must be careful. This alterity in Derrida does not mean that he is a philosopher of pure transcendence; he is a philosopher of the same, of impure, that is, contaminated immanence. Perhaps we must conceive the dative relation in Derrida not as a pure *à* but as an impure *à même:* transcendence *à même* immanence. Similarly, the dissolved self in Deleuze is a dissolution into the other that comes from the outside, and thus perhaps we must conceive the lack of the dative relation in Deleuze as impure transcendence. Always the diffraction threatens to disappear into the point.

But, at least, we can see always that the point of diffraction consists in the experience of death. When I suffer the erosion of my thought, this impotence forces me to think. This experience is fundamental for the great French philosophy of the Sixties, for Derrida, Deleuze, and Foucault. Of course, Derrida, Deleuze, and Foucault did not remain in this Sixties "archeological" phase. Yet, their most recent (and therefore supposedly most radical) thought flowed from this one point. The great French philosophers of the Sixties recognized that only the experience of life in death and death in life liberates thought from its immobility. It seems to me that the liberation of thought is no less urgent today. Perhaps it is even more so, since we are living in an epoch when the common opinion is that computers think, answer questions, solve problems, perhaps keep promises. For Derrida, Deleuze, and Foucault, the task of liberating thought was the reversal of Platonism. This was the task of modernity. But for both Deleuze and Derrida (indeed, for Foucault as well), this task did not consist in a mere reversal. For Deleuze, in the Sixties, the reversal of Platonism had to "extract" from modernity the "untimely" (LS 305/265).[34] For Derrida, in the Sixties, the reversal of Platonism had "to go beyond" absolute knowledge to something "older" (VP 116/103). For Foucault, in the

Sixties, the reversal of Platonism had to "hollow out" the foundations of history in order to make it actual (NGH 160/154). This extraction, this going beyond, this hollowing out requires a new kind of memory or even a new kind of "counter-memory." Perhaps this memory and counter-memory, an "awaiting forgetting," is what "post-modernism" really means.

Conclusion

The Point of Diffraction

> Philosophy . . . does not consist in choosing between concepts and in taking sides for one school, but in seeking a unique intuition from which one redescends as well to the diverse concepts, because one has placed oneself above the divisions of the school.
>
> —Bergson, "Introduction to Metaphysics"[1]

The popularity of the word "post-modernism" today indicates that ontology and phenomenology are coming to an end. As Foucault would say, there is an "erosion from the outside," which is producing a discontinuity. In other words, certain areas of non-philosophy are producing new needs for thinking. It is in light of these new needs for thinking that, here, I have attempted to determine the system of thought that arose in France in the Sixties. Here is the system in its most schematic and now most elaborated form. Derrida, Deleuze, and Foucault recognized that thought had become immobile. Thought could not move because "Platonism"—that is, any metaphysics of the transcendent—conceived thought as returning at the end to an idea that had already been present at the origin. Thought was caught between a beginning and an end. Thus in the Sixties a need is felt to liberate thought by reconceiving history without end and without origin.[2] The need motivates a convergence between phenomenology and structuralism, a convergence that becomes an archeological investigation. The archeology consists first in a reduction to sense, meaning the transformation of the metaphysical concept of essence (the transcendent) into the concept of sense. Unlike essence, sense is immanent to subjectivity. Immanence, however, must be made complete. Thus, sense or subjectivity itself must be reduced, since sense still implies directionality (transcendence) and thus end and origin. Sense is reduced down to something non-subjective or non-sensical, that is, to a structure whose elements themselves do not signify. The reduction to a non-signifying structure prioritizes spatiality over temporality, that is, it prioritizes a non-mundane space, a profound space, a rarefied space. This is the space of memory. And what is discovered in this memorial space is a defect or a lack. Within this place (*ce lieu*), time itself is out of joint. This disjointure is experienced as a question insofar as every question, in order to be what it is, lacks an answer. Within the question, there is silence, impotence, irresponsibility. The voice posing the question is asking the question of being, of existence, and thus of death. The great French philosophy of the Sixties depends fundamentally on the test (*une épreuve*), on the experience of the voice, which is the experience of death. But just as a question lacks an answer, it also demands an answer. Thus the question opens out onto an excess of answers, a potentiality of voices, responsibility. Where time is out of joint, the untimely (*l'intemporel*) is generated as an excess of life. The question implies: life in death, death in life. The doubling of life in death and of death in life is a paradox. The paradox of the double is what finally enables the genuine movement of thought. The paradox of the double is the point of diffraction.

We were interested in focusing on this point because it would allow us to see, as a kind of *optics*, the *options* that this system makes available to thinking. The idea of a diffraction implies that we are dealing here sometimes with oppositions and sometimes with gradual differences. Thus the determination of the options can occur at times in "more–less" formulas and at times in "this or that" formulas. If we simplify the point, we can see the extreme opposites of the diffraction. We can simplify the point of diffraction by saying that it consists in the experience of language. As Derrida says in *Of Grammatology*, "the problem of language has never been simply one problem among others" (DLG 15/6). If we start from Heidegger's imperative to investigate language as such, there are only two ways in which one can conceive language. On the one hand, there is the idea that communication defines language; language is the address or the apostrophe (or even the prayer). On the other hand, there is the idea that creation defines language; language is expression or novelty (or even noise). On the first side, we must say that language is conceived more as mediation; on the second side, language is conceived more as immediacy (that is, as closer to intuition). Nevertheless, the inclusion (mediation) or exclusion (immediacy) of the dative preposition "to" in the verb is the basis of this distinction. Following Deleuze (and Guattari's) definition in *What Is Philosophy?* the inclusion of the "to" implies transcendence; immanence is the exclusion of the "to" (QPH 46–47/44–45). We must recall, however, that, since the great French philosophy of the Sixties consists in a reversal of Platonism, it is uniformly a philosophy of immanence. The diffraction is a diffraction of immanence. Again at this point we could place a reflection on the French idiom "à même." Therefore all the options for thinking that this system makes available to us are options of immanence.[3] We can formulate the options in the following ways. The proper names in these formulas—Derrida, Deleuze, and Foucault—are being used to refer less to the corpus of each than to the individual options.

Thus we have the Derridean option. This option starts from the idea that the address defines language. To take the address as one's starting point implies that one is conceiving language by means of the mediation that unifies. The Derridean option is more unity than duality. The mediated unity means that there is no hierarchy, no *arche*. Yet this lack of *arche* occurs because language is formal. The Derridean option is more formal, less informal. The forms of language mediate between me and the other, implying that the other who sends these forms to me is never completely present. This lack of presence in the form is the silence behind the voice that says them. Yet, it is precisely the silence that allows for—indeed, demands—a surplus of voices. The experience of this silence is the experience of death, which means that more vocality is more life. Nevertheless, the Derridean option is more silent, less vocal. The Derridean option is more mortal, less vital: the refinition of death in life. We can make one last equation. If silence is equal to death and death is equal to memory, dead (rote) memory (*hypomneme*), then the Derridean option is more memorial and less forgetfulness.

The Deleuzian option starts from conceiving language as expression. To take expression as one's starting point means that one is conceiving language as the immediacy that divides. The Deleuzian option is more duality than unity. Like the Derridean option of mediated unity, the Deleuzian immediate duality means that there is no hierarchy, again no *arche*. Yet, in the Deleuzian option this lack of *arche* occurs because language is informal. The Deleuzian option is less formal, more informal. The informality of language is the immediate presence of noise. The noise becomes language by passing across silence. Again, it is precisely the silence that allows for the multiplicity of voices. But here, because silence actually allows noise and voice to contact one another immediately—Deleuze's "*clamor* of being"—we must say that the Deleuzian option is less silent and more vocal. There is a multiplicity of voices, which is a multiplicity of life. The Deleuzian option is more vital, less mortal: the recommencement of life in death. Finally, again, if voice is equal to life and life too is equal to novelty, then the Deleuzian option is more forgetfulness and less memorial.

Finally, we come to the Foucaultian option. The Foucaultian option starts from conceiving language as discourse. To take discourse as one's starting point means that one is conceiving language as immediately doubled. Like the Deleuzian option, the Foucaultian option is more duality than unity. As before, the Foucaultian immediate duplicity means that there is no hierarchy, again no *arche*. Paradoxically, the lack of *arche* is the fundamental sense of philosophical archeology. In the Foucaultian option this lack of *arche* occurs because discourse, as in the Deleuzian option, is informal. The Foucaultian option is less formal and more informal. The informality of discourse, its materiality, is the immediate presence of murmuring. This murmuring, how-ever, is accumulated into the archive. But if the murmur is accumulated into the archive, then we have to say that the murmur becomes silent in the docu-ments. If the Derridean option has silence behind the voice, and the Deleuz-ian option has silence in the middle of the voice, then the Foucaultian option has silence on the far side of the voice. But this placement of silence makes the Foucaultian option similar not to the Deleuzian option but to the Der-ridean one. In the Derridean option, the voice too gets accumulated into the archive. Although the silent archive is the place of dead memory (*hypomne-sis*), this memorial place means that the Foucaultian option is more memorial and less forgetfulness. Of course, Foucault has spoken of counter-memory, thus of forgetfulness. But this forgetfulness is a forgetfulness of the *arche,* which in turn allows us to await the future, "l'attente, l'oubli," as Blanchot would say. Waiting is remembering and remembering is thought and thought is remembering the future. The Foucaultian memory—but here we could say as well the concept of memory found in the entire system of the French phi-losophy of the Sixties—is a memory of the future. And we could conceive this memory of the future as either refinition or recommencement: death in life; life in death.

These investigations of the great French philosophy of the Sixties were done as a propaedeutic. I had to do these investigations, first, because, it seems to me, that the concepts forged in this period still determine the most recent writings by Derrida, Deleuze, and Foucault. These concepts are still deter-mining what we are doing today in Continental philosophy. But, more im-portantly, what I have done here is, so to speak, put tools in my toolbox to work on the central problem. It seems to me that new needs for thinking are arising from two areas, computer science and the life sciences. The life sci-ences have raised problems that demand philosophical reflection. The latest developments in the life sciences such as genetics constantly suggest a form of biologism, a way of thinking that reduces the body to physical, that is, irrational forces, drives, and instincts. How are we to conceive the body with-out this biologism? These reflections on the experience of language are rele-vant to these questions. One can combat biologism through the materialism of language. Computer technology too has raised problems that demand philosophical reflection. What kind of space is "cyber-space"? What kind of environment is the Internet? A "mi-lieu," a "non-lieu," a "lieu commun" which homogenizes everything according to the needs of the growth of capi-tal? Computer technology concerns entirely the question of intelligence (and memory), and the life sciences obviously concern the question of life (and death). It seems to me therefore that these two areas, areas that are politi-cally sensitive, demand an investigation into the relation between memory and life. And no philosopher has reflected more thoroughly on this relation, a relation that is thought itself, than Bergson. Like Heidegger, Bergson challenges us to stop conceiving being—life—in terms of the present. Thus *Thinking through French Philosophy* precedes an investigation into *The Challenge of Bergsonism*.[4]

Appendix 1

Interview for *Journal Phänomenologie*

Conducted by Silvia Stoller and Gerhard Unterthurner[1]

Q: In your article "The End of Ontology: Interrogation in Merleau-Ponty and Deleuze" you claim that "the phenomenological philosophy of Edmund Husserl is at an end."[2] Could you perhaps further elaborate what you mean by this? And if Husserl's phenomenology has come to an end, what are the consequences then for phenomenological research in general?

A: Let me begin by thanking you both for giving me this opportunity to speak about my own philosophical research. The questions that you have presented to me concern some of the most provocative things I have said in my recent writings, things that I am only now in the process of understanding well. In fact, the essay to which you are referring in this first question may be the most provocative text that I have ever written. When I presented it in Milan in 1998, some members of the audience were quite hostile to it. In fact, it is probable that the hostility arose from the very sentence that you quoted, which is the very first sentence of the essay.

In its complete form, the sentence reads: "Today, the phenomenological philosophy of Edmund Husserl is at an end." This sentence is overdetermined, a fact that the audience who heard this essay for the first time could not have recognized. The main part of the sentence—"the phenonenological philosophy of Edmund Husserl"—refers to the title of Eugen Fink's famous 1933 *Kantstudien* essay: "Die Phänomenologische Philosophie E. Husserl in der Gegenwärtigen Kritik." Some Husserl scholars think that Fink's interpretation of Husserl's philosophy, presented in this essay and in the *Sixth Cartesian Meditation,* is unfaithful to the "master" since it bears the mark of Heidegger's philosophy. But I think that, when Fink says that phenomenology consists in a "new idea of philosophy," a philosophy that describes "the origin of the world" in *non-mundane* terms, that is, as Heidegger would say, in non-ontic terms, this definition sets up all of twentieth-century Continental philosophy. When Merleau-Ponty in *The Visible and the Invisible* describes the paradoxical and thus non-mundane reversibility of the chiasm, it seems to me that he is working within this "new idea of philosophy." When Levinas in *Totality and Infinity* says that the relation between me and the other does not obey classical logic, that is, mundane logic, he is phenomenological in this sense. When Derrida utilizes negative theological language to describe *différance,* he too is relying on this definition. But let me take one other example, an example that is not usually seen as belonging to the phenomenological school. When Deleuze in *Difference and Repetition* says that conditions of experience cannot be "copied off" (*décalqué*) the objects that they condition (DR 176–77/135),[3] in other words, the conditions cannot be ontic, it seems to me that he is phenomenological in this sense. In any case, with the reference to Fink's famous *Kantstudien* essay, I was intending to place my whole discussion in this essay within the framework that Fink set up.

The two words on either side of "the phenomenological philosophy of Edmund Husserl," "today" and "end," refer to one another. Many of the questions that you have posed to me concern the philosophical situation *today.* Like all philosophers, I am interested in what the past and future of our current—today—philosophical (and political) situation may be. It *may be*— nothing is certain—that today something in philosophy is coming to an *end.* The English word "end" refers, by means of its being the translation of the French word "fin" and the German words "Zweck" and "Ende" to a large discourse about ends (Derrida's "The Ends of Man," for example). And, like Derrida, I was intending it in the double sense of termination point and purpose. But I did not pluralize the word as Derrida does, and I did not adopt Derrida's obscure use of the word "clôture" (closure) because I wanted the word to resound a little more sharply as a break. I think that the current— and at times interesting—resurgence in classical phenomenological research ignores certain developments in twentieth-century Continental philosophy that, as far as I am concerned, are irreversible: Heidegger's ontologization of phenomenology, then, following Heidegger, Merleau-Ponty's ontologization of phenomenology. But also we have then, in his Preface to Hesnard's *L'Œuvre de Freud,* Merleau-Ponty's suggestion of a convergence between phenomenology and psychoanalysis (HES 9). We have as well the convergence between phenomenology and structuralism enacted by Deleuze in *The Logic of Sense,* by Derrida in many of the essays in *L'Écriture et la différence,* by Foucault in *Les Mots et les choses.* And finally we have Levinas's conversion of ethical discourse into foundational discourse. All of these developments set up what we commonly call post-structuralism or post-modernism. It seems to me that these developments have made it quite impossible to engage in classical phenomenological research. To be as blunt and as succinct as possible, we must start to think in new ways, ways that are not strictly phenomenological.

Let me be more precise about this. To end phenomenology does not mean that we abandon the greatest phenomenological insights that Husserl brought to light. Here again the reference to Fink is crucial. When Fink says that phenomenology consists in a non-mundane description of the origin of the world, he is making the reduction absolutely necessary for phenomenological research. Thus he says in a note to the *Kantstudien* essay that "All phenomenology passes through the 'reduction.' A 'phenomenology' that renounced the reduction would in principle signify a mundane philosophy, that is (understood, of course, phenomenologically), a dogmatic philosophy."[4] I am wholly in agreement with this claim. In fact, as far as I am concerned, it is impossible to philosophize without some form of the reduction since, without it, as Fink says, we would be engaged in dogmatism. This means, as you can see, that every philosophy journal, no matter what, should be entitled "Journal Phänomenologie."

Yet, in his very early Introduction to his French translation of Husserl's "The Origin of Geometry," Derrida spoke of "une réduction de la réduction." And this "reduction of the reduction" was supposed to lead us to what he then called "une discursivité infinie" (infinite discursivity) (LOG 60n1/ 69n66). Here Derrida was suggesting that the experience of language forces a transformation of phenomenology. A transformation of what in phenomenology? Not the reduction but phenomenology's subjectivism. We must say even its metaphysical commitment to the subject or consciousness. I know that the best interpretations of Husserl, based on the Husserliana volumes, contest that phenomenology is a subjectivism—Merleau-Ponty showed this better than anyone in last writings on Husserl—but Husserl's programmatic statements in the published works support this charge. Thus, Derrida's transformation of phenomenology consists in a critique of phenomenology's subjectivism, which we see in *La Voix et le phénomène,* a text to which I have devoted a lot of time.[5] This Derridean critique depends fundamentally on generalizing another of Husserl's greatest phenomenological insights, that is, that I can never have a *Gegenwärtigung* (presentation) of the other's interior life, but only ever a *Vergegenwärtigung* (representation). This insight is the basis for Derrida's entire discussion of presence and non-presence in *Voice and Phenomenon.* Generalizing *Vergegenwärtigung* means that even my own interior *Erlebnis* (lived experience) is like the experience of an other. In other words, every experience in Derrida is an experience of the trace (or to use his more recent terminology, an experience of the specter). Or to eliminate this terminology and therefore to say it more simply, every experience in Derrida is an experience of language, "infinite discursivity" again, or more precisely the experience of a voice that is equivocal since it comes from the other to me. At the question of language, therefore, it seems to me that phenomenology must come to an end.

So, my claim about the end of phenomenology in "The End of Ontology" essay referred back to Derrida's critique of Husserl. But there is a companion essay to "The End of Ontology" called "The End of Phenomenology" (Chapter 5 above). In this essay's opening pages, I lay out Deleuze's challenge to (or critique of) phenomenology's subjectivism. In his very early *Empiricism and Subjectivity,* Deleuze says, "We embark upon a transcendental critique when, having situated ourselves on a methodologically reduced plane . . . we ask: how can there be a given, how can something be given to a subject, and how can the subject give something to itself? . . . The critique is empirical when, having situated ourselves in a purely immanent point of view . . . we ask: how is the subject constituted in the given?"[6] So far, the Deleuzian "empirical" critique looks very similar to that of Derrida: subjectivity is not foundational but is based on something other than it, on what Deleuze later calls "a plane of immanence." But we can make a difference between Deleuze and Derrida. Derrida's critique depends on the necessary inclusion of the other in the subject or in the same (*Vergegenwärtigung* in *Gegenwärtigung*), while Deleuze's depends on the necessary dissociation of the other from the same. So, when Husserl and then Merleau-Ponty go back to an *Urdoxa* as the fundamental condition, what Deleuze sees in this move is that they have "copied" (*décalqué*) the *Urdoxa* from common sense or from the natural attitude. In other words, Deleuze challenges phenomenology's subjectivism by making the conditions—that is, the origin of the world—as heterogeneous as possible to the conditioned, which is the subject. For Deleuze, when the other is dissociated from the subject as its condition or as its genesis, the other must be characterized as the voice of noise. And for Deleuze, this voice is univocal, not equivocal. It seems to me therefore that this Deleuzian "other" —Deleuze's "*clamor* of being"—is different from what Derrida calls the trace or specter.

Nevertheless, whether one follows Derrida's or Deleuze's critique of phenomenology—both have been extremely important for me—what one is doing is following the phenomenological reduction as far as one absolutely can, so far that phenomenology finds itself transformed into something else, something non-phenomenological. Can there *truly* be a phenomenology of the other when it manifests itself only ever as *Vergegenwärtigung,* when it manifests itself as noise, or to use Foucaultian terminology, when it manifests itself as the outside? One can of course continue to call these new kinds of investigations phenomenological, but, I think, that name does not acknowledge that a threshold has been crossed, that something has come to an end, and that we are starting to do something else. And it seems to me that new needs for thinking have *necessitated*—hence my use above of the word "must"—that we cross this threshold and start to do something else.

Q: With reference to Merleau-Ponty's notion of "flesh," you and Fred Evans have indicated two post-Merleau-Pontean ways for phenomenology: one with Levinas, that for you leads in the direction of theology, and the other in the direction of Deleuze and Foucault. You and Evans find the second way more attractive (*sympathisieren*), and even think that we should abandon Derrida and Levinas, at least for now, although you yourself have worked a lot on Derrida.[7] What do you understand by this "abandonment," and what do you find problematic in Levinas?

A: Yes, I have worked a lot on Derrida and I have learned a lot of philosophy from him. In fact, I often, without any hesitation, call myself a Derridean. It seems to me that Derrida is an incredibly powerful philosopher insofar as he is a philosopher *du tout*. This phrase "du tout," of course, means insofar as he is a philosopher "at all," insofar as he is a genuine philosopher. But also it means that Derrida is a philosopher "of the whole." This "whole" is where the power, for example, of his concept of contamination comes from. Only with the completion of my long study of Derrida's interpretation of Husserl did I come to understand how powerful this concept is. It means that, like Hegel, Derrida can absorb any other position that is opposed to his. In other words, one cannot find a position outside of his system. This inability to exit his system is what Derrida's infamous statement from the Sixties really means: "Il n'y a pas de hors-texte" (There is no outside the text [DLG 227/ 158]).

And yes, I have found Levinas's philosophy problematic. Given what I have said at the end of each of these three essays—"The End of Ontology" (Chapter 6 above), "We Need a Name for What We Do," and "The Value of Flesh" (the Introduction to *Chiasms* co-authored with Fred Evans)—in which I constantly associate Derrida and Levinas, you might find it surprising to learn that my "problems" with Levinas actually came from Derrida, that is, from Derrida's "Violence and Metaphysics." In relation to this important essay, one has to recognize first of all that Derrida is engaged in a *critique* of Levinas. I know that many Levinasians and some Derrideans have claimed that the deconstruction enacted in "Violence and Metaphysics" and even deconstruction in general is not a critique. Yet, if we say that deconstruction is not a critique, then it seems to me that we have reduced deconstruction to a meaningless verbal play. In short, we have "taken the teeth out of it." Moreover, it becomes impossible to understand what Derrida means when he says in the 1980s "deconstruction is justice." Even more, and this is really what was most important for me, if we say that there is no critique here, it is impossible to differentiate between Levinas and Derrida. Now, the critique in which Derrida is engaged in "Violence and Metaphysics" comes from onto-phenomenology, that is, from Husserl and Heidegger. As strange it might seem, the critique in the last two sections of "Violence and Metaphysics"—"Of Transcendental Violence" and "Of Ontological Violence"—relies on *presence*. Derrida says explicitly in these two sections that the other must enter the sphere of the phenomenon, the sphere of *das Seiende* (*l'étant*, "the being") in order for us to have an experience of the other and to be able to speak of it.[8] In other words, the alterity of the other, its non-presence, must be contaminated by presence. But this inclusion of the other in the same, of non-presence in presence, means that Derrida's critique of Levinas in "Violence and Metaphysics" is a critique from the standpoint of immanence.

It seems to me therefore that transcendence differentiates Levinas from Derrida. Let me present a quote from *Otherwise than Being or Beyond Essence:* "Before this anarchy [of the trace]—before this beginninglessness, the gathering of being fails. Its *essence* is undone in signification, in a Saying beyond being and its time, in the dia-chrony of transcendence."[9] As far as I can tell, Derrida would agree with everything that Levinas is saying here about the Heideggerian *Versammlung,* that is, that the trace of the other is the failure of the "gathering of being." But the quote continues: "in the diachrony of transcendence. A transcendence that cannot be converted into immanence." I think that, because of the concept of contamination, Derrida would have to say that transcendence is always included (*compris*) in immanence, that is, it is always necessarily converted into immanence. This is perhaps a very small difference between Levinas and Derrida. And I know that Levinas's concept of separation developed in *Totality and Infinity,* and still at work in *Otherwise than Being,*[10] implies some sort of priority of immanence over transcendence. Yet, it seems to me that we do not have the concept of contamination in Levinas, and this allows us to continue to insert a difference between Levinas and Derrida.

As you can see, I am struggling here to keep Levinas and Derrida separated ("insert a difference"). But I think, as well, that it is difficult, nearly impossible, to separate Derrida and Deleuze, Derrida and Foucault, Foucault and Deleuze, and, yes, even Levinas and Deleuze. Thus in order to be clear, I must say that now, after having investigated these differences more thoroughly, I would retreat from my suggestion in "We Need a Name for What We Do" that we need to "abandon" Levinas and Derrida at least for awhile. And I am not as certain as I used to be about finding Deleuze and Foucault more "attractive" than Levinas and Derrida. Again, as I was investigating these differences over the last few years, my thinking about these philosophers became much more confused, and as the confusion dissipated, what appeared to me was a different project, one that is not immediately interested in "sympathizing" more with one side than another. Instead, I have grown increasingly interested—this is my primary interest right now—in what philosophical *options* are still available in this entire system of "French" thought. I have put the word "French" in scare quotes because, obviously, Husserl and Heidegger strongly influenced this system. In any case, in order to determine the options for thinking, I have been trying to find what I am calling, following Foucault, "the point of diffraction" (AS 87/65) in this system. It seems to me that Heidegger's attempt in *Being and Time* to re-open the question of being is the defining event of twentieth-century Continental philosophy.[11] When Heidegger re-opens the question of being, he defines being itself as a question: the question of being is the being of the question. The experience of the question is the "point of diffraction" of this entire system of thought. The very idea of a diffraction implies that we must conceive the extremes of the diffraction by means of "more and less," even though such formulas seem imprecise. For example, Levinas's philosophy is less immanent, more transcendent, than Deleuze's philosophy. I also think that we can determine the extremes by means of two views of language (or of the voice). On the one hand (the less immanent side), language is conceived more as the address or the apostrophe, therefore as equivocal and yet always the same; on the other hand (the less transcendent side), language is conceived more as creative or expressive, therefore as univocal and yet always different. In other words, language is conceived either with or without the dative relation ("to").[12]

And, yes, we can determine the extremes of the diffraction by means of religion. I was initially troubled by the explicit turn that Derrida has taken in the last fifteen years toward the religious. I am less troubled now because I can see how his religious discourse flowed out of the point of diffraction—what he is now calling the religious is the experience of the question. In the experience of the question in Derrida one is demanded, or, better, commanded to make a response. Thus the experience of the question (which for Derrida is really the experience of the promise) immediately implies responsibility. This implication is extremely important for me. In fact, it seems to me that what is most important in Derrida's religious discourse is the sentence "tout autre est tout autre."[13] Within this sentence a commandment is concealed. We can see the commandment if we recall Kant's second formula of the categorical imperative. If every other is wholly other, then every other is a person. And if every other is a person, then we must respect every single other—including past and future others, others in the oceans and in the mountains and in the cities, others on other planets, rocks and computer chips, amoeba and humans. In other words, I must be responsible to everything. This remarkable universalism ultimately requires of us a lot of thinking.

By saying this ("requires of us a lot of thinking"), I mean that the point of diffraction in the experience of the question does not imply only responsibility. It ultimately implies thought. Or to be more precise, responsibility is thought. Thus, as far as I'm concerned, it is a mistake to say that the ultimate project of this "French" system of philosophy is "the deconstruction of the subject" or "the overcoming of humanism." These things are not truly what is at stake here. What is at stake here is a renewal of thought. Taking the reduction as far as possible leads us to the renewal of thought. The renewal of thought is really what I am interested in, not taking sides. Perhaps it is not necessary to say this, but I want to be clear. This renewal of thinking is not abstract. We must conceive thinking as Foucault does in *The Order of Things*, as "a certain mode of action": "thought . . . is in itself an action—a perilous act" (MC 339/328).

Q: In the United States there still exists a great tension (*eine große Diskrepanz*) between analytic and so-called Continental philosophy. With respect to this tension (*Auseinandersetzung*), you suggest that the word "phenomenology" not be used anymore, since analytic philosophers still identify phenomenology with "transcendental idealism." You advocate instead that we use terms like epistemology and genealogy.[14] Do you really believe that abandoning the concept of phenomenology is a productive alternative? In other words, to what extent can simply abandoning the concept of phenomenology clear up the misunderstandings between analytic philosophy and phenomenology?

A: No, I do not think that abandoning the concept of phenomenology will clear up the misunderstandings between analytic philosophy and what we call, especially in the United States, "Continental philosophy." In fact, the best reason for retaining the word and the concept of phenomenology is, as I have already noted, the reduction. If there is "eine große Diskrepanz" between analytic philosopher and so-called "Continental philosophy," this big divergence has occurred because of the reduction. I am not an expert in analytic philosophy, but it seems to me that there is no mechanism in it that is equivalent to the reduction. Indeed, until there is some mechanism like the reduction in analytic philosophy, the misunderstandings will continue. So, again, what is important for me in phenomenology is the reduction. And, again, we must push the concept of phenomenology as far as possible until it passes an endpoint and becomes something else.

As the title of my little essay suggests—"We Need a Name for What We Do"—my real interest there was in names. And my interest in names arose because of the "tensions" between analytic philosophy and Continental philosophy. "Tensions" is the English word you use to translate *Diskrepanz,* but also *Aufeinandersetzung* (confrontation). Yes, I think there are "confrontations" going on in the United States between analytic philosophy and Continental philosophy. As far as I can tell, the confrontations work this way. Because analytic philosophy hegemonically determines the rules of what counts as philosophy in the United States, analytic philosophers never really want to gain access to what we could call the "bastions" of Continental philosophy. Most analytic philosophers do not really care about Continental philosophy. And, if they concern themselves with Continental philosophy at all, they adopt Continental philosophy only according to the rules of analytic philosophy. The result is that they make Continental philosophy homogeneous with analytic philosophy. In short, they eliminate it. Thus the confrontations never come from the analytic philosophers. Instead, they always come from the Continental philosophers who do not obey the rules of analytic philosophy and therefore who want to change the rules of what counts for philosophy in the United States. This attempt to change the rules means that Continental philosophers in the United States are always trying to gain access to the "bastions" of analytic philosophy. These confrontations from the Continental philosophers are always delicate since if you gain access you risk being made homogeneous with analytic philosophy and thereby eliminated. It seems to me that these delicate confrontations take place at three levels.

First, the confrontations take place at the level of philosophical debates. To gain access to the "bastions" of analytic philosophy one must be able to participate in their debates. Thus names are important. How can we participate in analytic *epistemological* debates, when we immediately say—I've done this—that Heidegger in 1927 destroyed the entire epistemological endeavor? To be able to participate in these debates was one of the reasons why I suggested the word "epistemology" for what we do. (There were other reasons. There is Deleuze's claim, to which I refer at the end of "The End of Ontology," that Foucault converted phenomenology into epistemology. And I am interested in the French tradition of epistemology, for example, Cavaillès and Bachelard.) But one can ask, why would we Continental philosophers feel a need to participate in the analytic philosophy debates? This brings us to the second and more concrete level of the confrontations. In the United States, certain names have become synonymous with analytic philosophy. Here are three: metaphysics, epistemology, and ethics. The concrete result of this synonymy is that philosophy departments in American universities advertise teaching positions with these terms. If a philosophy department advertises that it needs a specialist in metaphysics, this advertisement means an "analytic metaphysician." Continental philosophers therefore feel the need to participate in analytic philosophy debates in order to break apart the synonymy between these terms and analytic philosophy. If we could break that synonymy, there would be more and more jobs available for the doctoral students that we train in Continental philosophy. And if we could place more and more of our doctoral students in teaching positions, we could start to change the rules of what counts for philosophy in the United States. Obviously, this second level of confrontation concerns the institution known as the university. But the university is situated within the much larger political realm. Thus we have the third and most concrete level: politics. It seems to me that today there are two areas to which we need to direct our philosophical reflection: computer technology and the life sciences. The stakes in these two areas are, as everyone knows, very high. Here we encounter the gravest danger. Pushing the reduction as far as we can means discovering a process of institution that is not "copied off" the natural attitude, off common opinions or off the status quo. It is only when we have reached this institution that genuine thinking can occur. If I am correct that analytic philosophy does not contain a mechanism of the reduction, then its analysis of these areas will end up by doing nothing more than *justifying by copying* the common opinions about intelligence (or memory) and life. I do not think I am exaggerating if I say that these common opinions result in the exploitation of certain groups of humans and of the environment. Therefore, as Continental philosophers, we must concern ourselves with these areas, and that means gaining access to the "bastions" of analytic philosophy since analytic philosophy has completely determined the philosophical discourse about these two areas. We need to gain access to the analytic debates surrounding these areas. And to do that, we need the right names.

What makes a name a good name? We must follow the example of the proper name and not the categorial name. A proper name at once designates a thing and yet does not define that thing. In other words, a proper name is at once determinate and indeterminate. A good name therefore designates something without reducing the plurality of its senses. It allows us to focus on a point without obliterating the diffraction. Under this definition, "Continental philosophy" is not a good name. It does not designate well, since the largest concentration of so-called Continental philosophers does not exist on the European continent but in the United States. Moreover, "phenomenology" is not a good name since it reduces the senses of what it is used to designate. It seems to me that Bergson, for example, is not a phenomenologist because of his concept of the unconscious, although his philosophy contains a mechanism equivalent to the reduction.[15] But there is one other characteristic to a good name. A good name is one that allows us to participate in a debate and affect the decisions that are based in it. If I am correct that the two most sensitive areas of politics today are computer technology and the life sciences, then a good name for what we do would allow us to intervene in the debates surrounding these areas. I have experimented with many names lately. Besides "epistemology" and "genealogy," I have suggested "lifeism" (see Chapter 7 above) and "archeology" (see Chapter 2 above). But I do not really think that any of these names are very good. Today, I still think that we need a name for what we do.

Q: In your appropriation (*Parteinahme*) of Deleuze and Foucault you propose a primacy of institution in place of Merleau-Ponty's primacy of perception.[16] How is institution more fundamental than perception, and what exactly do you mean by "institution"?

A: Let me say something again. Right now, I am no longer interested in "taking sides" (*Parteinahme*). I am interested in the "point of diffraction" of the entire system of "French" thought. Because of this interest, the concept of "institution" that Fred Evans and I introduced in our Introduction to the volume called *Chiasms* is very important to me. When we spoke of "institution" there, we were intending this word in a Merleau-Pontean sense. In fact, by saying that the primacy of perception must be replaced by the primacy of institution, we were referring to a development in Merleau-Ponty's own thinking. Merleau-Ponty conceived the project of *The Visible and the Invisible* as quite different from the project of *Phenomenology of Perception,* as certain well-known working notes to *The Visible and the Invisible* verify. We might say that the project of *Phenomenology of Perception* was "constitution," whereas the project of *The Visible and the Invisible* was "institution." I hope you can hear now the Husserlian resonance of these terms. When Evans and I spoke of institution, we were referring to Merleau-Ponty's later appropriation of the Husserlian concept of *Stiftung.* Here is the passage in the later Merleau-Ponty that we had in mind. It comes from "Indirect Language and the Voices of Silence": "Husserl has used the fine word *Stiftung*—foundation or establishment—to designate first of all the unlimited fecundity of each present which, precisely because it is singular and passes, can never stop having been and thus being universally. . . . It is thus that the world as soon as he has seen it, [there is] a *tradition . . . that is,* Husserl remarks, *the power to forget the origins* and to give to the past not a survival, which is the hypocritical form of forgetfulness, but a new life, which is the noble form of memory" (S 73–74/59, Merleau-Ponty's emphasis). Merleau-Ponty had developed this concept of *Stiftung,* "institution,"[17] in his reading of Husserl's "The Origin of Geometry." What Merleau-Ponty sees in this concept is a non-subjective version of what the early Husserl called "constitution." Institution means that there is a past that precedes and generates every subjective present experience. There is a tradition that has always already been before there is any individual work. As you know, in this passage Merleau-Ponty is referring to the art of painting. What he is saying is that there is a tradition of painting as soon as the world is seen, a tradition that exists as soon as cave-people started painting in the cave at Lascaux. How are we to conceive this "past that was never present"? Because it is not based in the present, it must be conceived through spatiality. This move from time to space should look familiar. It is precisely the move that defined French structuralism in the 1960s. In fact, I intended with the word "interobjectivity"[18]—I do not think that Fred Evans would want to take responsibility for this clumsy word—to replace both phenomenology's "intersubjectivity" and structuralism's "structure."

I do not think that I will retain this word "interobjectivity" in future works, because now I can see that what Merleau-Ponty calls "institution" must be conceived as a *place* (*un lieu*), and here we come across, once again, the point of diffraction to which I was referring above. Here's how the *diffraction* looks. For Merleau-Ponty and Deleuze, the place is the earth. For Derrida and Levinas, the place is the desert. For Foucault, the place is the archive. The *point* of the diffraction consists in the following. Since this past is not based on a present, it always involves a lack (*un manque*) or a defect (*un défaut*).[19] Insofar as the place involves a lack or defect, it is experienced as a question. A question always lacks an answer, a response. And in this way, through the experience of the question, we are led back to language or the voice. For me, however, following what Merleau-Ponty says in the passage I just quoted, this voice is the voice of memory. As Merleau-Ponty also says in the passage above, what is at issue in memory is life. When one pushes the reduction as far as possible, to the point where phenomenology turns into something else, then we find ourselves confronted with the relation between memory and life. Only this relation, it seems to me, can lead to a renewal of thought.

This phrase, "memory and life," has become increasingly important to me. It will probably be the title of a book that I hope to write over the next five years. But you can see, I hope, that this phrase refers back to the system of "French" thought, most obviously to the Merleau-Pontean concept of institution, but also back to Heidegger's reflections on Hölderlin, back to Foucault's concept of "counter-memory," back Derrida's concept of specter, back to Deleuze's concept of the virtual, and back to Levinas's concept of the immemorial. Moreover, this phrase refers back to what I was calling the "two most sensitive areas of politics today," computer technology and the life sciences. Computer technology concerns entirely the question of memory, and biology obviously concerns the question of life (and death). When I said that "new needs for thinking have *necessitated* . . . that we cross this threshold [of phenomenology] and start to do something else," I was thinking that these new needs have arisen from computer technology and the life sciences.

Let me add a word about Fred Evans's work on the concept of institution. Fred Evans, co-author of our joint essay, uses the notion of "voice" and the idea of society as a "multi-voiced body" to spell out how each of these "institutions" or voices is simultaneously the "other" and part of the identity of the rest, that is, mutually transcendent (heterogeneity) and mutually immanent (social solidarity) in relation to one another. He also shows how new voices are produced through the interplay of these voices—how the being of the multi-voiced body is ultimately its constant metamorphosis. He introduced these ideas in some of his earlier works,[20] has continued their development in a number of recent pieces,[21] and is currently working on a book that shows how they can be used to address philosophical issues concerning society, communication, and politics.[22]

Q: You have worked a great deal on Merleau-Ponty, recently editing a volume on Merleau-Ponty's later work and the concept of "chiasm." And your English translation of Merleau-Ponty's lecture "Husserl aux limites de la phénoménologie" will appear soon (see HL). You are a member of the Merleau-Ponty Circle, and since 1999 a co-editor of the journal *Chiasmi International*. In a report on contemporary Merleau-Ponty research in the U.S., you mention —along with traditional Merleau-Ponty scholarship—three areas that at present have important and productive connections with Merleau-Ponty: ecological philosophy, feminist philosophy, and philosophy of mind. In the German-speaking world there are still significant reservations and prejudices on the part of (male) phenomenologists with respect to feminist philosophy. In your opinion, to what extent does feminist philosophy represent a challenge for phenomenology, and in turn what can feminist philosophy learn from phenomenology? Finally, what do you think about the different research undertaken in the area of "feminist phenomenology" over the last ten years?

A: Over the last ten or twenty years, in the United States, "Continental feminism" has been quite diverse and rich. I think, as in German-speaking world, in the United States, there are still significant reservations and prejudices in philosophy in general (in both analytic and Continental philosophy) against feminist philosophy. Continental philosophy, however, has certainly been receptive to feminism. In fact, I would say that Continental philosophy in the United States now is feminist. In turn, feminism has invigorated Continental philosophy, bringing it back to more concrete political concerns. And it seems to me that this movement toward the concrete, done rigorously, is absolutely necessary.

Yet feminist philosophy in general in the United States has focused primarily on the problem of embodiment. This problem is one on which I have not worked a lot because of Heidegger. If Heidegger still counts as a phenomenologist, then I think feminist philosophy could learn a little from Heidegger. As you know, many feminist philosophers criticize Heidegger for not giving explicitly *Dasein* a body. It seems to me, however, that Heidegger has some good reasons for, so to speak "disembodying" *Dasein*. On the one hand, to move from the mind to the body, as the defining feature of existence, would amount to only a reversal of Platonism; as Heidegger would say, this mere *Umdrehung* (reversal) is not a *Herausdrehung* (a "twisting free").[23] On the other hand, Heidegger recognizes that, if one is going to have a philosophy of the body, then one is going to find oneself involved in the discourse of biologism, and biologism, as everyone knows too well, is a system of doctrines that can have dangerous political consequences. Again, because of biologism, I think the life sciences are a politically sensitive area. Thus if one is going to have a philosophy of the body, if one is going to reverse Platonism (or Cartesianism), then one must redefine the body in a way that does not necessarily reduce it to physical, and therefore to irrational, forces, drives, or instincts. This redefinition, it seems to me, can be done by calling the body the "fold" between matter and discourse.[24] We can conceive this "fold," however, in two ways. On the one hand, there is the Merleau-Pontean way (and here I think we could say Derridean way as well). In this first way, the body is "folded up" (*replié*). The body then is the "mi-lieu," the halfway place, where discourse and matter, hearing and seeing, are interlaced, woven closely together. It is the point in which discourse and matter are united in "contamination." On the other hand, there is the Foucaultian way (and here we could say Deleuzian way as well). In this second way, the body is "unfolded" (*déplié*). The body then is the "non-lieu," the non-place where discourse and matter, hearing and seeing, are untied and unwoven. It is the point in which discourse and matter are dissociated in order to form the "audio-visual battle." By describing this first way I am relying on the fourth chapter of Merleau-Ponty's *The Visible and the Invisible*, "The Intertwining—The Chiasm," but also Derrida's uses of the figure of the chiasm. By describing the second way I am relying on the second chapter of Foucault's *Discipline and Punish*, "The Spectacle of the Scaffold" ("L'Éclat des supplices"),[25] and Deleuze's uses of the figure of the fold. In particular, the following passage from Deleuze's Foucault book has been important for me to conceive this difference:

> Knowledge is Being, . . . but Being lies between two forms. Is this not precisely what Heidegger called the "between-two" or Merleau-Ponty termed the "interlacing or chiasmus"? In fact, they are not at all the same thing.

> For Merleau-Ponty, the interlacing or between two merges with the fold. But not for Foucault. There is an interlacing or intertwining of the visible and the stateable. . . . But this interlacing is in fact a stranglehold, or a battle between two implacable foes who are the two forms of knowledge-Being. . . . Everything takes place as though Foucault were reproaching Heidegger and Merleau-Ponty for going too quickly. (F 119/111–12)

I would like to add a more general observation here. Along with feminism, ecological philosophy and "race theory" are currently very important in philosophy. There are many lively debates in all three areas. And in these three areas, it seems to me, the delicate confrontations between analytic philosophy and Continental philosophy are taking place. But these debates in feminism, race theory, and environmental philosophy (level one), and the transformation of philosophy in the university (level two), really lead us to level three, concrete politics. These three areas of philosophy, it seems to me, really lead us back to what I called "the two most sensitive areas in politics today," computer technology and the life sciences. Feminism, race theory, and environmental philosophy engage the question of life and technology, indeed, computer technology. Computer technology has raised questions that we must ask. What kind of space is "cyber space"? What kind of environment is the Internet? A "mi-lieu," a "non-lieu," a "lieu commun" which homogenizes everything according to the needs of the growth of capital? What I am really trying to say, however, is that, if I am right that these questions from the life sciences and computer technology are necessitating new forms of thought, and these new forms of thought have started to appear as feminism, race theory, and environmentalism, then it seems to me that *ultimately today* we must investigate the relation between *memory and life*.

Appendix 2

"Reversing Platonism"

GILLES DELEUZE

Introduction and Translation by Heath Massey

Introduction

Deleuze originally published "Renverser le platonisme" in *Revue de Métaphysique et de Morale* 71, no. 4 (Oct.–Dec. 1966), pp. 426–38. Subsequently he revised the piece and included it in *Logique du sens* (Paris: Minuet, 1969) as "Platon et le simulacra," the first part of the first appendix, "Simulacre et philosophie antique." What follows here is a translation of the 1966 version. I have used boldface to indicate passages or phrases that Deleuze revised or omitted for the 1969 version, and where the two versions are identical, I have utilized the Lester-Stivale translation of *The Logic of Sense* (New York: Columbia University Press, 1990), indicated by regular typeface. This is intended to give readers access to the differences between the two versions and the opportunity to bring them into question.

Both versions of this essay begin with a discussion of Plato's dialectical procedure of division and its aim, to distinguish false pretenders from true ones, to find criteria for selection, that is, to articulate the foundation that makes a claim well or poorly founded. When Deleuze published *The Logic of Sense,* he maintained the first five paragraphs of this essay without alteration. Thereafter we find a number of significant omissions, additions, and other revisions, most of which alter Deleuze's original emphasis or language, but not the substance of the essay.

Among the parts omitted by Deleuze for publication in *The Logic of Sense* are a note at the end of paragraph 8 to pieces on Plato by Schuhl and Rodis-Lewis; the opening sentences of paragraph 9, which are made redundant by revisions to the preceding paragraph; a comment in note 9 of this translation, which is replaced by a second reference to Plato's *Sophist;* remarks on differences between the literary "procedures" of Joyce, Roussel, Robbe-Grillet, Klossowski, and Gombrowicz; certain passages, particularly in paragraphs 11–16, that do not survive the rearrangement of those discussions;

and most obviously, in the final paragraph, the long quotation from Henry Miller's *The Time of the Assassins: A Study of Rimbaud,* which reflects upon Rimbaud's remark "There is some destruction that is necessary." Whether Deleuze eliminated this quotation in order to conserve space or for other reasons, he replaced it with just a single sentence distinguishing between two kinds of destruction, thus giving a different character to the piece's conclusion.

More extensive are Deleuze's additions to the piece, although the essay as a whole is somewhat shorter (by about 150 words) than it appears in *The Logic of Sense.* One example is the insertion of two early notes, one referring to Derrida's "Le Pharmacie de Platon" (pp. 257, 361) and the other to Plato's *Theaetetus* and *Timaeus* (pp. 258, 361). Also worth noting is Deleuze's expansion of the discussion of knowledge and opinion found in paragraph 9 of the 1966 version presented here. In 1969 Deleuze characterizes imitative reproduction as veritable production for Plato, as opposed to what Plato views as the nonproductive effect of the simulacrum, which is a becoming mad, becoming unlimited, becoming other, becoming subversive of profundity and evasive of the Same and the Similar. Also, whereas Deleuze concludes this paragraph in the 1966 version with a comment on the foreignness of the simulacrum to knowledge or representation, in 1969 he continues with a discussion of Platonism's development of "the power of the representation" and further contributions by Aristotle and Christianity to its domination. The discussion of Leibniz and Hegel that constitutes paragraph 15 of the 1966 version was significantly revised by Deleuze and relocated to precede his remarks on modern literature. In the 1969 version, Deleuze emphasizes the dominance of Leibniz's and Hegel's thought by the Same and the Similar and their teleological exclusion of eccentricity and divergence. Other additions to the 1969 version of the essay include an allusion to Joyce's *Finnegans Wake* with respect to chaos (p. 260); a note to Blanchot's "Le Rire des dieux" (pp. 262, 362); a comment about Greek, particularly Platonistic, loathing of the eternal return in its latent signification (p. 264); and two pregnant remarks about Socrates, concerning his distinguishability from the Sophist (p. 263) and his fate "under the blade" of Platonism (p. 265). Other noteworthy additions made by Deleuze for *The Logic of Sense* are addressed in the notes to this translation.

In general, the most significant revisions to the essay involve paragraphs 11–16 of the 1966 version. Although the concluding paragraphs of the essay received attention as well, its central paragraphs show the greatest effort. I leave it to readers to decide whether and how these revisions signify changes in Deleuze's thinking during that period.

Reversing Platonism
(Simulacra)

1. What does it mean "to reverse Platonism"? This is how Nietzsche defined the task of his philosophy or, more generally, the task of the philosophy of the future. The formula seems to mean the abolition of the world of essences and of the world of appearances. Such a project, however, would not be peculiar to Nietzsche. The dual denunciation of essences and appearances dates back to Hegel or, better yet, to Kant. It is doubtful that Nietzsche meant the same thing. Moreover, this formula of reversal has the disadvantage of being abstract; it leaves the motivation of Platonism in the shadows. On the contrary, "to reverse Platonism" must mean to bring this motivation out into the light of the day, to "track it down"—the way Plato tracks down the Sophist.

2. In very general terms, the motive of the theory of Ideas must be sought in a will to select and to sort. It is a question of "making a difference," of distinguishing the "thing" itself from its images, the original from the copy, the model from the simulacrum. But are all these expressions equivalent? The Platonic project comes to light only when we turn back to the method of division, for this method is not just one dialectical procedure among others. It assembles the whole power of the dialectic in order to combine with it another power, and represents thus the entire system. One might at first want to say that this method amounts to the division of a genus into contrary species in order to subsume the thing investigated under the appropriate species: this would explain the process of specification, in the *Sophist,* undertaken for the sake of a definition of the angler. But this is only the superficial aspect of division, its ironic aspect. If one takes this aspect seriously, Aristotle's objection would clearly be in order: division would be a bad and illicit syllogism, since the middle term is lacking, and this would make us conclude, for example, that angling is on the side of the arts of acquisition, of acquisition by capture, etc.

3. The real purpose of division must be sought elsewhere. In the *Statesman,* a preliminary definition is attained according to which the statesman is the shepherd of men. But all sorts of rivals spring up, the doctor, the merchant, the laborer, and say, "I am the shepherd of men." Again, in the *Phaedrus,* the question is about the definition of delirium and, more precisely, about the discernment of the well-founded delirium or true love. Once again, many pretenders rise up to say, "I am the inspired one, the lover." The purpose of division then is not at all to divide a genus

into species, but, more profoundly, to select lineages: to distinguish pretenders; to distinguish the pure from the impure, the authentic from the inauthentic. This explains the constancy of the metaphor assimilating division to the testing of gold. Platonism is the philosophical Odyssey and the Platonic dialectic is neither a dialectic of contradiction nor of contrariety, but a dialectic of rivalry (amphisbetesis), a dialectic of rivals and suitors. The essence of division does not appear in its breadth, in the determination of the species of a genus, but in its depth, in the selection of the lineage. It is to screen the claims (pretensions) and to distinguish the true pretender from the false one.

4. To achieve this end, Plato proceeds once again by means of irony. For when division gets down to the actual task of selection, it all happens as though division renounces its task, letting itself be carried along by a myth. Thus, in the *Phaedrus,* the myth of the circulation of the souls seems to interrupt the effort of division. The same thing happens in the *Statesman* with the myth of archaic ages. This flight, this appearance of flight or renunciation, is the second snare of division, its second irony. In fact, myth interrupts nothing. On the contrary, it is an integral element of division. The characteristic of division is to surmount the duality of myth and dialectic, and to reunite in itself dialectical and mythic power. Myth, with its always circular structure, is indeed the story of the establishment of a foundation. It permits the construction of a model according to which the different pretenders can be judged. What needs a foundation, in fact, is always a pretension or a claim. It is the pretender who appeals to a foundation, whose claim may be judged well-founded, ill-founded, or unfounded. Thus, in the *Phaedrus,* the myth of circulation explains that before their incarnation souls had been able to see the Ideas. At the same time, it gives us a criterion of selection according to which the well-founded delirium or true love belongs only to souls which have seen many things, and which have within them many slumbering but revivable memories. The souls which are sensual, forgetful, and full of petty purposes are, on the contrary, denounced as false pretenders. It is the same in the *Statesman:* the circular myth shows that the definition of the statesman as "shepherd of men" literally applies only to the ancient god; but a criterion of selection is extracted from the myth, according to which the different men of the city participate unequally in the mythic model. In short, an elective participation is the response to the problem of a method of selection.

5. To participate is, at best, to rank second. The celebrated Neoplatonic

triad of the "Unparticipated," the participated, and the participant follows from this. One could express it in the following manner as well: the foundation, the object aspired to, and the pretender; the father, the daughter, and the fiancé. The foundation is that which possesses something in a primary way; it relinquishes it to be participated in, giving it to the suitor, who possesses only secondarily and insofar as he has been able to pass the test of the foundation. The participated is what the unparticipated possesses primarily. The unparticipated gives it out for participation, it offers the participated to the participants: Justice, the quality of being just, and the just men. Undoubtedly, one must distinguish all sorts of degrees, an entire hierarchy, in this elective participation. Is there not a possessor of the third or the fourth rank, and on to an infinity of degradation culminating in the one who possesses no more than a simulacrum, a mirage—the one who is himself a mirage and simulacrum? In fact, the *Statesman* distinguishes such a hierarchy in detail: the true statesman or the well-founded aspirer, then relatives, auxiliaries, and slaves, down to simulacra and counterfeits. Malediction weighs heavily on these last—they incarnate the evil power of the false pretender.

6. **But if it is true that the myth, in the dialectical method of division, is necessary in the erection of a model-foundation according to which the pretenders must be judged and their pretensions measured, it is surprising that, of Plato's three major texts—the *Phaedrus,* the *Statesman,* and the *Sophist*—the *Sophist* introduces no myth that establishes a foundation.** The reason for this is simple. In the *Sophist,* the method of division is employed paradoxically, not in order to evaluate the just pretenders, but, on the contrary, in order to track down the false pretender as such, in order to define the being (or rather the nonbeing) of the simulacrum. The Sophist himself is the being of the simulacrum, the satyr or centaur, the Proteus who meddles and insinuates himself everywhere. For this reason, it may be that the end of the *Sophist* contains the most extraordinary adventure of Platonism: as a consequence of searching in the direction of the simulacrum and of leaning over its abyss, Plato discovers, in the flash of an instant, that the simulacrum is not simply a false copy, but that it places in question the very notions of copy and model. The final definition of the Sophist leads us to the point where we can no longer distinguish him from Socrates himself—the ironist working in private by means of brief arguments. Was it not necessary to push irony to that extreme? Was it not Plato himself who pointed out the direction for the reversal of Platonism?

*

7. We started with an initial determination of the Platonic motivation: to distinguish **the thing itself from its images,**[1] original from copy, and model from simulacrum. But we already see that these expressions are not equivalent, **and that the** distinction wavers between two sorts of images. Copies are secondary possessors. They are well-founded pretenders, guaranteed by resemblance; simulacra are like false pretenders, built upon a dissimilarity, implying an essential perversion or a deviation. It is in this sense that Plato divides in two the domain of images-idols: on one hand there are copies-icons, on the other there are simulacra-phantasms.[2] We are now in a better position to define the totality of the Platonic motivation: it has to do with selecting among the pretenders, distinguishing good and bad copies or, rather, copies (always well-founded) and simulacra (always engulfed in dissimilarity). It is a question of assuring the triumph of the copies over simulacra.[3]

8. **It is relatively easy to define copies and icons: they are images endowed with resemblance. Yet this resemblance submits to two conditions. The resemblance must not be an exterior relation, but an interiorized resemblance; the copy is all the better as it obtains the resemblance through procedures themselves, which are similar to those that constitute the model. And since it is interior, the resemblance is sprititual, ideal.** It goes less from one thing to another than from one thing to an Idea, since it is the idea which contains these relations and proportions constitutive of the internal essence. **Therefore, in order to judge a copy, it is not sufficient to know [*savoir*] what it resembles; one must know [*connaître*] the Idea of that to which the copy bears a resemblance. It is even in this sense that every copy exhibits a *pretension* as far as it resembles something, but this pretension can be founded only by an Idea, in a more profound relation with the Idea as such. The copy is a copy of an Idea and, at the same time, a copy of what presents the Idea. The well-founded pretension is defined only by this interior and ideal resemblance.**[4]

9. **Yet it seems much more difficult to define the simulacrum or the phantasm. Doubtless it still produces an effect of resemblance, but as a unifying and totally exterior effect.** If we say[5] that it is a copy of a copy, an infinitely degraded icon, an infinitely relaxed resemblance, we miss what is essential: the difference in nature between simulacrum and copy, the aspect through which they form two halves of a division. The simulacrum, in fact, is an image without resemblance. The catechism, so much

inspired by **Platonist Fathers,**[6] has familiarized us with this notion: God made man in His image and in His resemblance, but through sin man lost the resemblance while keeping the image. **Through sin** we have become simulacra, **phantasms. Have we not lost moral existence in order to enter into aesthetic existence?**[7] This remark about the catechism has the advantage of accentuating the demonic character of the simulacrum. **Plato defines it precisely through three characteristics. First, even if the simulacrum produces an exterior effect of resemblance, it does so by means entirely different from those that are at work in the model. The simulacrum is constructed on a disparity; it has interiorized a dissemblance. It has interiorized a dissimilarity. This is even why the simulacrum cannot be defined by the totally exterior effect of resemblance; its interiority and essence are elsewhere, in the interiorized dissimilarity. This is why it is apt to define the essence of the false pretender, like the "copy," that of the well-founded pretender. But in the second place, the simulacrum implies a work of great dimensions, of depths and distances that the observer cannot master. Because the observer cannot master them, he experiences an impression of resemblance. This to say that the observer takes part in the work itself, that the work is deformed and transformed with the point of view of the observer. The simulacrum includes in itself, it interiorizes, the differential point of view.**[8] **Finally, the last characteristic, perhaps the most mysterious, concerns the mode of apprehension of the simulacrum. We can call knowledge [**savoir**] the apprehension of the model or of the Idea. Strictly, only what possesses primarily, possesses thereby a genuine knowledge. The copy, the icon, must therefore imply solely a "right opinion." However, the copy itself participates in knowledge inasmuch as it interiorizes the resemblance with the Idea, and inasmuch as its pretension is well-founded. Consequently, let us reserve the name of right opinion for the apprehension of the simple, exterior resemblance, to the extent that the exterior resemblance finds itself guaranteed by a more profound similarity. What is left over for the simulacrum, for its internal dissemblance and its false resemblance? Neither knowledge nor even right opinion. In this sense, Book X of the** *Republic* **reserves knowledge [***le savoir***] for "the user" and right opinion for the maker (when he listens to the advice of the user), but Book X refers the man of the simulacrum to a strange encounter, outside of knowledge [***savior***] and opinion. A species of ruse and irony, an art of encounters that takes the place of the mode of knowledge [***connaissance***] or representation.**[9]

10. We would like to speak of some things well known in the contemporary arts, which have, it seems, nothing to do with Platonism, nor even
with the reversal of Platonism. We know that several literary procedures (the same holds for other arts) permit several stories to be told at
once.[10] It is not at all a question of different points of view on one story
supposedly the same; for points of view would still be submitted to
a rule of **possible** convergence. It is rather a question of different and
divergent stories, as if an absolutely distinct landscape corresponded
to each point of view. **The unity of divergent series, insofar as they
are divergent, exists, but necessarily constitutes a *chaos* which is itself
identical with the Great Work. This informal chaos is not just any
chaos. This chaos holds "complicated" within itself all the divergent
series; it complicates all the series at the same time as each actual series explicates it, and as all the virtual series implicate it.[11] (It is not
surprising that Joyce took such an interest in Bruno, the theoretician
of the *complicatio*.) We can cite a couple of the literary procedures that
make both this divergence of series and their communication in a
chaos-work of art possible: the concerted employment of esoteric
words (of which "portmanteau words" are one instance), and the directed utilization of phantasms. We can also cite certain authors who
have constructed their work of art on one or another of these procedures: obviously Joyce, Roussel, Robbe-Grillet, Klossowski, Gombrowicz. No less obviously, it would be necessary to distinguish the procedures of each of them. From a linguistic perspective, the esoteric
words of Joyce do not at all resemble the common words of Roussel.
From a phantasmatic perspective, the organization of series or divergences refers to a technique that is very different in Robbe-Grillet,
Klossowski, and Gombrowicz. There is only a commonality sufficient
enough to be able to say: the work itself has become the simulacrum.[12]**

11. **The ability to simultaneously affirm heterogeneous and divergent series testifies to a positive power, which is that of language as well as
that of the phantasm. Freud showed how the phantasm is established
between two series, or rather Freud found the condition of the phantasm in the coexistence of two series, one infantile, the other post-
pubescent. It is possible that the phantasm and language have, in this
regard, a common structure: that every word and every phantasm
would be constructed on such heterogeneous series, and institute a
sort of *coupling* between these series, from whence derives an internal
resonance within the system, a *forced movement* whose amplitude**

overflows the basic series themselves. Placing disparates in communication, resonance, forced movement would thus be the characteristic of the phantasm-language or the simulacrum. The affective charge linked to simulacra would be explicated by the internal resonance which the simulacra carry, like the impression of death, like the impression of rupture or dismemberment of life; it would be explicated by the amplitude of the forced movement. At the most, one would be able to distinguish two poles, according to whether the difference between the heterogeneous series is posited as very small or as very large. For example, the originary difference is very small in certain phantasms of Robbe-Grillet, and very large in certain phantasms of Gomborwicz. And in general, the properly linguistic pole ensures differences much greater than the properly phantasmic pole.

12. However, this distinction itself remains secondary. In the case of very small differences, it seems that each series becomes a variant of the other, and that a dominant effect of resemblance emerges from their being placed in communication. But it is precisely not this—that is to say, the degree of external resemblance—that matters. Let us consider the following two formulas: "only that which resembles differs," and "only differences resemble." These are two distinct readings of the world: one invites us to think difference from the standpoint of a previous similitude or identity; whereas the other invites us to think similitude and even identity as the product of a fundamental disparity. The first reading precisely defines the world of copies or representations; it posits the world **itself as representation.**[13] **The second, contrary to the first, defines the world of simulacra; it posits the world as itself being simulacrum.** Now, from the point of view of this second formula, it matters little whether the original disparity, upon which the simulacrum is constructed, is very small or very large.[14] It suffices that the constitutive disparity be judged in itself, **that it be called small or large because and as a function of criteria which do not prejudge from any prior identity. It suffices** that it has "the disparate" [*le dispars*] as unit of measurement and communication. Then the resemblance **is never thought of but** as the product of this internal difference. It matters little whether the system consists "in large external resemblance and small internal difference," or the opposite, since resemblance is always on the exterior, and difference, small or large, occupies the center of the system.[15]

13. Such systems, constituted by placing disparate elements or heterogeneous series in communication, are in a sense quite common. They are signal-sign systems. The signal is a structure in which differences of potential

are distributed, **ensuring the communication of the heterogeneous:**[16] the sign is what flashes across the boundary of two levels, between two communicating series. Indeed, it seems that all phenomena respond to these conditions inasmuch as they find their ground **in a dissymmetry, a constitutive difference.**[17] All physical systems are signals; all qualities are signs. It is true, however, that the **heterogenous** series which border them remain external. By the same token, the conditions of their reproduction remain external to phenomena. In order to speak of simulacra, it is necessary for the heterogeneous series to be really internalized in the system.[18] **It is necessary that these series be interiorized as long as they are heterogeneous. It is necessary, therefore, that their difference itself be _included._ Under this condition the series are not simply heterogeneous, but really divergent. And under this condition of interiority, divergence itself is not the opposite of convergence, but posits convergence as an internal chaos which, as we have seen, keeps all the series "complicated." So each series is able to pass into actuality, and to bring out an instant of chaos which retains the series, only by affirming its divergence or its original difference, however small it may be, from all the other series.**

14. Something living is more a simulacrum than a thing. But the perfect state of the simulacrum is only approached by certain machines or certain works of art. What is essential is to turn the difference, as such, into an object of affirmation—and thereby to affirm chaos? It is in this sense that the world of simulacra manifests its irreducibility to the world of copies, or more generally, of _representations._ When one considers the history of representation, one must note two particularly important moments, where representation has seemed to be on the verge of ovecoming its own limits: with Leibniz, then with Hegel. For in these two cases, representation became infinite representation. It became infinite through diverse procedures, concerning with Leibniz the infinitely small, and with Hegel the infinitely large. And yet, if one remained finally in the domain of representation, if the limits were only exceeded in appearance, it is because Leibniz and Hegel were not free from a condition of convergence of the series, or a condition of monocentricity of the circles. A notion as rich as the Leibnizian notion of incompossibility is not reduced to simple contradiction; it is defined by divergence. (For each world, the monads representing so many remarkable points, a series which converges around one of these points is capable of extending itself in all directions, into other series converging around other points, the incompossibility of the worlds being defined in the vicinity of the points which would cause the series

obtained to diverge.) We therefore see how Leibniz excludes divergence by distributing it into the incompossibles, and conserves the maximum of convergence as the criterion for the chosen world, that is, of the real world. Likewise in Hegel it has recently been shown at what point the circles of dialectic revolved around or rested on a single center, so their intoxication was feigned.[19] In fact, infinite representation has only invented particularly subtle means for assuring the triumph of identity as principle of representation in general in the existent. Representation continued to think difference as a function of the identical, and to subordinate the world, the "pretender," to conditions of convergence and monocentricity.

15.   Inasmuch as the conditions of experience are determined as conditions of possible experience, their grids are too loose and they let everything pass through. At the same time, aesthetics suffers from an insurmountable duality. On the one hand, it designates the theory of sensibility as the form of possible experience; on the other hand, the theory of art as the reflection of real experience. For these two meanings to be tied together, the conditions of experience[20] themselves become conditions of real experience. The work of art then appears from this perspective for what it is—an "experimentation." The conditions of real experience, which are also structures of the work of art, seem to us to be the conditions of experience: divergence of the series, decentering of the circles, constitution of the chaos which contains them. It is a matter of liberating difference from all subordination to the similar and the identical, in order to make from the similar and the identical, to the contrary, a second power which derives from difference itself. It is only in this sense that the world of representation is actually reversed. These conditions are fulfilled in the simulacrum. We define the simulacrum as a sign-signal system, having interiorized its difference, constructed on at least two divergent series, establishing between the series an internal resonance, operating from one to the other a forced movement.

*

16.   Reversing Platonism consequently means affirming the right of simulacra, of phantasms, against icons or copies. Such is the sense of the expression "twilight of the idols." Reversing Platonism is not simply to dispute the Platonic distinction Essence-Appearance, Model-Image. It is to value the rights of one kind of image against another kind of image. The simulacrum is not a degraded copy. It harbors a positive

power which denies the original and the copy, the model and the repro-duction. The Platonic **original**[21] is the Same, in the sense that Plato says that **only** Justice is just, **only** Courage courageous, only Piety pious[22]—the abstract determination of the foundation as that which possesses in a primary way [*en premier*]. The Platonic copy is the Similar: the pre-tender who **participates in the same or who receives secondarily.**[23] The similarity called exemplary corresponds to the pure identity of the origi-nal; the similarity called imitative corresponds to the pure resemblance of the copy. **But the simulacrum abolishes both. For, of the two diver-gent series which it interiorizes, *none can be assigned as the original, none as the copy.* There is no privileged point of view, just as there is no object common to all points of view.** There is no possible hierarchy: no second, no third. Resemblance subsists, but it is produced as an ex-ternal effect of the simulacrum, since it is constructed upon divergent series and makes them resonate. Identity subsists, but it is produced as the law that **maintains**[24] all the series **within each one and *makes the whole return.***[25] In the reversal of Platonism, resemblance is said of inte-riorized difference, and identity of the Different as primary power. The same and the similar no longer have an essence except as *simulated,* that is, as expressing the functioning of the simulacrum.[26] It is the triumph of the false pretender. **It simulates both the father and the fiancé, in a strange incest which undoes the order of participations.**[27] But the false pretender cannot be called false in relation to a presupposed model of truth, no more than the simulation can be called an appearance.[28] It in-volves the false as power, Pseudos, in the sense in which Nietzsche speaks of the highest power of the false. The simulacrum makes both the Same and the Similar, both model and copy, to fall under the power of the false **(under its own power)**.[29] It makes both the fixity of distribution and the determination of hierarchy impossible. It institutes the world of nomadic distributions or crowned anarchies. Far from being a new foun-dation, it engulfs every foundation, it assures a universal breakdown [*ef-fondrement*], but as a joyful and positive event, as *un-founding* [*effonde-ment*]: "behind each cave another that opens more deeply, and beyond each surface a subterranean world yet more vast, more strange. Richer still . . . and under all foundations, under every ground, a subsoil still more profound."[30]

17. **There is a being of simulacra. And it is the most secret point in the reversal of Platonism—the point that Nietzsche determined as be-ing the eternal return. There are so many misunderstandings concern-ing the eternal return because, in itself, the latent content is opposed to the manifest content.** The manifest content of the eternal return

can be determined in conformity with Platonism in general. **So it represents the manner in which chaos is organized under the action of the demiurge and receives the similar, or the effect of the Same.** The eternal return in this sense is the vanquished chaos, the mastered mad-becoming; it forces becoming to copy the eternal. It is under this form that the eternal return is myth that establishes a foundation. It establishes the copy in the image, and subordinates the image to resemblance. **Clearly it is not in this sense that Nietzsche considers the eternal return. Otherwise, why would he treat it as his, Nietzsche's own vertiginous idea? And why would this serene and translucent idea be enough to make Zarathustra ill? In Nietzsche we find statements of the manifest content of the eternal return; it is even fair to say that we find only that. But, at the same time, these manifest statements are there in order to be challenged by Zarathustra, who does not want moreover to speak about them, and who will not have time moreover to speak about them. In effect, they are not formulated by Zarathustra himself, but once by the dwarf, and another time by Zarathustra's animals. Thus Zarathustra challenges them by scolding them for** transforming into a natural platitude what is otherwise profound, into an "old tune" what is an other music, and into circular simplicity what is otherwise sinuous. In the eternal return, one must pass through the manifest content[31] in order to attain the latent content, situated a thousand feet below (the cave behind every cave . . .).[32]

18. The secret of the eternal return is that it does not express an order opposed to the chaos that subordinates it. **It is not anything** other than chaos, **than** the power of affirming chaos **(of making chaos an object of affirmation). The genius common to Nietzsche and Joyce was to show that the "vicus of recirculation" could** not affect and cause a "chaosmos" to revolve.[33] Between the eternal return and the simulacrum, there is such a profound link that the one cannot be understood except through the other. Only the divergent series, insofar as they are divergent, return; that is, **insofar as each implicates its differences along with the others, and all are complicated within chaos. This is why Pierre Klossowski can say** of the eternal return that it is a "simulacrum of a doctrine": it is indeed **being** [*l'être*], but only when "being" [*étant*] is the simulacrum.[34] **The eternal return is the way of the *sub*- or *supra*-representative world. It does not make everything return. It makes nothing return of what pretends to correct the divergence or recenter the circles. It makes nothing return of what pretends to subordinate, to assess the different in relation to the Same and the Similar. Yet the eternal return is itself the same and the similar. But it is the same and the similar which are**

never presupposed in that of which they are said, which are said solely of difference and the different: same and similar insofar as simulated. The eternal return, as selective thought and being, thus makes the difference, but makes it in a manner opposed to that of Plato. It is under the power of the false pretender that it makes everything that is pass. The eternal return has no essence other than univocal Being. It is the univocity of being. Being is said in one and the same sense of all that of which it is said—but that of which it is said is the simulacrum, the chaosmos. But that of which it is said differs, interiorizes the difference and makes it diverge (the world of the will to power as "simulation," as the fantastic machine of Dionysus).

19. **We can define modernity** by the power of the simulacrum. It behooves philosophy not to be modern at any cost (no more than to be nontemporal), but to extract from modernity something that Nietzsche designated as "the untimely," which pertains to modernity, but which must also be turned against it—"in favor (I hope) of a time to come." **As well, it is not in the great forests and footpaths, but in the towns and streets, including what there is most *artificial* in them, that philosophy is elaborated.** The untimely is attained in relation to the most distant past, by the reversal of Platonism; in relation to the present, by the simulacrum conceived as the edge of critical modernity; in relation to the future, by the eternal return as belief in the future.[35] The artificial and the simulacrum are not the same thing. They are even opposed to each other. The artificial is always a copy of a copy, which should be pushed to the point where it changes its nature and is reversed into the simulacrum.[36] Artifice and simulacrum are opposed at the heart of modernity, at the point where modernity settles all of its accounts, as two modes of destruction. **In modern life, the simulacrum is a destroyer, but in a completely different manner than our modern destructions: *the two nihilisms.* There is a great difference between sustaining or instituting a chaos which negates and affirming chaos itself. In his admirable book on Rimbaud, Henry Miller comments: "There is some destruction that is necessary." Miller knows how to find the radical tone of philosophical-poetic prophesy—"and what a fuss has been made over that simple statement! He was speaking then of the destruction incidental to creation. But governments destroy without the slightest excuse, and certainly with never a thought of creation. What Rimbaud the poet desired was to see the old forms go, in life as well as in literature. What governments desire is to preserve the status quo, no matter how much slaughter and destruction it entails. . . . I don't think he would have brought about quite the destruction which [Hitler,**

Stalin, Mussolini, Churchill, and Roosevelt] visited upon the world. He would have kept something up his sleeve for a rainy day, so to speak. He would not have shot his bolt. He would not have lost track of the goal, as our brilliant leaders seem to have done. No matter what a fiasco he made of his own life, oddly enough I believe that if he had been given the chance he would have made the world a better place to live in. I believe that the dreamer, no matter how impractical he may appear to the man in the street, is a thousand times more capable, more efficient, than the so-called statesman. All those incredible projects which Rimbaud envisaged putting into effect, and which were frustrated for one reason or another, have since been realized in some degree. He thought of them too soon, that was all. He saw far beyond the hopes and dreams of ordinary men and statesmen alike. He lacked the support of those very people who delight in accusing him of being the dreamer, the people who dream only when they fall asleep, never with eyes wide-open. For the dreamer who stands in the very midst of reality all proceeds too slowly, too lumberingly—even destruction"[37]—even the most innocent of all destructions, the destruction of Platonism.[38]

Notes

Introduction

1. Everyone associates with this moment not only Deleuze, Derrida, and Foucault, but also Althusser, Ricoeur, Lyotard, Bourdieu, and Kristeva. Nevertheless, even the small amount of historical distance that we have already from this moment shows that Deleuze, Derrida, and Foucault have had the most wide-ranging influence. This influence, however, was not the principle on which I based my selection. Concerning the relation between Derrida and Ricoeur, for example, see my *Imagination and Chance: The Difference between the Thought of Ricoeur and Derrida* (Albany: SUNY Press, 1992).

2. See Luc Ferry and Alain Renaut, *La Pensée 68* (Paris: Gallimard, 1985); English translation by Mary Schnackenberg Cattani as *French Philosophy of the Sixties* (Amherst: University of Massachusetts Press, 1990).

3. I am borrowing this phrase from Foucault; see AS 87/65.

4. Martin Heidegger, *Was heisst Denken?* (Tübingen: Max Niemeyer Verlag, 1961), p. 2; English translation from the first 1954 edition by J. Glenn Gray as *What Is Called Thinking?* (New York: Harper and Row, 1968), p. 4.

5. For a very similar interpretation of this connection between Derrida, Deleuze, and Foucault with Heidegger, see Giorgio Agamben, "Absolute Immanence," in *Potentialities*, ed. and trans. Daniel Heller-Roazen (Stanford: Stanford University Press, 1999).

6. If one used, not Merleau-Ponty, but Sartre or Lacan or Lévi-Strauss as a partner in the dialogue, one might be required to construct the French Sixties philosophical system differently. Undoubtedly changing the partner would bring to light a different aspect of the point of diffraction. Thomas Flynn's two-volume study of the relation of Sartre and Foucault will make a major contribution to this question. See Thomas Flynn, *Sartre, Foucault, Historical Reason: Toward an Existentialist Theory of History*, vol. 1 (Chicago: University of Chicago Press, 1997). Volume 2 is forthcoming.

7. Michel Foucault, *Dits et écrits*, vol. IV, *1980–1988* (Paris: Gallimard, 1994), p. 574; English translation in *Ethics: Subjectivity and Truth*, ed. Paul Rabinow (vol. 1 of *The Essential Works of Michel Foucault, 1954–84*) (New York: New Press, 1997), p. 315.

8. It was impossible to take *Le Toucher* into account in these essays, since it was published only in 2000.

9. Jacques Derrida, *Le Toucher—Jean-Luc Nancy* (Paris: Galilée, 2000), p. 218.

10. Derrida, *Le Toucher*, p. 223.

11. Derrida, *Le Toucher*, p. 241.

12. See the Interview for *Journal Phänomenologie* (Appendix 1) for an explanation of this sentence. The interview with *Journal Phänomenologie* was conducted in August 2001 and published in German in the autumn of 2001. No English language version exists. The interview took place after this book was almost entirely completed, so it is the most recent text in the book (except for the Introduction and Conclusion). Therefore, it contains my most mature reflections on the issues in this book; it presents in a more informal manner the general philosophical orientation of this entire book. That is one of the main reasons

why I decided to include it. Indeed, since it discusses directly two of the essays ("The End of Phenomenology" and "The End of Ontology"), it functions as a kind of guide to a basic reading of *Thinking through French Philosophy*. But there is a second main reason. I included the interview because it extends the discussions found in the essays in new directions, in the direction of the body and in the direction of politics. But beyond these new issues, it shows how these investigations are the foundation for a major philosophical book (*Memory and Life*) that I am about to begin. So the interview (more than any one of the essays) is the bridge to my future work. But there is a third reason. The two Viennese philosophers who conducted the interview wanted to learn more about the Analytic-Continental division in the United States. This is the first time I have ever published anything on this division, on this *Auseinandersetzung*, as Stoller and Unterthurner say.

13. Friedrich Nietzsche, *Zur Genealogie der Moral*, vol. 5 of the *Kritische Studienausgabe* (Munich: Deutscher Taschenbuch Verlag de Gruyter, 1988), p. 309; English translation by Walter Kaufmann as *On the Genealogy of Morals*, in *Basic Writings of Nietzsche* (New York: Modern Library, 1968), p. 509 (second essay, paragraph 10). The emphasis is Nietzsche's.

14. Although I think one could include Levinas in the great French philosophy of the Sixties, I have not included him directly in any of my investigations. At least at a superficial level, Levinas is a philosopher of transcendence. Clearly transcendence is at work in both Merleau-Ponty and Derrida, and indeed, it is difficult to differentiate between Derrida and Levinas. Nevertheless, it seems to me that Derrida is more immanentist than Levinas. And then we have to say that Foucault and Deleuze are even more immanentist.

1. "If Theory Is Gray, Green Is the Golden Tree of Life"

1. This essay continues my "Translator's Preface" to Jean Hyppolite, *Logic and Existence*, trans. Leonard Lawlor and Amit Sen (Albany: SUNY Press, 1997), pp. vii–xvi, and my "Gray Morning," in *Research in Phenomenology* 27 (1997), pp. 234–45. The following texts have been consulted in the writing of this paper: Rudi Visker, *Michel Foucault: Genealogy as Critique*, trans. Chris Turner (London: Verso, 1995); Alan Schrift, *Nietzsche's French Legacy: A Genealogy of Poststructuralism* (New York: Routledge, 1995); Michael Mahon, *Foucault's Nietzschean Genealogy: Truth, Power, and the Subject* (Albany: SUNY Press, 1992); James Bernauer, *Michel Foucault's Force of Flight: Toward an Ethics for Thought* (Atlantic Highlands, N.J.: Humanities Press, 1990); Hubert Dreyfus and Paul Rabinow, *Michel Foucault: Beyond Structuralism and Hermeneutics*, 2nd ed. (Chicago: University of Chicago Press, 1983); Didier Eribon, *Michel Foucault*, trans. Betsy Wing (Cambridge, Mass.: Harvard University Press, 1991); Arnold Davidson, ed., *Foucault and His Interlocutors* (Chicago: University of Chicago Press, 1997); Susan J. Hekman, ed., *Feminist Interpretations of Michel Foucault* (University Park: Pennsylvania State University Press, 1996); Arnold Davidson, "Archeology, Genealogy, Ethics," in *Foucault: A Critical Reader*, ed. David Couzens Hoy (New York: Blackwell, 1986), pp. 221–33.

2. Hyppolite is obviously the source of the title of Gilles Deleuze's *Logique du sens* (Paris: Minuit, 1969).

3. Martial Gueroult, *Descartes selon l'ordre des raisons*, vol. 1 (Paris: Aubier, 1968), p. 9; English translation by Roger Ariew as *Descartes' Philosophy Interpreted according to Order of Reasons* (Minneapolis: University of Minnesota Press, 1984), p. xvii.

4. For more on the "paradox of repetition," see below, Chapter 8.

5. The question might be "What difference is there?" Cf. Deleuze, DR 142/107.

6. Michel Foucault, *Naissance de la clinique* (Paris: Presses Universitaire de France, 1963), p. 147; English translation by A. M. Sheridan Smith as *The Birth of the Clinic* (New York: Vintage, 1973), p. 145.

7. See Ian Hacking, "Self-improvement," in *Foucault: A Critical Reader*, pp. 235–40.

8. This comment, made by Foucault in the 1983 course "The Culture of the Self," is very important: "I never stopped doing archeology. I never stopped doing genealogy. Genealogy defines the target and the finality of the work and archeology indicates the field with which I deal to make a genealogy." Quoted in Mahon, *Foucault's Nietzschean Genealogy*, p. 212.

9. See QPH 107–8/112–13.

10. For Foucault on the concept of form, see AS 134/101–2.

11. Cf. Michel Foucault, "Nietzsche, Freud, Marx," in *Dits et écrits*, vol. I, *1954–1988* (Paris: Gallimard, 1994), p. 570; English translation by Jon Anderson and Gary Hentzi as "Nietzsche, Freud, Marx," in *Critical Texts* 3, no. 2 (1986), p. 3.

12. Here Foucault is alluding to paragraph 7 of the Preface to *The Genealogy of Morals*, where Nietzsche says that gray is a "color a hundred times more important for a genealogist of morals than blue." See Friedrich Nietzsche, *On the Genealogy of Morals*, in *Basic Writings of Nietzsche*, ed. and trans. Walter Kaufmann (New York: Modern Library, 1968), p. 457.

13. Jacques Derrida, "Le Puits et la pyramid: introduction à la sémilogie de Hegel," in *Marges de la philosophie* (Paris: Minuit, 1972), pp. 79–128; "The Pit and the Pyramid: Introduction to Hegel's Semiology," in *Margins of Philosophy*, trans. Alan Bass (Chicago: University of Chicago Press, 1982), pp. 69–108. Published in 1972, this essay was first delivered on January 16, 1968, in a seminar directed by Jean Hyppolite at the Collège de France.

14. Jacques Derrida, *Spectres de Marx* (Paris: Galilée, 1993); English translation by Peggy Kamuf as *Specters of Marx* (New York: Routledge, 1994).

15. Michel Foucault, "Qu'est-ce qu'un auteur?" in *Dits et écrits*, vol. I, p. 795; English translation by Donald F. Bouchard and Sherry Simon as "What Is an Author?" in *Language, Counter-memory, Practice*, ed. Donald F. Bouchard (Ithaca: Cornell University Press, 1977), pp. 113–38.

16. I have deliberately avoided entering into the Derrida-Foucault debate because my purpose here is to define certain logics. Nevertheless, it is clear that, when one examines the documents, Derrida is accusing Foucault of being a metaphysician of presence and Foucault is accusing Derrida of being an metaphysician of the supra-historical perspective. For Foucault's accusation of metaphysics, see Michel Foucault, "My Body, This Paper, This Fire," in *Oxford Literary Review* 4, no. 1 (1979), p. 27; the French version is in *Dits et écrits*, vol. II. It is also clear that the logic of contamination is at the basis of Derrida criticism, even most recently; see Jacques Derrida, "'Être juste avec Freud," in *Penser la folie* (Paris: Galilée, 1992); English translation by Pascale-Anne Brault and Michael Nass as "To Do Justice to Freud," in *Foucault and His Interlocutors*.

17. See also Derrida, *Spectres de Marx*, p. 102; *Specters of Marx*, p. 59.

18. Jacques Derrida, *Apories* (Paris: Galilée, 1996); English translation by Thomas Dutoit as *Aporias* (Stanford: Stanford University Press, 1993).

19. Michel Foucault, *Histoire de la folie à l'âge classique* (Paris: Gallimard, 1972), p. 26; partial English translation by Richard Howard as *Madness and Civilization* (New York: Vintage, 1965), p. 11.

20. But, as we shall see in the next chapter, the prioritization of time turns the moment into a place.

2. The Chiasm and the Fold

1. See Burkhard Liebsch, "Archeological Questioning: Merleau-Ponty and Ricoeur," and Françoise Dastur, "Merleau-Ponty and Thinking from Within," both in *Merleau-Ponty in Contemporary Perspectives*, ed. Patrick Burke and Jan van der Veken (Dordrecht: Kluwer, 1993), pp. 19 and 25. Both of these essays were extremely helpful for the formulation of the ideas presented here. But the interpretation of Foucault that we are putting forward owes much to that of Deleuze: Gilles Deleuze, *Foucault* (Paris: Minuit, 1986); English translation by Paul Bové as *Foucault* (Minneapolis: University of Minnesota Press, 1992). See especially pp. 105–106, especially n12 (English translation, pp. 98–99, n12), and p. 117 (English translation, p. 110). One aspect of Deleuze's book on Foucault that we find difficult to accept is his use of the word "expression" to discuss Foucault. Nothing seems clearer in *The Archeology of Knowledge* that Foucault is not a philosopher of expression (as Merleau-Ponty is). Yet Deleuze seems to have his own reasons for speaking of expression, that is, that the "ex" of "ex-pression" suggests the outside and the becoming-other. We shall return to this question of expression in Deleuze in an upcoming essay concerning the relation of Derrida and Deleuze. Another essay that was helpful was Paul Veyne's "Foucault Revolutionizes History," trans. Catherine Porter in *Foucault and His Interlocutors*, ed. Arnold Davidson (Chicago: University of Chicago Press, 1997).

2. Jacques Derrida, "Force et signification," in *L'Écriture et la différence* (Paris: Minuit, 1967); English translation by Alan Bass as "Force and Signification," in *Writing and Difference* (Chicago: University of Chicago Press, 1978).

3. The use of this term is not consistent across the texts from the Sixties; yet its use is regular enough to justify the general way I am using it here. For example, in Foucault, see MC 353/342; then see AS 145/110 and 156/118. Deleuze uses both *défaut* and *manque*; see LS 83/66 and 88–89/70–71. Deleuze undoubtedly adopted his use of the term "manque" from Lacan; see LS 52–56/38–41. See, of course, Jacques Lacan, *Écrits* (Paris: Seuil, 1966), p. 25. See also Gilles Deleuze, "A quoi reconnait-on le structuralisme?" in François Châtelet, *La Philosophie au XXe siecle* (Paris: Marabout, Hachette, 1973), pp. 317–18; English translation by Melissa McMahon and Charles Stivale as "How Do We Recognize Structuralism?" an appendix to Charles Stivale, *The Two-fold Thought of Deleuze and Guattari* (New York: Guilford Press, 1998), p. 295.

4. Deleuze, "A quoi reconnait-on le structuralisme?" p. 300; "How Do We Recognize Structuralism?" p. 263.

5. Deleuze says that genealogy is one of the forms of "active science." See Gilles Deleuze, *Nietzsche et la philosophie* (Paris: PUF, 1962), p. 85; English translation by Hugh Tomlinson as *Nietzsche and Philosophy* (New York: Columbia University Press, 1983), p. 75. The entire chapter "Critique" is relevant to the question of what genealogy is.

6. Here I am borrowing from Jacques Derrida's excellent analysis of this term at the beginning of *Mal d'archive* (Paris: Galilée, 1995), p. 11; English translation by Eric Prenowitz as *Archive Fever* (Chicago: University of Chicago Press, 1996), p. 1.

7. In fact, Merleau-Ponty was using it as early as 1952, in his candidacy text for the Collège de France. See "Un Inédit de Maurice Merleau-Ponty," in *Revue de Métaphysique et de Morale* 67, no. 4 (1962), p. 403; English translation by Arleen B. Dallery as "An Unpublished Text by Maurice Merleau-Ponty," in *The Primacy of Perception*, ed. James Edie (Evanston: Northwestern University Press, 1964), p. 5. Merleau-Ponty also uses the word "archeology" in a 1960 note on Claude Simon. See Maurice Merleau-Ponty, *Texts and Dialogues*, ed. Hugh J. Silverman and James Barry Jr. (Atlantic Highlands, N.J.: Humanities

Press, 1991), p. 142. See also RC 51/72, and Maurice Merleau-Ponty, *Parcours deux, 1951–1961* (Lagrasse: Verdier, 2000), p. 228 and p. 228n68. My thanks to Ted Toadvine for reminding me of these other occurrences of "archeology" in Merleau-Ponty.

8. See Alwin Dienner, *Edmund Husserl* (Meisenheim am Glan: Verlag Anton Hain, 1965), p. 11n6.

9. See Liebsch, "Archeological Questioning," pp. 16–17 and n15.

10. Michel Foucault, "Monstrosities in Criticism," *diacritics* (fall 1971), p. 60.

11. Typescript page 4 of Michel Foucault, *Introduction à l'anthropologie de Kant*, Thèse Complémentaire pour le Doctorat des Lettres, Université de Paris, Faculté de Lettres et des Sciences Humaines, Directeur d'Études: M. Jean Hyppolite. The manuscript is housed at the Institut mémoires de l'édition contemporaine (IMEC), Paris. Perhaps the most important thing Foucault says here is on typescript pages 88–89: "The Anthropology is systematic. It is systematic by virtue of a structure that is that of the Critique, a structure that the Anthropology repeats. But what the Critique states as a determination in the relation between passivity and spontaneity, the Anthropology describes across a temporal dispersion, which is never complete and never begun. What the Anthropology concerns is always already there, and never entirely given. Primarily, the Anthropology devotes itself to a time, which in every way envelops it from afar and generally. The problem of origins is not foreign to it. On the contrary, the Anthropology restores to the origin its true sense. Origin does not mean to bring to light and isolate in the instant, in the first, but to rediscover a temporal web that has already begun but that is nevertheless radical. The originary is not the *really* primitive, it is the *truly* temporal. That is, the origin is where, in time, truth and freedom belong together. There would be a false anthropology. We know it only too well. It would be an anthropology that attempted to shift the structures of the *a priori* toward a beginning, toward an in fact and in principle archaism. Kant's Anthropology tells us something else: to repeat the *a priori* of the critique in the originary, that is, in a truly temporal dimension" (translation mine, Foucault's emphasis).

12. Immanuel Kant, *Critique of Judgment,* trans. Werner S. Pluhar (Indianapolis: Hackett, 1987), pp. 315n20 and 304–305.

13. *La Nature, notes, cours du Collège de France,* établi et annoté par Dominique Séglard (Paris: Seuil, 1995), pp. 45–46. Here, according to the Notes, Merleau-Ponty refers to Kant's idea of an *Urmutter,* which occurs on p. 418 of the Academie edition; the phrase "archeology of nature" occurs on p. 419 (English translation, pp. 304–305). Here Merleau-Ponty also speaks of "un autre fondement de la Nature, en circonscrivant les phénomènes autour d'un *intellectus archetypus* qui verrait le multiple de l'intérieur." We could compare this *intellectus archetypus* to what Husserl calls *Vorhabe,* and this "other foundation" to what Husserl calls "the earth" in his late fragment.

14. Ludwig Binswanger, *Le Rêve et l'existence,* trans. Jacqueline Verdeaux, Introduction and notes by Michel Foucault (Paris: Desclée de Brouwer, 1954), p. 93n1 (reference to Fink), p. 40 (confrontation between phenomenology and psychoanalysis), and p. 87n2 (reference to Husserl's "The Origin of Geometry").

15. Sigmund Freud, *Civilization and Its Discontents,* trans. James Strachey (New York: Norton, 1961), pp. 16–20. My thanks to Sara Beardsworth and Greg Horowitz for assembling these references to archeology in Freud.

16. See Paul Ricoeur, *Freud and Philosophy,* trans. Denis Savage (New Haven: Yale University Press, 1970), p. 442.

17. Sigmund Freud, "The Unconscious," in *General Psychological Theory* (New York: Simon and Schuster, 1997), p. 135.

18. Sigmund Freud, "The Aetiology of Hysteria," in *The Complete Psychological Works of Sigmund Freud*, vol. 3, trans. James Strachey (London: Hogarth Press, 1962), p. 192. Jacques Derrida discusses this comparison in *Mal d'archive*, pp. 144–46; *Archive Fever*, pp. 92–94. Here Freud is expanding on a comparison he made earlier, that the analysis of hysteria resembles "the technique of excavating a buried city." See Josef Breuer and Sigmund Freud, *Studies in Hysteria*, trans. James Strachey (New York: Basic Books, 2000), p. 139.

19. Ricoeur, *Freud and Philosophy*, p. 423.

20. This essay, "Das Problem der Phänomenologie Edmund Husserls," was later collected into Eugen Fink, *Studien zur Phänomenologie 1930–1939* (The Hague: Nijhoff, 1966). I have relied on the French translation of this volume: Eugen Fink, *De la Phénoménologie*, trans. Didier Franck (Paris: Minuit, 1974).

21. Fink, "Le Problème," p. 215; "Das Problem," p. 195.

22. Fink, "Le Problème," p. 212; "Das Problem," p. 193.

23. Fink, "Le Problème," p. 215; "Das Problem," p. 195.

24. Fink, "Le Problème," p. 215; "Das Problem," p. 195.

25. Fink, "Le Problème," p. 217; "Das Problem," pp. 197–98.

26. Fink, "Le Problème," p. 217; "Das Problem," p. 198.

27. Fink, "Le Problème," p. 218; "Das Problem," pp. 198–99.

28. Fink, "Le Problème," p. 217; "Das Problem," p. 198.

29. Fink, "Le Problème," p. 209; "Das Problem," p. 189.

30. Eugen Fink, "Was will die Phänomenologie Edmund Husserls?" in Fink, *Studien zur Phänomenologie*, p. 174. I have relied on the French translation, "Que veut la phénoménologie d'Edmund Husserl? in Fink, *De la Phénoménologie*, p. 193.

31. Fink, "Que veut," p. 194n2; "Was will," p. 175n1.

32. Fink, "Que veut," p. 195; "Was will," p. 175.

33. Fink, "Que veut," p. 196; "Was will," p. 177, my emphasis.

34. Immanuel Kant, Academie Edition, vol. 7, pp. 193, 323n; French translation by Michel Foucault as *Anthropologie du point de vue pragmatique* (Paris: Vrin, 1988), pp. 65–66, 162n4.

35. Immanuel Kant, Academie Edition, vol. 20, pp. 340–41: "Von einer philosophierenden Geschichte der Philosophie." James Bernauer's *Michel Foucault's Force of Flight* (Atlantic Highlands, N.J.: Humanities Press, 1990) cited this Kant fragment as the source of Foucault's archeology; see p. 202n113. See also Liebsch, "Archeological Questioning," for a discussion of Kant and archeology. My thanks to Hoke Robinson for translating the fragment and for finding other references in Kant to archeology. The translation of the fragment follows:

Concerning a Philosophizing History of Philosophy

All historical knowledge is empirical, and therefore it is knowledge of things as they are; not that they must necessarily be this way.—Rational knowledge represents things according to its necessity. A historical representation of philosophy thus relates how [thinkers] have philosophized up until now, and in what order. But philosophizing is a gradual development of human reason, and such a development cannot have proceeded or even begun following the empirical path, that is, through mere concepts. It must have been a need of reason (a theoretical or practical need) that first obliged reason to rise above its judgments about things and consider their grounds, up to the first grounds; at first through common reason, for example, concerning the heavenly bodies and their motions. But [thinkers] also encountered purposes [*teloi*]: And, finally, as they noted that they find rational grounds concerning all things, they began to list our rational concepts (or those of the understanding), but first to articulate thinking in general into its parts, without object. The former [i.e., the listing of rational and intellectual concepts] was accomplished by Aristotle; the latter [the articulation of thinking] even earlier by the logicians.

A philosophical history of philosophy is itself not possible historically or empirically, but only rationally, that is, *a priori* possible. For whether or not it sets up facts [*Facta*] of reason right away, it does not borrow them from historiography, but rather draws them from the nature of human reason as philosophical archeology. What [kind of crazy things] were the people's thinkers capable of conjuring up concerning the origin, the goal and the end of things in the world? Was it the purposive element in the world, or only the chain of causes and effects, or was it the purpose of humanity itself with which they began?

36. See above, n34.

37. Cf. Foucault's discussion of natural history in *Les Mots et les choses* (Paris: Gallimard, 1966), pp. 140–44; English translation as *The Order of Things*, no translator given (New York: Random House, 1970), pp. 128–32. Here Foucault stresses that history changes its sense when it becomes natural.

38. In fact, the Course Notes on "The Origin of Geometry" could be seen as a sort of continuation of Merleau-Ponty's famous later essay on Husserl, "The Philosopher and His Shadow": Maurice Merleau-Ponty, "Le Philosophe et son ombre," in *Signes* (Paris: Gallimard, 1960], pp. 201–28; English translation by Richard C. McCleary as "The Philosopher and His Shadow," in *Signs* (Evanston: Northwestern University Press, 1964), pp. 159–81. "The Philosopher and His Shadow" begins in effect with a quote from "The Origin of Geometry": "Tradition is the forgetfulness of origins" (S 201/159). Also, in "The Philosopher and His Shadow," Merleau-Ponty quotes the same passage from Heidegger's *Der Satz vom Grund* (*Signes*, p. 202; *Signs*, p. 160), that the greater the work accomplished by a thinker the greater the un-thought; see p. 14 of the Notes.

39. See also "Un Inédit de Maurice Merleau-Ponty," p. 403; "An Unpublished Text," in *The Primacy of Perception*, p. 5.

40. See Merleau-Ponty's *La Nature*, pp. 110–13.

41. This quote is an allusion to "Appendix IX" of *The Crisis:* "Denial of Scientific Philosophy. Necessity of Reflection. The Reflection [Must Be] Historical. How Is History Required?" At the end of this fragment Husserl speaks of a "*Dichtung* of the history of philosophy" (p. 394 of the English translation).

42. For the "unthought," see Michel Foucault, *L'Ordre du discours* (Paris: Gallimard, 1971), pp. 54–55; English translation by A. M. Sheridan Smith as "The Discourse on Language," an appendix to *The Archeology of Knowledge* (New York: Pantheon, 1972), p. 229.

43. That the historical a priori are conditions of the existence of discourse distinguishes Foucault's archeology from structuralism in the popular sense.

44. If we look at Foucault's essay "Nietzsche, Genealogy, History," we can see that, according to Foucault, genealogy is concerned with actual history (*wirkliche Geschichte*): "Nietzsche, la généalogie, l'histoire," in *Homage à Jean Hyppolite* (Paris: Presses Universitaires de France, 1971), pp. 145–72; English translation by Donald F. Bouchard and Sherry

Simon as "Nietzsche, Genealogy, History," in *Language, Counter-memory, Practice,* ed. Donald F. Bouchard (Ithaca: Cornell University Press, 1977), pp. 139–64.

45. This is why Dreyfus and Rabinow subtitle their chapter on *The Archeology of Knowledge* as "A Phenomenology to End All Phenomenology." See Hubert L. Dreyfus and Paul Rabinow, *Michel Foucault: Beyond Structuralism and Hermeneutics* (Chicago: University of Chicago Press, 1983).

46. Cf. Deleuze, *Foucault,* p. 105; *Foucault,* p. 98.

47. Cf. Michel Foucault, *La Naissance de la clinique* (Paris: PUF, 1063), p. xii; English translation by A. M. Sheridan Smith as *The Birth of the Clinic* (New York: Vintage, 1973), p. xvi.

48. See also Maurice Merleau-Ponty, *L'Œil et l'esprit* (Paris: Gallimard, 1964), p. 92; English translation by Michael B. Smith as "Eye and Mind," in *The Merleau-Ponty Aesthetics Reader,* ed. Galen Johnson (Evanston: Northwestern University Press, 1993), p. 149.

49. When my right touches my left hand, I can never grasp with my right hand the work of my left hand as it is touching. As soon as I try to do grasp my left hand touching, it becomes the "touched." In other words, if I try to grasp the subjective or interior side of my left hand, it becomes the object of my grasp and loses its subjectivity. Of course, this relation is reversible. I can start from my left hand and try to grasp my right in the act of touching, but the result is the same: the right hand becomes the touched and is no longer the touching.

50. See also Maurice Merleau-Ponty, "Notes de lecture et commentaires sur *Théorie du champ de la conscience* de Aron Gurwitsch," in *Revue de Métaphysique et de Morale* 101, no. 3 (1997), p. 329, where Merleau-Ponty also defines essence as "charnière."

51. See Chapter 1 above, ""If Theory Is Gray, Green Is the Golden Tree of Life."

52. This word "fraternité" comes from Merleau-Ponty's "Indirect Language and the Voices of Silence," in *Signes* (Paris: Gallimard, 1960), p. 77; English translation by Richard C. McCleary as *Signs* (Evanston: Northwestern University Press, 1964), p. 62. But the word is interesting here in the context of Foucault's idea of the heteroclite since it suggests friendship. In Foucault's *Le Souci de soi,* it is clear that the friendship relation does not take place in the heterosexual relation between a man and a woman (marriage), but rather it takes place only in the homosexual relation between a man and a boy, and this relation itself takes place only in the heteroclite.

53. Michel Foucault, *Raymond Roussel* (Paris: Gallimard, 1963), pp. 28–29; English translation by Charles Ruas as *Death and the Labyrinth: The World of Raymond Roussel* (Berkeley: University of California Press, 1986), p. 19.

3. Eliminating Some Confusion

1. As is well known, over the last two decades Derrida has developed an ethical discourse, for example, his discourse on law. And Merleau-Ponty promised an ethical discourse on the basis of his metaphysics, the metaphysics for which *The Visible and the Invisible* was to be the start; see Merleau-Ponty, "Un Inédit de Maurice Merleau-Ponty," in *Revue de Métaphysique et de Morale* 67, no. 4 (1962), p. 409; English translation by Arleen B. Dallery as "An Unpublished Text by Maurice Merleau-Ponty: A Prospectus of His Work," in *The Primacy of Perception,* ed. James Edie (Evanston: Northwestern University Press, 1964), p. 11. See below, Chapter 4.

2. Patrick Burke, "Listening at the Abyss," in *Ontology and Alterity in Merleau-Ponty,*

ed. Galen A. Johnson and Michael B. Smith (Evanston: Northwestern University Press, 1990), pp. 81–97.

3. Cf. RC 162/188, where Merleau-Ponty says that "The true cannot be defined outside of the *possibility* of the false" (my emphasis). This essay does not take into account the recent publication of Merleau-Ponty's Course Notes on "The Origin of Geometry" (in HL; see below, Chapter 4). Neither of the Merleau-Ponty–Derrida essays (neither Chapter 3 nor Chapter 4) takes into account Derrida's recent *Le Toucher—Jean-Luc Nancy* (Paris: Galilée, 2000), in which Derrida examines corporeality in Merleau-Ponty. We intend to devote an essay to *Le Toucher* at a later date.

4. Derrida's starting point in structuralism, in the precomprehension of the meaning of a word, his privilege of the question "What is?" can be seen as early as the 1953–54 *Le Problème de la genèse dans la philosophie de Husserl* (Paris: Presses Universitaires de France, 1990): "If we do not begin with a description of a priori essences, never will we be able to claim any rigor. In its most originary upsurge, existence itself will not be able to appear to philosophic contemplation. Also, every reproach addressed to this Husserlian essentialism in the name of an empirical or existential originality or in the name of some prior genetic moment, in order to make sense, will have to suppose an already constituted eidetics. This postulate of all philosophy has opened, in all of its depth, the primary phenomenological procedure. The absolute beginning of philosophy must be essentialist. This law, insofar as it is 'methodological,' insofar as it not founded on the actual movement of the genesis constituting and prior to the essences and where it rules all philosophic elucidation, makes of formalism or of idealism or, if you will, of eideticism, the inaugural moment of all real or possible philosophy. Every reflection must begin by assuming this idealism, without which it will always remain in confusion and in inauthenticity" (225–26, my translation). It can be seen as recently as *Given Time: 1. Counterfeit Money,* trans. Peggy Kamuf (Chicago: University of Chicago Press, 1992): "For the gift to be possible, for there to be gift event, according to our common language and logic, it seems that this compound structure is indispensable. Notice that in order to say this, I must already suppose a certain precomprehension of what gift means. I suppose that I know and that you know what 'to give,' 'gift,' 'donor,' 'donee' mean in our common language. As well as 'to want,' 'to desire,' 'to intend.' This is an unsigned but effective contract between us, indispensable to what is going on here" (11). Moreover, "it is a matter of . . . responding faithfully but also as rigorously as possible both to the injunction or the order of the gift ('give') as well as to the injunction or the order of meaning (presence, science, knowledge): Know still what giving wants to say, know how to give" (30).

5. For more on Derrida's interpretation of Husserl see Leonard Lawlor, *Derrida and Husserl: The Basic Problem of Phenomenology* (Bloomington: Indiana University Press, 2002).

6. And this non-ontic duplicity is why we will be able to say that Derrida's concept of contamination is a mediated unity as opposed to Deleuze's immediate duality. See below, Chapter 8.

7. Again, this milieu will actually make Derrida's philosophy be closer to Merleau-Ponty (see below, Chapter 4), and more distant from that of Deleuze. See below, Chapter 8.

8. In a note to "Violence and Metaphysics," Derrida says, "Pure difference is not absolutely different (from nondifference). Hegel's critique of the concept of pure difference is for us here, doubtless, the most uncircumventable theme. Hegel thought absolute difference and showed that can be pure only by being impure" (ED 227n1/320n91).

9. See below, Chapter 8, for more on the experience of the voice in Derrida and in Deleuze.

10. This entire discussion of the circle must lead us to the figure of the chiasm. See above, Chapter 2, and below, Chapter 8.

11. Or perhaps even into something like *Otherwise than Being or Beyond Essence.*

4. The Legacy of Husserl's "The Origin of Geometry"

1. It is this thematic and terminological overlap that has allowed me to construct, in schematic form, the system of the great French philosophy of the Sixties.

2. Jacques Derrida, *Mémoires d'aveugle* (Paris: Editions de la Réunion des Musées Nationaux, 1990), p. 56; English translation by Pascale-Anne Brault and Michael Naas as *Memoirs of the Blind* (Chicago: University of Chicago Press, 1993), pp. 51–52, Derrida's emphasis.

3. Edmund Husserl, *Die Krisis der europaischen Wissenschaften und die transzendentale Phänomenologie,* Beilage III, heraugegeben von Walter Biemel (The Hague: Nijhoff, 1962), pp. 365–86; English translation as "The Origin of Geometry," in *The Crisis of European Sciences and Transcendental Phenomenology* (Evanston: Northwestern University Press, 1970), pp. 353–78. The abbreviation used is HUS with reference first to the original German, then to the English translation.

4. For the importance of the experience of the other in Merleau-Ponty, see Renaud Barbaras, *De l'être du phénomène: l'ontologie de Merleau-Ponty* (Grenoble: Millon, 1991); English translation by Theodore Toadvine and Leonard Lawlor forthcoming as *The Being of the Phenomenon: Merleau-Ponty's Ontology* (Indiana University Press). What is most remarkable about Derrida's Introduction, when one compares it to his earlier 1953–54 *Mémoire* called *The Problem of Genesis in Husserl's Philosophy,* is that the Introduction frequently discusses intersubjectivity (LOG 83n1/86n90; cf. LOG 129n2/121n134, 46/57–58, 49–50/60–61). This interest in the experience of intersubjectivity will only intensify for Derrida especially after his 1964 encounter with Levinas in "Violence and Metaphysics" (in *Writing and Difference*), and, as a result of this encounter, the interest dominates *Voice and Phenomenon*. See Leonard Lawlor, *Derrida and Husserl: The Basic Problem of Phenomenology* (Bloomington: Indiana University Press, 2002).

5. See Jacques Derrida, *Spectres de Marx* (Paris: Galilée, 1993), p. 215n2; English translation by Peggy Kamuf as *Specters of Marx* (New York: Routledge, 1994), p. 135n6. Again see Leonard Lawlor, *Derrida and Husserl,* especially Chapter 8, for more on *Specters of Marx.*

6. Cf. Maurice Merleau-Ponty, *L'Œil et l'esprit* (Paris: Gallimard, 1964), p. 22, where Merleau-Ponty speaks of "un visible à deuxième puissance"; English translation by Michael B. Smith as "Eye and Mind," in *The Merleau-Ponty Aesthetics Reader,* ed. Galen A. Johnson (Evanston: Northwestern University Press, 1993), p. 126.

7. See Paola Marrati-Guénoun's excellent *La Trace et le genèse: Derrida lecture de Husserl et Heidegger* (Dordrecht: Kluwer, 1997), p. 48, for a very illuminating discussion of this difficult concept in the early Derrida; see also my review of her book in *Husserl Studies* 16, no. 1 (1999), pp. 77–81.

8. Here it would be necessary to take into account Merleau-Ponty's comments on the "museum" as the "historicity of death" in "Indirect Language and the Voices of Silence." See above, Introduction and Chapters 2 and 3. It is not possible to find this Merleau-Pontean "fallen" kind of historicity in Derrida because of the concept of supplementarity.

9. Martin Heidegger, "Was ist Metaphysik?" in *Wegmarken* (Frankfurt: Klostermann, 1978), pp. 105, 115–16; English translation by David F. Krell as "What Is Metaphysics?" in *Martin Heidegger: Basic Writings* (New York: HarperCollins, 1993), pp. 95, 105.

10. Here Merleau-Ponty alludes to Heidegger discussion of the *Etwas* in *Der Satz vom Grund*.

11. This kind of negativity defines what above (Chapter 2) we called Merleau-Ponty's negativism.

12. Here we rejoin the thesis of Chapter 3.

13. See also Maurice Merleau-Ponty, *La Prose du monde* (Paris: Gallimard, 1969), p. 17; English translation by John O'Neill as *The Prose of the World* (Evanston: Northwestern University Press, 1973), p. 10.

14. This "jointure" would be another place into which one could insert a difference between Derrida and Merleau-Ponty. For Derrida, the two necessities form not a jointure (a *Fuge*, as Heidegger would say), but a disjointure or disjunction. Thus the chiasm in Derrida is always defined by dissymmetry.

15. It is at this point—at the point of ghostly presence—that one could make the transition to what Merleau-Ponty, in the Notes, calls "vertical being" (HL BN 33) and "the paradox of the horizon" (HL BN 22).

16. See below, Chapter 5.

17. Jacques Derrida, *De l'esprit* (Paris: Galilée, 1987), pp. 36, 59, 87; English translation by Geoffrey Bennington and Rachel Bowlby as *Of Spirit* (Chicago: University of Chicago, 1989), pp. 17, 35, 56.

18. Maurice Merleau-Ponty, "Un Inédit de Maurice Merleau-Ponty," in *Revue de Métaphysique et de Morale* 67, no. 4 (1962), p. 409; English translation by Arleen B. Dallery as "An Unpublished Text by Maurice Merleau-Ponty: A Prospectus of His Work," in *The Primacy of Perception,* ed. James Edie (Evanston: Northwestern University Press, 1964), p. 11.

5. The End of Phenomenology

1. Jean Greisch, "Reading Heidegger in the Third Generation," unpublished manuscript, pp. 6–7.

2. See, for example, Natalie Depraz, *Transcendence et incarnation* (Paris: Vrin, 1995).

3. Gilles Deleuze, *Empirisme et subjectivité* (Paris: Presses Universitaires de France, 1988 [1953]), p. 92; English translation by Constantin V. Boundas as *Empiricism and Subjectivity* (New York: Columbia University Press, 1991), p. 87.

4. If there is a shortcoming to Michael Hardt's *Gilles Deleuze: An Apprenticeship in Philosophy* (Minneapolis: University of Minnesota Press, 1993), it is his failure to see Heidegger's overwhelming influence on Deleuze; for example, Hardt says, "Even without close examination, the most general facts of Deleuze's biography, particularly the things he did not do, indicate his difference from nearly all other major French philosophical voices to emerge from his generation. He was never a member of the French Communist Party, he did not attend the exclusive École Normal Supérieure, and he was never fascinated by the work of Martin Heidegger" (p. 125n6).

5. Fichte formulates this principle in his *The Science of Knowledge* (trans. Peter Heath and John Lachs [New York: Cambridge University Press, 1982 (1794)]), where he says, "By virtue of its mere notion, the ground falls outside of what it grounds; both ground and grounded are, as such, opposed and yet linked to each other, so that the former explains the latter" (p. 8). For other formulations of this principle by Deleuze see BER 100/97–98,

and SPE 39/48. Cf. also Rodolphe Gasché's analysis of Werner Flach's "pure heterology" in *The Tain of the Mirror* (Cambridge, Mass.: Harvard University Press, 1986): "Flach is compelled to follow such a direction because he recognizes that Hegel's determination of the ground of reflection—of the originary synthetic unity—is not accompanied by a determination of that ground as ground. Instead of determining that ground as radically heterogeneous to what, as ground, it is supposed to make possible, Hegel's concept of the reflection of reflection understands ground in the sense of homogeneity, that is, in the sense of what the ground is to account for. Yet if a ground is to be an absolute ground, it must be heterogeneous" (p. 89).

6. Ludwig Landgrebe has also characterized Husserl's phenomenology as a "transcendental empiricism"; see Landgrebe, "The Phenomenological Concept of Experience," in *Philosophy and Phenomenological Research* 34 (1973–74), pp. 1–13.

7. Michel Foucault, "Theatrum Philosophicum," in *Language, Counter-memory, Practice,* ed. Donald F. Bouchard, trans. Donald F. Bouchard and Sherry Simon (Ithaca: Cornell University Press, 1977), p. 170.

8. See Gilles Deleuze and Claire Parnet, *Dialogues* (Paris: Flammarion, 1977), pp. 18–19; English translation by Hugh Tomlinson and Barabara Habberjam (New York: Columbia University Press, 1987), p. 12; see also Deleuze's review of Hyppolite's *Logique et existence* in *Revue Philosophique de la France et l'Étranger* 144 (1954), pp. 457–60; the English translation is an appendix to *Logic and Existence,* trans. Leonard Lawlor and Amit Sen (Albany: SUNY Press, 1997).

9. Cf. also LS 126n3/344n3, where Deleuze says that Gilbert Simondon's *L'Individu et sa genèse physico-biologique* (Paris: Presses Universitaires de France, 1964) provides "a new conception of the transcendental." Simondon's book, by the way, is dedicated to Merleau-Ponty.

10. Deleuze here also stresses Sartre's "invocation of Spinoza."

11. Jean-Paul Sartre, *The Transcendence of the Ego* (New York: Noonday Press, 1957 [1936]).

12. According to Sartre, the principle for the unity of an object identified by an indefinite number of consciousnesses lies in the object itself. See Sartre, *The Transcendence of the Ego,* p. 38.

13. According to Sartre, consciousness is self-unifying and self-individuating; see Sartre, *The Transcendence of the Ego,* pp. 38–39.

14. Sartre says, "All the results of phenomenology begin to crumble if the *I* is not, by the same title as the world, a relative existent: that is to says, an object *for* consciousness" (Sartre, *The Transcendence of the Ego,* p. 42, Sartre's emphasis).

15. Sartre, *The Transcendence of the Ego,* pp. 36–37.

16. See Jean Hyppolite's comments on Fr. Van Breda's "La Réduction phénoménologique," in *Husserl: cahiers du Royaumont* (p. 323) where he speaks of a "subjectless transcendental field."

17. Gilles Deleuze and Félix Guattari, *Mille plateaus* (Paris: Minuit, 1980), pp. 356–57; English translation by Brian Massumi as *A Thousand Plateaus* (Minneapolis: University of Minnesota Press, 1987), pp. 407–408; see also p. 367.

18. Edmund Husserl, *Ideas Pertaining to a Pure Phenomenology and to a Phenomenological Philosophy,* book I, trans. F. Kersten (The Hague: Nijhoff, 1982).

19. The notion of cause in Deleuze is based on his reading of the Stoics and cannot be associated with the modern notion of causality. Deleuze says, "[The Stoics] are in the process of bringing about, first, an entirely new cleavage of the causal relation. They dis-

member this relation, even at the risk of recreating a unity on each side. They refer causes to causes and place a bond of causes between them (destiny). They refer effects to effects and pose certain bonds of effects between them. But these two operations are not accomplished in the same manner. Incorporeal effects are never themselves causes in relation to each other; rather, they are only 'quasi-causes' following laws which perhaps express in each case the relative unity or mixture of bodies on which they depend for their real causes" (LS 15/6).

20. Cf. Constantin Boundas's excellent article "Deleuze: Serialization and Concept Formation," in *Gilles Deleuze and the Theater of Philosophy*, ed. Constantin Boundas and Dorothea Olkowski (New York: Routledge, 1994), pp. 99–115, but especially pp. 103–106. Cf. also Dorothea Olkowski-Laetz, "Merleau-Ponty: The Demand for Mystery in Language," in *Philosophy Today* 31 (winter 1987), pp. 353–58.

21. Importantly, according to Deleuze, because a structure includes two distributions of singularities, it is unnecessary to oppose structure and event (or structure and genesis) (LS 88/71; DR 237–38/183); he says, "the structure includes a record of ideal *events*, that is, an entire *history* internal to it" (LS 66/50, Deleuze's emphasis).

22. Deleuze also defines the paradoxical element as that toward which the two heterogeneous series converge, while belonging to neither series; nevertheless, the paradoxical element articulates or differentiates the two series, reflects the one into the other, makes them communicate, coexist, and resonate (LS 66/51).

23. For more on this concept of repetition, see below, Chapter 8.

24. Gilles Deleuze, *Proust et les signes* (Paris: PUF, 1970), pp. 69–74, 168; English translation by Richard Howard as *Proust and Signs* (New York: Braziller, 1972), pp. 55–60, 136.

25. What is also crucial is that a logic of sense not treat sense as a proposition and therefore as a predicate. We do not express the sense of a perception in the form of "The tree is green," but rather in the form of "The tree greens." A sense, for Deleuze, is always expressed in the infinitive form of the verb; the infinitive form allows the sense to become, to be an event; it allows it to be free and nomadic (cf. LS 130–31/107, 33/21).

26. The lack of resemblance between expression and expressed entirely distinguishes Deleuze's notion of expression from that of Husserl found in paragraph #124 (LS 119–20/97–98, 147–48/122–23).

27. Cf. PHP 249/215, 275/238, 400/348, 511–13/448–50. Cf. also Rudolf Bernet's excellent "The Subject in Nature: Reflection on Merleau-Ponty's *The Phenomenology of Perception*," in *Merleau-Ponty in Contemporary Perspective* (The Hague: Kluwer, 1993), p. 57, where Bernet says, "When *Phenomenology of Perception* talks about the 'anonymous' (215, 238) character of a natural life governed by an indeterminate and general 'They' (*On*) (215, 240), these terms borrowed from Husserl and Heidegger have a new meaning: prepersonal life is neither the life of a transcendental subject that accomplishes its activity of constitution of objects without being conscious of this activity, nor the inauthentic existence of a *Dasein* that flees from its personal responsibility by identifying with a silent majority." He continues on p. 58: "The 'They' of prepersonal life is not a personal subject that melts into the anonymity of the masses, but is a subject interwoven with the natural world because it lives only through its body." This remarkable essay ends by saying, "If *Phenomenology of Perception* reveals a common flesh of the world, things and body, it still tries to understand this within the horizon of bodily subjectivity. This is why the philosophy of nature leads to a naturalization of the perceiving subject that, in its turn, goes hand in hand with a subjectivization of nature. However, this philosophy of nature, surmounting the opposition between nature and subject, and providing a genealogy of the subject,

also gives birth to a new conception of the subject as well as of nature. Arising out of things within a common world and affirming its identity through its difference from things, the human subject is at once itself and another, one and manifold, present and absent, visible and invisible. Within the universal intersubjectivity or 'intercorporeity' of the world, the subject is that singularity by which the world is articulated as an open system of diacritical differences" (p. 67).

28. Cf. Deleuze's use of the phrase "stylistic Idea," DR 34–35/22.

29. For more on the use of this phrase in twentieth-century French philosophy, see Robert Bernasconi, "The Trace of Levinas in Derrida," in *Derrida and Différance*, ed. David Wood and Robert Bernasconi (Evanston: Northwestern University Press, 1988), pp. 13–29.

30. M. C. Dillon, "The Unconscious: Language and World," in *Merleau-Ponty in Contemporary Perspective*, ed. P. Burke and J. Van der Veken (The Hague: Kluwer, 1993), p. 72.

31. Cf. Renaud Barbaras, *De l'être du phénomène* (Grenoble: Millon, 1991), p. 122n21; Claude Lefort, *Sur une colonne absente* (Paris: Gallimard, 1978), pp. 26–27, 27n12. See also Maurice Merleau-Ponty, *In Praise of Philosophy and Other Essays*, trans. John Wild, James Edie, and John O'Neill (Evanston: Northwestern University Press, 1970), pp. 9–33, especially p. 23; also S 229–41/182–91; VI 165/124, 170/128. See also Jean Hyppolite, "Aspects divers de la mémoire chez Bergson," in *Figures de la pensée philosophique*, vol. I, pp. 468–88, especially p. 482.

32. Henri Bergson, *Matter and Memory*, trans. Nancy Margaret Paul and W. Scott Palmer (London: George Allen and Unwin, 1911), p. 179; this translation has been reissued by Zone Books (New York), 1988, p. 139.

33. Bergson, *Matter and Memory*, p. 179 (Zone Books, p. 139).

34. Cf. Barbaras, *De l'être du phénomène*, pp. 80–88.

35. Merleau-Ponty also uses the word "realization." Deleuze distinguishes virtuality from possibility because possibility is separate from being; therefore, possibility's companion term is "realization." Virtuality is not separate from being, and its companion term is "actualization." In *The Phenomenology of Perception*, Merleau-Ponty, however, also uses the word "virtual" (cf. PHP 126/109). It is unclear whether Merleau-Ponty is aware of such fine distinctions: possibility–realization, virtuality–actualization.

36. Cf. Yves Thierry, *Du corps parlant* (Brussels: Editions Ousia, 1987), p. 33. Cf. also Barbaras, *De l'être du phénomène*, pp. 64–65. For this discussion of expression I have also consulted Jean-Pierre Charcosset, *Approches phénoménologiques* (Paris: Hachette, 1981); Maurice Rainville, *L'Expérience et l'expression* (Montreal: Bellarmin, 1988); M. C. Dillon, *Merleau-Ponty's Ontology* (Bloomington: Indiana University Press, 1988), pp. 186–223.

37. Cf. Thierry, *Du corps parlant*, p. 33.

38. Quoted in Deleuze, LS 80/63, and in Derrida, DIS 156/175.

39. Here, in a famous working note from July 1959, Merleau-Ponty makes the famous comment that "The problems posed in *The Phenomenology of Perception* are insoluble because I start there from the 'consciousness'-'object' distinction." In a working note from February 1959, Merleau-Ponty says, "I must show that what one might consider to be 'psychology' (*Phenomenology of Perception*) is in fact ontology" (VI 230/176).

40. This piece was originally published as the preface to *Les Philosophes célèbres*, ed. Maurice Merleau-Ponty (Paris: Mazenod, 1956). Deleuze wrote the essay on Bergson for this volume, and he cites this passage in SPE 28/22.

41. Here Deleuze says, "No longer content with handing over immanence to transcendence, we want to discharge it, reproduce it, and fabricate it itself. In fact this is not

difficult—all that is necessary *is for movement to be stopped.* Transcendence enters as soon as movement of the infinite is stopped."

42. Maurice Merleau-Ponty, "Philosophy and Non-philosophy since Hegel," trans. Hugh J. Silverman, in *Philosophy and Non-philosophy since Merleau-Ponty* (New York: Routledge, 1989), p. 52; see also translator's note 86.

43. Maurice Merleau-Ponty, "An Unpublished Text by Maurice Merleau-Ponty," trans. Arleen B. Dallery, in *The Primacy of Perception,* ed. James M. Edie (Evanston: Northwestern University Press, 1964), p. 11.

44. No one has come closer to resolving the issue of expressionism in Merleau-Ponty than Renaud Barbaras. See his "Perception and Movement: The End of the Metaphysical Approach," in *Chiasms,* ed. Fred Evans and Leonard Lawlor (Albany: SUNY Press, 2000).

6. The End of Ontology

1. See Appendix 1 for an explication of this first sentence.

2. Edmund Husserl, *Ideen zu einer reinen Phänomenologie und phänomenologischen Philosophie,* I. Buch (The Hague: Nijhoff, 1976), paragraph 58; English translation by Fred Kersten as *Ideas Pertaining to a Pure Phenomenology and a Phenomenological Philosophy,* First Book (The Hague: Nijhoff, 1983), paragraph 58.

3. Martin Heidegger, *Sein und Zeit* (Tübingen: Niemeyer, 1979); English translation by John Macquarrie and Edward Robinson as *Being and Time* (New York: Harper and Row, 1962).

4. Martin Heidegger, "Was ist Metaphysik?" in *Wegmarken* (Frankfurt: Klostermann, 1978), p. 113; English translation by David F. Krell as "What Is Metaphysics?" in *Martin Heidegger: Basic Writings* (New York: HarperCollins, 1983), p. 105.

5. Cf. Jacques Derrida, *De l'esprit* (Paris: Galilée, 1987), pp. 80–89; English translation by Geoffrey Bennington and Rachel Bowlby as *Of Spirit* (Chicago: University of Chicago Press, 1989), pp. 50–57.

6. Cf. Michael Hardt, *Gilles Deleuze: An Apprenticeship in Philosophy* (Minneapolis: University of Minnesota Press, 1993), p. 125n6, where Hardt says that Deleuze was "never fascinated by Heidegger."

7. See Jacques Derrida, "Foi et savoir," in *La Religion* (Paris: Seuil, 1996), pp. 9–86. See also Dominque Janicaud, *Le Tournant théologique de la phénoménologie française* (Combas: L'Éclat, 1991).

8. Deleuze establishes five theses for Heidegger's ontological difference: (1) "The *not* expresses not the negative but the difference between Being and being." (2) "This difference is not 'between' in the ordinary sense of the word. It is the Fold, *Zwiefalt.*" (3) "Ontological difference corresponds to question." (4) "Difference is not an object of representation. As the element of metaphysics, representation subordinates difference to identity, if only in relating it to a third term as the center of comparison *between* two supposedly different terms (Being and being)." (5) "Difference cannot, therefore, be subordinated to the identical or the equal but must be thought as the same, in the same" (DR 90–91/64–65).

9. Martin Heidegger, "Die ewige Wiederkehr des Gleichens," in *Nietzsche,* vol. I (Pfullingen: Neske, 1961), pp. 462–72; English translation by David F. Krell as *The Eternal Recurrence of the Same* (New York: Harper and Row, 1984), pp. 198–208.

10. Heidegger, *Nietzsche,* vol. I, pp. 231–42; translated by David F. Kress in *Nietzsche,* vol. I (New York: Harper and Row, 1987), pp. 200–210.

11. Cf. Gilles Deleuze, "La Conception de la différence chez Bergson," in *Les Études*

bergsoniennes 4 (1956), p. 111; English translation by Melissa McMahon as "Bergson's Conception of Difference," in *The New Bergson,* ed. John Mullarkey (Manchester: Manchester University Press, 1999).

12. What is conserved, however, from Platonism is the simulacrum which is the power of the false, the power to destroy Platonism, which, according to Deleuze, subordinates difference in itself to the same. For more on Platonism see Chapter 8.

13. See also Renaud Barbaras, *De l'être du phénomène: l'ontologie de Merleau-Ponty* (Grenoble: Millon, 1991), pp. 364–65.

14. Direct ontology would be an attempt to go up to being without going through the mediations of beings, without starting in the domains of nature or culture. Having bypassed beings, the direct ontologist would apparently have to forego the use of language, which predominantly refers to beings. So, Merleau-Ponty says, "If we call philosophy the investigation of Being . . . is not philosophy quickly led up to silence—that very silence which from time to time breaks into Heidegger's essays? But does not this silence come from the fact that Heidegger has always sought a direct expression of the fundamental at the very moment during which he was in the process of showing that such a direct expression is impossible" (RC 156/179–80). This comment sounds, of course, as though Merleau-Ponty is—this is a comment from Claude Lefort—"firm in his criticism of direct ontology" (NC 9). But we must be careful here. Merleau-Ponty is describing Heidegger's procedure as a contradiction. To seek a direct expression of Being at the very moment of showing its impossibility is equivalent to saying that what cannot be vocalized is vocalized. If this equivalence is true, then we must conclude that what Heidegger is doing is precisely what Merleau-Ponty himself calls indirect language. So, instead of Merleau-Ponty "being firm in his criticism" of Heidegger's ontology, he is actually saying that Heidegger's essays are voices of silence. There is textual evidence to support this claim if one examines the *Notes de cours, 1959–1961.* There, speaking of the malaise that one finds in Heidegger's writings, Merleau-Ponty says, "[Heidegger] seeks a direct expression of being about which moreover he shows that it is not susceptible to direct expression." But, he continues, "One has to attempt an indirect expression, i.e., to make being be seen across the *Winke* of life, of science, etc. Thus, philosophy is perhaps possible as 'das rechte Schweigen' mentioned in *The Letter on Humanism*" (NC 148). According to this comment, Heidegger's ontology is a sign in the exact sense that Merleau-Ponty gives this word in the book of the same name; it is a sign of the "right silence." Therefore, Heidegger's ontology in fact functions as the very model for the "indirect ontology" found in *The Visible and the Invisible*. But, as we shall see, it is not Heidegger's but Husserl's influence that is decisive for Merleau-Ponty.

15. In regard to the necessary indirectness of ontology, Merleau-Ponty seems to be taking very seriously the paradoxes that Fink describes at the end of his landmark 1933 essay "The Phenomenological Philosophy of Edmund Husserl and Contemporary Criticism." See Eugen Fink, "Die Phänomenologische Philosophie E. Husserl in der Gegenwärtigen Kritik," originally published in *Kantstudien* 38, nos. 3/4 (Berlin, 1933), and collected in Fink, *Studien zur Phänomenologie 1930–1939* (The Hague: Nijhoff, 1966); English translation as "The Phenomenological Philosophy of Edmund Husserl and Contemporary Criticism," in *The Phenomenology of Husserl,* ed. and trans. R. O. Elveton (Chicago: Quadrangle Books, 1970), pp. 73–147.

16. Cf. Renaud Barbaras, *Le Tournant de l'expérience* (Paris: Vrin, 1998).

17. Cf. Patrick Burke, "Listening at the Abyss," in *Ontology and Alterity in Merleau-*

Ponty, ed. Galen A. Johnson and Michael B. Smith (Evanston: Northwestern University Press, 1990), pp. 81–97, especially pp. 83 and 93–94.

18. Heidegger, *Nietzsche,* vol. I, pp. 318–25; Heidegger, *Nietzsche,* vol. II, pp. 62–69. It is unlikely, of course, that Merleau-Ponty possessed an advance copy of Heidegger's lectures as early as February 1959, but he seems to be aware of what is contained in them prior to their publication in 1961; see *Notes de cours 1959–1961,* p. 165, where in 1960 Merleau-Ponty alludes to the forthcoming publication of the lectures.

19. In *The Phenomenology of Spirit,* paragraph 658, Hegel, of course, appropriates this concept from Goethe. Cf. Jean Hyppolite's discussion of it in *Genèse et structure de la Phénoménologie de l'esprit* (Paris: Aubier, 1946); English translation by Samuel Cherniak and John Heckman as *Genesis and Structure of Hegel's Phenomenology of Spirit* (Evanston: Northwestern University Press, 1974), pp. 501, 508; also see LE 22–23/18–19.

20. On silence in Deleuze, see below, Chapter 8.

21. Cf. Barbaras, *De l'être du phénomène,* p. 166.

22. Eugen Fink, *VI, Cartesianische Meditation,* Teil 1 (The Hague: Kluwer, 1988); English translation by Ronald Bruzina as *Sixth Cartesian Meditation* (Bloomington: Indiana University Press, 1995), paragraphs 4, 8, and 10.

23. Cf. Jacques Derrida, *Mémoires d'aveugle* (Paris: Editions de la Réunion des Musées Nationaux, 1990), pp. 56–58; English translation by Pascale-Anne Brault and Michael Naas as *Memoirs of the Blind* (Chicago: University of Chicago Press, 1993), pp. 52–53.

24. See also Mauro Carbone, "The Thinking of the Sensible," in *Chiasms: Merleau-Ponty's Notion of the Flesh,* ed. Fred Evans and Leonard Lawlor (Albany: SUNY Press, 2000).

25. Edmund Husserl, *Cartesianische Meditationen* (Hamburg: Meiner, 1995); English translation by Dorian Cairns as *Cartesian Meditations* (The Hague: Nijhoff, 1977).

26. See also Bernhard Waldenfels's "The Paradox of Expression," in *Chiasms.*

27. See *Cartesian Meditations,* paragraph 50. Cf. also Derrida, ED 181/123. See also Bernhard Waldenfels, "Experience of the Alien in Husserl's Phenomenology," trans. Anthony Steinbock, in *Research in Phenomenology* 20 (1990), pp. 19–31; see also Waldenfels's four-volume study of *Fremderfahrung: Studien zur Phänomenologie des Fremden.* Vol. 1: *Topographie des Fremden* (Frankfurt: Suhrkamp, 1997); *Studien zur Phänomenologie des Fremden.* Vol. 2: *Grenzen des Normalisierung* (Frankfurt: Suhrkamp, 1998); *Studien zur Phänomenologie des Fremden.* Vol. 3: *Sinneschewellen* (Frankfurt: Suhrkamp, 1999); *Studien zur Phänomenologie des Fremden.* Vol. 4: *Vielstimmigkeit der Rede* (Frankfurt: Suhrkamp, 1999).

28. See Edmund Husserl, *Ideen zu einer reinene Phänomenologie und phänomenologischen Philosophie,* Zweites Buch (The Hague: Nijhoff, 1952); English translation by Richard Rojcewicz and André Schuwer as *Ideas Pertaining to a Pure Phenomenology and to a Phenomenological Philosophy,* Second Book (Boston: Dordrecht, 1989), paragraph 56, but also paragraphs 46–47.

29. Concerning sympathy, see also Maurice Merleau-Ponty, *La Nature: notes cours du Collège de France,* edited and annotated by Dominique Seglard (Paris: Seuil, 1995), p. 65. See also *Phénoménologie de la perception* (Paris: Gallimard, 1945), p. 247, English translation by Colin Smith as *Phenomenology of Perception* (London: Routledge & Kegan Paul, 1962), p. 214. See also Maurice Merleau-Ponty, "Christianity and *Ressentiment* (1935)," in *Texts and Dialogues,* ed. Hugh J. Silverman and James Barry (Atlantic Highlands, N.J.: Humanities Press, 1991), pp. 85–100. Although "Christianity and *Ressentiment*," which re-

views Scheler's book on Nietzschean *ressentiment,* appears early in Merleau-Ponty's career, one could perhaps argue that it sets up a trajectory for Merleau-Ponty which ends the concept of the flesh; here Merleau-Ponty defends Christianity from Nietzscheanism, indeed, defends the Christian idea of love, and speaks of sympathy (see, in particular, p. 91). Here he also says that "true Christianity . . . is the Cross" (p. 98), which perhaps anticipates the concept of chiasm.

30. To determine Merleau-Ponty's use of *personne* and his discussions of *Einfühlung,* one will have to investigate Merleau-Ponty comments about Scheler. It is particularly interesting to see Schutz's discussion of Scheler in *Les Philosophes célèbres* (Paris: Mazenod, 1956), pp. 330–35. Here Schutz stresses Scheler's religious interests, his concept of *Personne* (which takes its inspiration from Kant, "Persona cogitans"), and his concept of sympathy (see especially pp. 331–32).

31. See DR 139/105, where Deleuze defines intersubjectivity by means of the virtual object: "[The former present and the actual one] put a variety of terms and subjects into play in a complex intersubjectivity in which each subject owes its role and function in the series to the timeless position it occupies in relation to the virtual object."

32. On the use of *personne,* see also Derrida, *Mémoires d'aveugle,* pp. 89–90; *Memoirs of the Blind,* p. 88; Jacques Derrida, *Spectres de Marx* (Paris: Galilée, 1993), p. 250; English translation by Peggy Kamuf as *Specters of Marx* (New York: Routledge, 1994), p. 157.

33. Edmund Husserl, *Meditations Cartesiennes,* trans. Gabrielle Pfeiffer and Emmanuel Levinas (Paris: Vrin, 1992), in particular p. 152. In *Transcendence et incarnation* (Paris: Vrin, 1995), Natalie Depraz, like Levinas, refuses to translate the word "Einfühlung" into French; moreover, she rejects the word "empathie" as a possible translation because it "colors *Einfühlung* with a Lippsian but not Husserlian affective (indeed pathetic) tenor" (pp. 343–44). But she uses the word "sym-pathie" on p. 189. The entire discussion of *Einfühlung* is inspired by Levinas's two short notes on Merleau-Ponty: "Two Texts on Merleau-Ponty by Emmanuel Levinas," trans. Michael B. Smith, in *Ontology and Alterity by Emmanuel Levinas* (Evanston: Northwestern University Press, 1990), pp. 53–66. Here Levinas stresses that "intropathy," which is how Levinas translates *Einfühlung,* is cognitive and tries to show how the touching–touched relation refers to a sociality below knowledge. Here I have tried to utilize Levinas's descriptions as though they were those of Merleau-Ponty in order to determine a strain of philosophy that runs from Merleau-Ponty to Levinas and up to Derrida. It seems to me particularly important that Levinas says, "As expressed by Husserl in the personal form of a reflexive verb, *Ich fühle mich ein,* does it not already resonate like a feeling of sympathy, already like a friendship and almost like a kind of fraternal compassion?" (p. 64); and, speaking again of *Einfühlung,* Levinas says, "It is an affectivity that carries within itself affection and love—secret structure or concretization of feeling. Should we say a waiting for God in this anticipatory feeling of the absolutely other?" (p. 65). But it is interesting to note also that Levinas associates Merleau-Pontean "intropathy" with knowledge; it is interesting because this association makes Merleau-Ponty's position in the confrontation with the Nietzschean-Deleuzian-Foucaultian strain of contemporary philosophy ambiguous. See also Emmanuel Levinas, *Totalité et infini* (The Hague: Nijhoff, 1961), p. 39; English translation by Alphonso Lingis as *Totality and Infinity* (Pittsburgh: Duquesne University Press, 1969), p. 67; here Levinas makes an analysis of Husserl's Fifth Cartesian Meditation which is virtually identical to what he says about Merleau-Ponty in these two texts.

34. See again Depraz, *Transcendence et incarnation,* pp. 180–92, especially, pp. 189–90.

35. Cf. Derrida, *Mémoires d'aveugle*, pp. 12–15; *Memoirs of the Blind*, pp. 4–5.

36. Cf. Levinas, "Two Texts on Merleau-Ponty by Levinas," in *Ontology and Alterity in Merleau-Ponty*, p. 59.

37. On p. 192/146 of *The Visible and the Invisible*, Merleau-Ponty speaks of a "pact"; it also seems that one could develop an analysis of the eyes in Merleau-Ponty similar to this analysis of the hands.

38. NP 172/149, p. 149, where Deleuze says that pity is nothing more than tolerance for the weak. In reference to these claims about strength and weakness, we must recall that in Nietzsche, in the second essay of *The Genealogy of Morals*, says that the greatest sign of strength is not revenge but mercy.

7. The Beginnings of Post-modernism

1. See Eugen Fink's authorized essay on Husserl's philosophy: "Die phänomenologische Philosophie E. Husserl in der gegenwärtigen Kritik," originally published in *Kant-studien 38*, nos. 3/4 (Berlin, 1933), and collected in Fink, *Studien zur Phänomenologie 1930–1939* (The Hague: Nijhoff, 1966); English translation as "The Phenomenological Philosophy of Edmund Husserl and Contemporary Criticism," in *The Phenomenology of Husserl*, ed. R. O. Elveton (Chicago: Quadrangle Books, 1970), 73–147.

2. Edmund Husserl, "Philosophie als strenge Wissenscaft," in *Husserliana*, Band XXV (The Hague: Nijhoff, 1987), pp. 15 and 11; English translation by Quentin Lauer as "Philosophy as a Rigorous Science," in *Phenomenology and the Crisis of Philosophy* (New York: Harper and Row, 1965), pp. 89 and 83.

3. Henri Bergson, *Matière et mémoire*, in *Œuvres, Édition du centenaire* (Paris: Presses Universitaires de France, 1959), p. 321; English translation by M. M. Paul and W. S. Palmer as *Matter and Memory* (New York: Zone Books, 1991), p. 184.

4. Edmund Husserl, *Vorlesungen zur Phänomenologie des inneren Zeitbewusstsen* (Halle: Niemeyer, 1929), section 36; English translation by James S. Churchill as *The Phenomenology of Internal Time-Consciousness* (Bloomington: Indiana University Press, 1964).

5. Henri Bergson, *Pensée et mouvant* in *Oeuvres, Édition du centenaire*, pp. 1394–96; English translation by Mabelle L. Andison as *The Creative Mind* (New York: Philosophical Library, 1946), pp. 188–90.

6. Edmund Husserl, *Phänomenologische Psychologie* (The Hague: Nijhoff, 1962), p. 343. The word rendered as "concealment" is *Deckung*.

7. Henri Bergson, *Essai sur les données immédiates de la conscience*, in *Œuvres, Édition de centenaire*, p. 15; English translation by F. L. Pogson as *Time and Free Will* (Kila, Mont.: Kessinger, n.d. [original date of translation is 1910]), p. 17.

8. Edmund Husserl, *Ideen zu einer reinen Phänomenologie und phänomenologischen Philosophie, I (Husserliana*, Band III, Part I) (The Hague: Nijhoff, 1976), section 70, p. 132; English translation by F. Kersten as *Ideas Pertaining to a Pure Phenomenology and to a Phenomenological Philosophy, First Book* (Boston: Kluwer, 1982), section 70, p. 160.

9. Bergson, *Pensée et mouvant* in *Œuvres, Édition du centenaire*, pp. 1341–42; *The Creative Mind*, p. 120.

10. Marcel Proust, *À la recherche du temps perdu, Le Temps retrouvé* (Paris: Gallimard, 1954), p. 230; English translation as *Remembrance of Things Past, Time Regained*, vol. III, by C. K. Scott Moncrieff and Terrence Kilmartin and by Andreas Mayor (New York: Random House, 1981), p. 906.

11. One can, of course, see the development of the concept of the simulacrum in Baudrillard. See, in particular, Jean Baudrillard, "The Precession of Simulacra," in *Simulacra and Simulation* (Ann Arbor: University of Michigan Press, 1994), pp. 3–42.

12. Perhaps this dissipation explains Deleuze's abandonment of the concept of simulacrum. See Jean-Clet Martin, *Variations,* Préface par Gilles Deleuze (Paris: Payot, 1993), p. 8. Derrida has continued to use the concept. See Jacques Derrida, *Spectres de Marx* (Paris: Galilée, 1993), p. 268; English translation by Peggy Kamuf as *Specters of Marx* (New York: Routledge, 1994), p. 169. I return to the concept of the simulacrum in Derrida and Deleuze in Chapter 8.

13. See my "We Need a Name for What We Do," in *Chiasmi International* 1 (1999), pp. 27–36.

14. Cf. VP 59/53, where Derrida himself seems to make a distinction between Platonism and the metaphysics of presence.

15. To resolve with some certainty this question of the relation of "reversing Platonism" to "the deconstruction of the metaphysics of presence," one would have to compare carefully Derrida's "Plato's Pharmacy" with Deleuze's "Renverser le platonisme." "Plato's Pharmacy" was first published in 1968, one year after Deleuze's "Renverser le platonisme." See below, Chapter 8.

16. Jacques Derrida, *Spurs,* bilingual edition, English translation by Stefano Agosto (Chicago: University of Chicago Press, 1979), pp. 127, 133, 139.

17. There are other ways to describe this fundamental diffraction. Whereas Derridean deconstruction distances the presence that had been close-by, Deleuzian destruction brings close-by the presence that had been distant; whereas Derridean deconstruction is a contamination, Deleuzian destruction is a purification. Indeed, whereas *Voice and Phenomenon* demonstrates, by means of Husserl's phenomenology, the impossibility of exiting the metaphysics of presence (VP 16/16, 53/48), Deleuze's *Bergsonism* determines the progress Bergson made in the actualization of a new ontology outside of Platonism (BER 1/13, 27/34–35; see also Gilles Deleuze, "La Conception de la différence chez Bergson," in *Les Études bergsoniennes* 4 (1965), p. 111; English translation by Melissa McMahon as "Bergson's Conception of Difference," in *The New Bergson,* ed. John Mullarkey (Manchester: Manchester University Press, 1999). In other words, whereas Derridean deconstruction, in Husserl, aims at showing that the functions of the sign, indication and expression, are not distinct, Deleuzian destruction, in Bergson, aims at establishing a difference in nature between extensity (and its illusion) and duration. Indicative of this diffraction between Derridean deconstruction and Deleuzian destruction is the fact that, in *Voice and Phenomenon,* Derrida always seeks contradictions in Husserl's argumentation (VP 64n1/57n6)—contradictions that imply a fundamental contamination or unity—whereas in *Bergsonism* Deleuze always seeks consistency in Bergson's argumentation (BER 95/94)—a consistency which implies a fundamental purity or duality.

18. Henri Bergson, *La Pensée et le mouvant,* in *Œuvres, Édition du centenaire* (Paris: Presses Universitaires de France, 1959), pp. 1428–30; English translation by Mabelle L. Andison as *The Creative Mind* (New York: Philosophical Library, 1946), pp. 232–33. In *Creative Evolution,* Bergson openly approves of Plato's image of the dialectician as the good carver, cutting at the articulations of the real. See Henri Bergson, *L'Évolution créatrice,* in *Oeuvres, Édition du centenaire,* p. 627; English translation by Arthur Mitchell as *Creative Evolution* (Mineola, N.Y.: Dover, 1998), p. 156.

19. Deleuze, "La Conception de la différence," p. 111; also DR 83/59.

20. Deleuze, "La Conception de la différence," p. 84.

21. Deleuze, "La Conception de la différence," p. 96.

22. Deleuze, "La Conception de la différence," p. 87.

23. See BER 38/44; see also Deleuze, "La Conception de la différence," p. 96.

24. Undoubtedly, this claim is too unequivocal, since Derrida like Deleuze claims to distinguish his concept of *différance* from the Hegelian concept of contradiction. But Derrida makes this distinction while keeping himself, as he says, "at the point of almost absolute proximity to Hegel." Derrida's "almost absolute proximity" (one never finds comments like this in Deleuze) allows me to make such an unequivocal claim. See Jacques Derrida, *Positions* (Paris: Minuit, 1972), pp. 58–59; English translation by Alan Bass as *Positions* (Chicago: University of Chicago Press, 1981), pp. 43–44.

25. Derrida always focuses on the reduction because of Fink's interpretation of Husserl.

26. See ED 196–224/134–51.

27. See also Jacques Derrida, Review of Edmund Husserl, *Phänomenologische Psychologie: Vorlesungen Sommersemester 1925,* in *Les Études philosophiques* 18, no. 2 (1963), pp. 203–206.

28. Gilles Deleuze, *La Philosophie critique de Kant* (Paris: Presses Universitaires de France, 1963), p. 37; English translation by Hugh Tomlinson and Barbara Habberjam as *Kant's Critical Philosophy* (Minneapolis: University of Minnesota Press, 1984), p. 24.

29. What here in 1966 Deleuze is calling a virtual image will become what he and Guattari call a concept in *What Is Philosophy?*

30. Deleuze, "La Conception de la différence," p. 85.

31. Gilles Deleuze, "Bergson," in *Les Philosophes célèbres,* ed. Maurice Merleau-Ponty (Paris: Mazenod, 1956), p. 298.

32. Deleuze, "La Conception de la différence," p. 90; see also LS 303/262.

33. The word Deleuze uses is *tracer.*

34. Deleuze discusses Husserl's concept of noema in LS 32–33/20–21.

35. See, for example, Derrida, *Spectres de Marx,* pp. 123–24; *Specters of Marx,* pp. 73–74.

36. Derrida, *Spurs,* p. 127.

37. Derrida, *Spectres de Marx,* pp. 123–24; *Specters of Marx,* p. 73.

38. There is no discussion of the Fifth Meditation in Derrida's earlier, 1953–54 *Le Problème de la genèse dans la philosophie de Husserl* (Paris: Presses Universitaires de France, 1991). And he only alludes to the Fifth Meditation in his *Introduction to The Origin of Geometry.*

39. For the most recent discussion of Husserlian appresentation, see Jacques Derrida, *Le Toucher—Jean-Luc Nancy* (Paris: Galilée, 2000), pp. 222–23.

40. See Derrida, *Spectres de Marx,* p. 268; *Specters of Marx,* p. 169.

41. Deleuze, "La Conception de la différence," p. 85.

42. Deleuze, "La Conception de la différence," p. 81.

43. I am alluding to the recent work of Edward S. Casey on the glance. See, for example, "Taking a Glance at the Environing World," in *Confluences: Phenomenology and Postmodernity, Environment, Race, and Gender* (Pittsburgh: Simon Silverman Phenomenology Center, Duquesne University, 2000), pp. 3–38; and Edward S. Casey, "The World at a Glance," in *Chiasms,* ed. Fred Evans and Leonard Lawlor (Albany: SUNY Press, 2000), pp. 147–64.

44. Deleuze, "La Conception de la différence," p. 98.

45. Cf. Gilles Deleuze and Félix Guattari, *Mille plateaus* (Paris: Minuit, 1980), pp. 356–57; English translation by Brian Massumi as *A Thousand Plateaus* (Minneapolis: University of Minnesota Press, 1987), p. 291.

46. In fact, the opposition that I am proposing here between intuition and language, an opposition I adopted from *Voice and Phenomenon*, must be understood as a slight difference of emphasis going from form (Derrida) to formless (Deleuze), a slight difference of emphasis that is inside the word "in-formal."

47. See Jacques Derrida, "La Loi du genre," in *Parages* (Paris: Galilée, 1986), pp. 249–87.

48. See Jacques Derrida, *La Vérité en peinture* (Paris: Flammarion, 1978); English translation by Geoff Bennington as *The Truth in Painting* (Chicago: University of Chicago Press, 1987). As Derrida shows in *Spurs*, a masculine style can also at the same time be feminine.

49. I am again alluding to the recent work of Edward S. Casey on the glance.

50. See Jacques Derrida, *Aporias*, trans. Thomas Dutoit (Stanford: Stanford University Press, 1993).

51. See Zeynep Direk, "Derrida's Renovation of Experience," Ph.D. dissertation, University of Memphis, 1999.

52. Jacques Derrida, "I'm Going to Have to Wander All Alone," trans. Leonard Lawlor, in *Philosophy Today* 42, no. 1 (spring 1998), pp. 3–5.

53. Jacques Derrida, *De l'esprit* (Paris: Galilée, 1987), p. 147; English translation by Geoffrey Bennington and Rachel Bowlby as *Of Spirit* (Chicago: University of Chicago Press, 1989), p. 94.

54. See Hans-Georg Gadamer, *Wahrheit und Methode* (Tübingen: Mohr, 1960), division 2; English translation revised by Joel Weisheimer and Donald G. Marshall as *Truth and Method* (New York: Crossroads, 1990), division 2.

55. Martin Heidegger, *Nietzsche*, vol. III (Pfullingen: Neske, 1961), p. 522; English translation by David F. Krell as *Nietzsche*, vol. III (New York: Harper and Row, 1987), p. 43.

56. Fred Evans, *Psychology and Nihilism: A Genealogical Critique of the Computational Model of Mind* (Albany: SUNY Press, 1993).

8. The Beginnings of Thought

1. Cf. Luc Ferry and Alain Renault, *French Philosophy of the Sixties*, trans. Mary Schnackenberg Cattani (Amherst: University of Massachusetts Press, 1990); and Vincent Descombes, *Le Même et l'autre* (Paris: Minuit, 1979); English translation by L. Scott-Fox and J. M. Harding as *Modern French Philosophy* (New York: Cambridge University Press, 1980).

2. The English translation of *Difference and Repetition* does not contain the passage that I just quoted. Deleuze and Guattari's final book, *Qu'est-ce que la philosophie?* (Paris: Minuit, 1991), indicates that thought was always Deleuze's prime concern. See also Gilles Deleuze, *Cinéma 2: l'image-temps* (Paris: Minuit, 1985), pp. 218–19; English translation by Hugh Tomlinson and Robert Galeta as *Cinema 2: The Time-Image* (Minneapolis: University of Minnesota Press, 1989), pp. 167–68.

3. This need to re-conceive history without beginning and end is what Descombes calls "hypothèse d'un éternel retour." See *Le Même et l'autre*, p. 212; *Modern French Philosophy*, p. 182.

4. See Jacques Derrida, "Force et signification," in *L'Écriture et la différence* (Paris:

Minuit, 1967); English translation by Alan Bass as "Force and Signification," in *Writing and Difference* (Chicago: University of Chicago Press, 1978). This essay is very important for understanding French philosophy of the Sixties.

5. The use of these terms varies across the texts from the Sixties. For example, in Foucault, see MC 353/342; in *The Archeology of Knowledge*, Foucault uses both *manque* and *déficit*; see AS 145/110 and 156/119. In *Logique du sens* Deleuze uses both *manque* and *défaut*. Derrida uses *manque*. See VP 98/88 and 109/97. Derrida's use of the word "manque" derives from his translation of Edmund Husserl's "The Origin of Geometry" in 1962. There Derrida translates Husserl's "es felht das verharrende Dasein" as "Il lui manque la présence perdurante." See Edmund Husserl, *L'Origine de la géométrie, traduction et introduction par Jacques Derrida* (Paris: Presses Universitaires de France, 1962), p. 185.

6. "A nearly total affinity" is the phrase Derrida used in his memorial piece for Deleuze to describe the relation between them. See Jacques Derrida, "Il me faudra errer tout seul," in *Liberation* (November 7, 1995), translated by Leonard Lawlor as "I'm Going to Have to Wander All Alone," in *Philosophy Today* 42, no. 1 (1998), pp. 3–5. See also Leonard Lawlor, "A Nearly Total Affinity: The Deleuzian Virtual Image versus the Derridean Trace," in *Angelakai* 5, no. 2 (August 2000), pp. 59–72.

7. See, for example, Jacques Derrida, "To Unsense the Subjectile," in Jacques Derrida and Paule Thévenin, *The Secret Art of Antonin Artaud* (Cambridge, Mass.: MIT Press, 1998).

8. Antonin Artaud, *Œuvres complètes*, vol. I (Paris: Gallimard, 1970), pp. 35–36. Also quoted in ED 264/177.

9. Antonin Artaud, *Le Théâtre et son double* (Paris: Folio/Essais, Gallimard, 1964), pp. 158–59, my translation.

10. Artaud, *Le Théâtre et son double*, p. 36.

11. This image occurs in Derrida and Deleuze during the Sixties. But it would be a mistake not to recognize this image at work in Part I ("le supplice") of Foucault's *Surveiller et punir* (Paris: Gallimard, 1975), pp. 56 and 76; English translation by Alan Sheridan as *Discipline and Punish* (New York: Vintage, 1977), pp. 46 and 63. Foucault mentions Artaud in *Les Mots et les choses* (Paris: Gallimard, 1966), pp. 59 and 395; English translation as *The Order of Things*, no translator listed (New York: Random House, 1970), pp. 43 and 383.

12. The idea of this paradox comes from both Deleuze and Derrida, but Descombes explicitly points to it. See *Le Même et l'autre*, pp. 170–71; *Modern French Philosophy*, p. 145.

13. See Michel Foucault, "La Prose d'Actéon," in *Dits et écrits*, vol. I, 1954–1969 (Paris: Gallimard, 1994), pp. 326–37. The essay was originally published in 1964.

14. See Gilles Deleuze, "Renverser le platonisme," in *Revue de Métaphysique et de Morale* 71, no. 4 (October-December 1966), pp. 426–38. The citation for this article in *Logique du sens* (and therefore also in the English translation) is incorrect. Deleuze also revised the article for its inclusion in *Logique du sens*.

15. The page parallel to LS 296n2 in the original version of "Renverser le platonisme" is pp. 428–29. See Jacques Derrida, "La Pharmacie de Platon," in *Tel Quel* 32–33 (1968), pp. 3–48, 38–75. Deleuze also removed a note to Foucault's essay on the simulacrum in Klossowski, "La Prose d'Actéon" in *Nouvelle Revue Française* of March 1964. Eric Alliez has commented on this note in his "Ontologie et logographie, la pharmacie, Platon et le simulacre," in *Nos Grecs et leurs modernes* (Paris: Seuil, 1992), p. 215.

16. It also seems to me that Foucault critique of Derrida's concept of "textual trace"

indicates that the Deleuzian simulacrum is not identical to the Derridean simulacrum. See Michel Foucault, "My Body, This Paper, This Fire," in *Michel Foucault,* vol. 2 (*Aesthetics, Method, and Epistemology*), ed. James D. Faubion (New York: New Press, 1998), p. 416.

17. Here Derrida speaks of three epochs of the repetition of Platonism.

18. In his *Le Platonisme* (Paris: Presses Universitaires de France, 1971) Vincent Descombes says, citing Derrida's "Plato's Pharmacy," that "Dans un texte qui, malheureusement, attribue à l'imitation selon Platon une sorte de péché originel, faute de distinguer les sens de la rectitude" (p. 48n1). But, as we shall see, what is at stake in "Plato's Pharmacy" is precisely the ability to distinguish different senses (of the word "pharmakon," for example) and keep the different senses from contaminating one another in a "mixture." That we cannot distinguish well in such a mixture is, indeed, like being in the state of sin, "malheureux."

19. One should keep in mind that Chapter 1 of *Difference and Repetition* is called "difference in itself."

20. One finds a similar statement in *Anti-Oedipus.* See Gilles Deleuze and Félix Guattari, *L'Anti-Oedipe* (Paris: Minuit, 1972), pp. 323–24; English translation by Robert Hurley, Mark Seem, and Helen R. Lane as *Anti-Oedipus* (New York: Viking Press, 1977), p. 271. When Deleuze here speaks of making the simulacra rise to the surface, as if they were buried in caves (cf. LS 304/263), he is implying that the reversal of Platonism consists in a kind of philosophical archeology. Similarly, in "Plato's Pharmacy," Derrida defines reversing Platonism as the "*exhumation* of the conceptual monuments erected by Platonism" (DIS 122–23/107, my emphasis; see also DIS 149/129). We should keep in mind Deleuze's close connection to Foucault. It is possible to read *The Logic of Sense* as an extension of *Les Mots et les choses.* See LS 83–84/66–67. And Deleuze uses the word "archeology" to describe a double thinking (LS 53/39). Also, one should not overlook Derrida's constant use of the word "archive." See DIS 122/107; VP 15/15. See also Derrida's recent *Mal d'archive* (Paris: Galilée, 1995); English translation by Eric Prenowitz as *Archive Fever* (Chicago: University of Chicago Press, 1966). It is at this point that we can see the connection to Foucault and even to the later Merleau-Ponty; see above, Chapter 2.

21. Cf., for example, Jacques Derrida, "Donner la mort," in *L'Ethique du don, Jacques Derrida et la pensée du don* (Paris: Transition, 1990), p. 54; English translation by David Wills as *The Gift of Death* (Chicago: University of Chicago Press, 1995), p. 51.

22. Cf. Jacques Derrida, "Nous autres Grecs," in *Nos Grecs et leurs modernes,* p. 259.

23. See also Jacques Derrida, "Form and Meaning: A Note on the Phenomenology of Language," in *Margins of Philosophy,* trans. Alan Bass (Chicago: University of Chicago Press, 1982).

24. Derrida begins his 1993 *Specters of Marx* with this phrase from Hamlet. See Jacques Derrida, *Spectres de Marx* (Paris: Galilée, 1993), pp. 43–44; English translation by Peggy Kamuf as *Specters of Marx* (New York: Routledge, 1994), pp. 19–20.

25. Here Deleuze is calling the "paradoxical element" "the dark precursor."

26. Eric Alliez has pointed to this distinction in his "Ontologie et logographie," in *Nos Grecs et leurs modernes,* p. 217.

27. For a more detailed analysis of Derrida and Husserl see my *Derrida and Husserl: The Basic Problem of Phenomenology* (Bloomington: Indiana University Press, 2002).

28. Jacques Derrida, "Survivre," in *Parages* (Paris: Galilée, 1986), p. 181; English translation by James Hulbert as "Living On: Borderlines," in *Deconstruction and Criticism* (Boston: Seabury Press, 1979), p. 138. This non-place is also, for Derrida, Plato's *chora.* See Jacques Derrida, *Khôra* (Paris: Galilée, 1993), especially p. 74, where Derrida places em-

phasis on the word "milieu"; English translation by Ian McLeod as "Khôra," in *On the Name* (Stanford: Stanford University Press, 1995), p. 116. Cf. also Francis Wolff, "Trios: Deleuze, Derrida, Foucault, historiens du platonisme," in *Nos Grecs et leurs modernes*, p. 245. For another use of this "non-lieu," see Foucault, NGH 145–72/139–64.

29. In his early writings Derrida uses Merleau-Ponty figure of the chiasm to speak of this undecidable point; see DIS 145/127. Cf. also Derrida's later *De l'esprit* (Paris: Galilée, 1987), pp. 23–24; English translation by Geoffrey Bennington and Rachel Bowlby as *Of Spirit* (Chicago: University of Chicago Press, 1989), pp. 8–9. Here Derrida is speaking of the four threads he is following in his reading of Heidegger. He says, "Following the trace of Heidegger's spirituality would perhaps approach, not a central point of this knot—I believe there is none—but approach what gathers a nodal resistance in its most economical torsion."

30. Cf. Deleuze's comment at F 119/112. Here Deleuze is speaking of the fold in Foucault. He says, "being is between two forms. Is this not precisely what Heidegger had called the 'between-two' or Merleau-Ponty termed the 'interlacing or chiasmus'? In fact, they are not at all the same thing. . . . Everything takes place as if Foucault were reproaching Heidegger and Merleau-Ponty for going too quickly."

31. See Gilles Deleuze, *Le Pli* (Paris: Minuit, 1988), p. 43; English translation by Tom Conley as *The Fold* (Minneapolis: University of Minnesota Press, 1993), p. 30.

32. On the concept of "aveu," see Jacques Derrida, *Politique de l'amitié* (Paris: Galilée, 1994), pp. 72–73; English translation by George Collins as *Politics of Friendship* (London: Verso Books, 1997), pp. 54–55.

33. For more on the positive and negative in Derrida and Deleuze, see Gordon C. F. Bearn, "Differentiating Derrida and Deleuze," in *Continental Philosophy Review* 33 (2000), pp. 441–65.

34. Speaking here of extracting the untimely from the simulacrum, Deleuze anticipates what he is going to say in 1993 in his Preface to Jean-Clet Martin's *Variations* (Paris: Payot, 1993): "'Rhizome' est le meilleur mot pour désigner les multiplicités. En revanche, il me semble que j'ai tout à fait abandonné la notion de simulacre, qui ne vaut pas grand-chose" (p. 8). However, Deleuze continues to speak of the untimely. See *Qu'est-ce la philosophie?* co-authored with Félix Guattari (Paris: Minuit, 1991), p. 107; English translation by Hugh Tomlinson and Graham Burchell as *What Is Philosophy?* (New York: Columbia University Press, 1994), p. 112. Thus when we speak of the simulacrum in Deleuze what we must hear is the untimely or the concept. Similarly, when we speak of the simulacrum in Derrida what we must hear is the older or the specter.

Conclusion

1. See Henri Bergson, *Œuvres, Édition du centenaire* (Paris: Presses Universitaires de France, 1959), p. 1408; English translation by Mabelle L. Andison in *The Creative Mind* (New York: Citadel Press, 1946), pp. 175–76.

2. This need to re-conceive history without beginning and end is what Descombes calls "hypothèse d'un éternel retour." See Vincent Descombes, *Le Même et l'autre* (Paris: Minuit, 1980), p. 212; English translation by L. Scott-Fox and J. M. Harding as *Modern French Philosophy* (New York: Cambridge University Press, 1980), p. 182.

3. That all the options are options of immanence explains the absence of Levinas from this system.

4. See Leonard Lawlor, *The Challenge of Bergsonism: Phenomenology, Ontology, Ethics*

(forthcoming, Continuum Books). *The Challenge of Bergsonism* is itself a propaedeutic to another book to be called *Memory and Life*.

Appendix 1

1. Stoller and Unterthurner posed the questions in German with an English translation. The answers were in English, which were then translated into German.

2. See above, Chapter 6.

3. For a more current statement of this principle see Gilles Deleuze, "Lettre-Préface" to Jean-Clet Martin, *Variations* (Paris: Payot, 1993), p. 8.

4. Eugen Fink, *Studien zur Phänomenologie 1930–1939* (The Hague: Nijhoff, 1966), p. 105n1; English translation as "The Phenomenological Philosophy of Edmund Husserl and Contemporary Criticism," in *The Phenomenology of Husserl*, ed. R. O. Elveton (Chicago: Quadrangle Books, 1970), p. 99n11.

5. See my *Derrida and Husserl: The Basic Problem of Phenomenology* (Bloomington: Indiana University Press, 2002).

6. Gilles Deleuze, *Empirisme et sujectivité* (Paris: Presses Universitaires de France, 1953), p. 92; English translation by Constantin V. Boundas as *Empiricism and Subjectivity* (New York: Columbia University Press, 1991), p. 87.

7. "We Need a Name for What We Do: Report on Contemporary Merleau-Ponty Research in the United States," in *Chiasmi International* 1 (1999), p. 32.

8. See ED 183/125: "What authorizes him [that is, Levinas] to say 'infinitely other' if the infinitely other does not appear as such in the zone he calls the same and which is the neutral level of transcendental description?"; and ED 202/138: "The 'letting-be' [of Heidegger] concerns all possible forms of the existent, and even those which, *by essence*, cannot be transformed into 'objects of understanding.' If it belongs to the essence of the Other first and foremost to be an 'interlocutor' and to be 'interpellated,' then the 'letting-be' will let the Other be what it is" (Derrida's emphasis).

9. Emmanuel Levinas, *Autrement qu'être ou au-delà de l'essence* (The Hague: Nijhoff, 1974 [Le Livre de poche, 1990]), p. 220, Levinas's emphasis; English translation by Alphonso Lingis as *Otherwise than Being or Beyond Essence* (The Hague: Nijhoff, 1981), p. 140. The translation here is modified.

10. See Levinas, *Autrement qu'être ou au-delà de l'essence*, p. 127; *Otherwise than Being*, p. 79.

11. One is tempted to say that Heidegger's re-opening of the question of being is the event of twentieth-century philosophy, without the qualification "Continental." But obviously, to be able to say this depends on what happens between Continental philosophy and analytic philosophy, and the development of this divergence is hard to predict. This divergence will be addressed below.

12. It may be the case that the French idiom *à même* is at the center of this difference.

13. This sentence cannot be translated without remainder. Perhaps it can be translated as "every other is every other" or "every other is wholly other."

14. "We Need a Name for What We Do," p. 32.

15. This mechanism is what Bergson calls "the turn of experience" in *Matter and Memory*. See Chapter 7 above. See also Leonard Lawlor, *The Challenge of Bergsonism: Phenomenology, Ontology, Ethics* (forthcoming, Continuum Books).

16. Fred Evans and Leonard Lawlor, "The Value of Flesh: Merleau-Ponty's Philosophy

and the Modernism/Postmodernism Debate," in *Chiasms: Merleau-Ponty's Notion of Flesh*, ed. Fred Evans and Leonard Lawlor (Albany: SUNY Press, 2000), p. 15.

17. Recent French Merleau-Ponty scholars such as Renaud Barbaras have used the word "institution" to render in French "Stiftung."

18. See "The Value of Flesh," in *Chiasms*, p. 15. See also Chapter 6 above.

19. The use of these terms varies across the texts that compose the system of "French" thought. See, for example, Foucault, MC 353/342. In AS, Foucault uses both *manque* and *déficit*, pp. 145/110 and 156/118. Deleuze uses both *manque* and *défaut;* see LS 83/66 and 88–89/70–71. Derrida uses *manque* in VP 98/88 and 109/97. Derrida's use of the word "manque" derives from his translation of Edmund Husserl's "The Origin of Geometry" in 1962. There Derrida translates Husserl's "es felht das verharrende Dasein" as "Il lui manque la présence perdurante." See Edmund Husserl, *L'Origine de la géométrie, traduction et introduction par Jacques Derrida*, p. 185.

20. See especially his *Psychology and Nihilism: A Genealogical Critique of the Computational Model of Mind* (Albany: SUNY Press, 1993).

21. See, for example, his "Genealogy and the Problem of Affirmation in Nietzsche, Foucault, and Bakhtin," *Philosophy and Social Criticism* 27, no. 3 (2001), pp. 41–65; "Voices of Chiapas: The Zapatistas, Bakhtin, and Human Rights," *Philosophy Today* 42 (2000), pp. 196–210 (SPEP Supplement, vol. 25); and "Bakhtin, Communication, and the Politics of Multiculturalism," *Constellations: An International Journal of Critical and Democratic Theory* 5, no. 3 (1998), pp. 403–23.

22. *The Multi-voiced Body: Society, Communication, and the Age of Diversity.*

23. Martin Heidegger, *Nietzsche*, vol. I (Pfullingen: Verlag Günther Neske, 1961), p. 233; English translation by David F. Krell as *Nietzsche*, vol. 1 (*The Will to Power as Art*) (New York: Harper and Row, 1979), p. 201.

24. I think this "fold" is the direction of Judith Butler's work. See, for example, Judith Butler, *Bodies That Matter* (New York: Routledge, 1993).

25. In reference to the First Part of Foucault's *Surveiller et punir* (Paris: Gallimard, 1975), English translation by Alan Sheridan as *Discipline and Punish* (New York: Vintage, 1977), called simply "supplice"—the English title is "Torture"—it is important to see the little word "pli" at work in the title. It is also important to recognize that "l'éclat" in the title to Chapter 2 could be rendered as "unconcealment" (*Entborgenheit*); this translation would allow us to see how much Foucault here is contesting Heidegger's account of "the essence of truth."

Appendix 2

1. In the 1969 *Logic of Sense* (trans. Mark Lester with Charles Stivale, ed. Constantin Boundas [New York: Columbia University Press, 1990]) version, Deleuze changes this phrase to "to distinguish essence from appearance" (p. 256). Trans.

2. *Sophist* 236b, 264c.

3. In the 1969 version, Deleuze continues the sentence: "of repressing simulacra, keeping them completely submerged, preventing them from climbing to the surface, and 'insinuating themselves' everywhere" (p. 257). Trans.

4. Schuhl has shown, in *Platon et l'art de son temps*, that Plato opposed not only techniques of illusion, but also realist techniques of thoroughly exterior imitation (p. 54). Cf. also the remarks of Rodis-Lewis in *Platon et la chasse de l'être*, pp. 46–47.

5. Here Deleuze adds the qualification "of the simulacrum" in the 1969 version (p. 257). Trans.

6. Deleuze changes "Platonist Fathers" to "Platonism" (p. 257). Trans.

7. Deleuze transforms this question into a declarative statement in the 1969 version. Trans.

8. X. Andouard, who marks the necessity of bringing together the Platonic phantasm and the phantasm in the psychoanalytic sense, says that unlike copies, phantasms-simulacra "are constructions which include the angle of the observer, so that illusion is produced at the very point where the observer is found. . . . It is not really on the status of nonbeing that the emphasis is placed, but rather on this slight gap [*pétit ecart*], this slight distortion of the real image, which happens at the particular point of view of the observer, and which constitutes the possibility of constructing the simulacrum, work of the sophist" ("Le Simulacre," *Cahiers pour l'analyse*, no. 3).

9. *Republic* X, 602a. **And doubtless the Sophist seems to accord a certain "opinion" to the man of the simulacrum; but it is in order to distinguish two cases, that of the native from that of the ironist, which keep their distance with regard to opinion (268a).**

10. Here Deleuze adds in the 1969 version "This is, without a doubt, the essential characteristic of the modern work of art" (p. 260). Trans.

11. In English, the terms "implicate" and "explicate" do not immediately convey the sense of enfolding and unfolding they do in French, where *le pli* means "the fold." "Complicate" may also be read with this in mind. Trans.

12. On these characteristics of the work of art, cf. Umberto Eco, *The Open Work*, trans. Cancogni (Cambridge, Mass.: Harvard University Press, 1989). On the theme of the simulacrum in the stories of Pierre Klossowski, refer in particular to the article of Michel Foucault, "La Prose d'Actéon, *N.R.F.,* March 1964. As for Gombrowicz, he prefaces his novel *Cosmos* with remarks about the constitution of divergent series and about the manner in which they resonate and communicate in the midst of chaos (cf. in *Cosmos,* the series of *mouths* and *hanged things,* the phantasm of *the murder of the cat* ensures their communication).

13. Deleuze replaces "the world itself as representation" with "the world as icon" in the 1969 version (p. 261). Trans.

14. In the 1969 version, Deleuze continues: "it may happen that the basic series have only a slight difference between them" (p. 261). Trans.

15. Deleuze changes this to "the center of the thus decentered system" in the 1969 version (p. 262). Trans.

16. In the 1969 version, Deleuze adds "assuring the communication of disparate components" (p. 261). Trans.

17. Here Deleuze writes in 1969 "they find their ground in a constitutive dissymmetry, difference, or inequality" (p. 261). Trans.

18. In the 1969 version, Deleuze adds "comprised or complicated in the chaos" (p. 261). Trans.

19. Cf. Louis Althusser, *For Marx,* trans. Brewster (London: Verso, 1996), p. 102: "Circle of circles, consciousness has but one center which alone determines it: it would be necessary for circles having another center than consciousness, for decentered circles, in order that consciousness be affected in its center by their efficacy, briefly that its essence be over-determined by them."

20. Here Deleuze adds "in general" in the 1969 version (p. 260). Trans.

21. Deleuze replaces "original" with "model" in 1969 (p. 259). Trans.

22. In the 1969 version Deleuze changes this to "in the sense that Plato says that Justice is nothing more than just, Courage nothing other than courageous, etc." (p. 259). Trans.

23. Deleuze replaces this in the 1969 version with "the pretender who possesses in a secondary way" (p. 259). Trans.

24. Here Deleuze replaces "maintains" with "complicates" in the 1969 version (p. 262). Trans.

25. Deleuze changes the end of this sentence to "and makes them all return to each one in the course of the forced movement" in the 1969 version (p. 262). Trans.

26. In the 1969 version, Deleuze adds "There is no longer any possible selection. The non-hierarchized work is a condensation of coexistences and a simultaneity of events" (p. 262). Trans.

27. Deleuze changes this sentence in the 1969 version to "It simulates at once the father, the pretender, and the fiancé in a superimposition of masks" (p. 262). Trans.

28. At the end of this sentence, Deleuze adds ", an illusion" in the 1969 version (p. 263). Then he writes "Simulation is the phantasm itself, that is, the effect of the functioning of the simulacrum as machinery—a Dionysian machine" (p. 263). Trans.

29. In the 1969 version, Deleuze begins this sentence with "By rising to the surface," and he concludes it with only the word "phantasm" in parentheses (p. 263). Trans.

30. Friedrich Nietzsche, *Beyond Good and Evil*, trans. R. J. Hollingdale, section 289. [In the 1969 version, Deleuze adds "How would Socrates be recognized in these caverns, which are no longer his? With what thread, since the thread is lost? How would he exit from them, and how could he still distinguish himself from the Sophist? (p. 263). Trans.]

31. Here Deleuze adds ", but only" in the 1969 version (p. 264). Trans.

32. In 1969 Deleuze adds "Thus, what appeared to Plato to be only a sterile effect reveals in itself the intractability of masks and the impassibility of signs" (p. 264). Trans.

33. In the 1969 version, Deleuze continues by saying "To the coherence of representation, the eternal return substitutes something else entirely—its own chaodyssey [*chaoerrance*]" (p. 264). Trans.

34. Pierre Klossowski, *Nietzsche, le polythéism et la parodie* (Un si funeste désir, *N.R.F.*, p. 226). Cf. also pp. 216–18, where Klossowski comments on the *Gay Science*, section 361: "The pleasure of simulation, exploding as power, driving back the so-called character, submerging it at times to the point of extinguishing it." [In the 1969 version, Deleuze uses the upper case: "l'Être" (p. 264). Trans.]

35. In the 1969 version, Deleuze changed this phrase and said, "in relation to the future, it is attained by the phantasm of the eternal return as belief in the future" (p. 265). Trans.

36. Here Deleuze inserts "the moment of Pop Art" between parentheses in the 1969 version (p. 265). Trans.

37. Henry Miller, *The Time of the Assassins: A Study of Rimbaud* (New York: New Directions, 1956), pp. 26–28. Trans.

38. In the 1969 version, instead of the quote from Miller, Deleuze writes, "For there is a vast difference between destroying in order to conserve and perpetuate the established order of representations, models, and copies, and destroying the models and copies in order to institute the chaos which creates, making the simulacra function and raising a phantasm" (p. 266). Trans.

Index

LEONARD LAWLOR is Dunavant Distinguished Professor of Philosophy at the University of Memphis. He is author of *Derrida and Husserl: The Basic Problem of Phenomenology.*